THE REAL WORLD

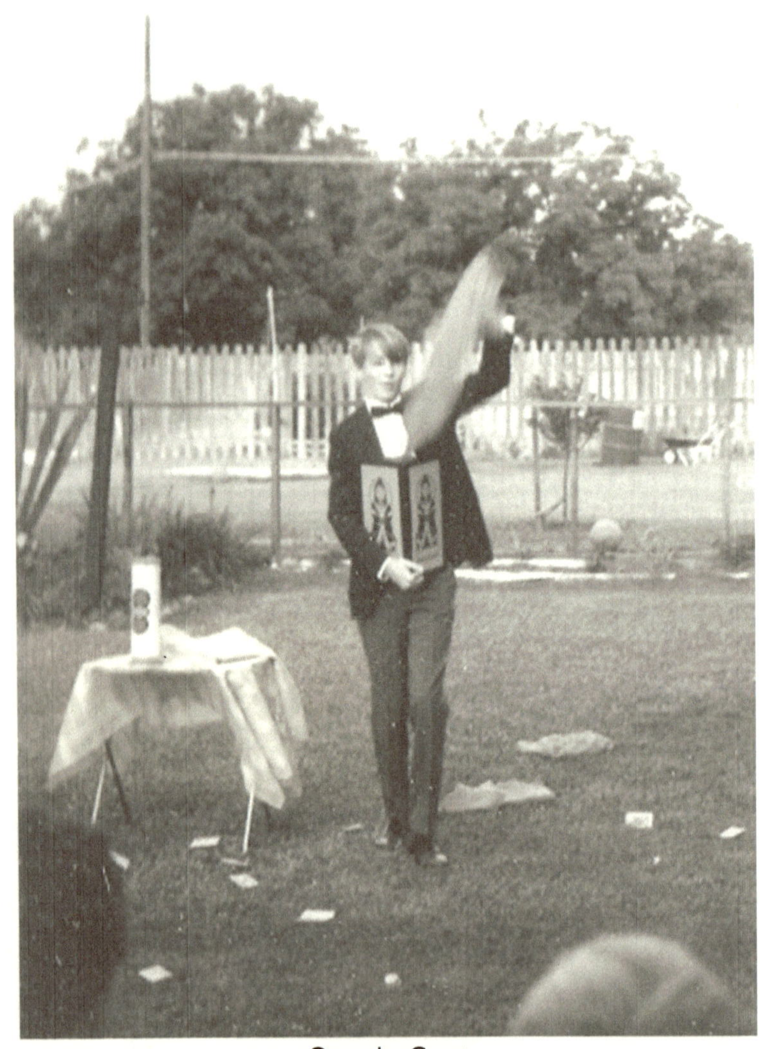

Gary the Great

THE REAL WORLD

by Gary Comenas

FAST BOOKS

For Bill

Photos courtesy of the author unless otherwise noted.

Fast Books are edited and published by Michael Smith
P. O. Box 1268, Silverton, OR 97381

ISBN 978-0-9982793-6-7

Contents

Part IV

Part V

THE REAL WORLD

Part I

1. Delirium

I HAVE ALWAYS BEEN AFRAID OF DEATH, but when it finally came, I barely noticed. Before I died I sometimes told myself it wasn't death I was afraid of, it was the pain leading up to it that worried me. But I don't remember the pain either.

I didn't stay dead, of course. It only lasted a few minutes. Survival took a lot longer. I spent four months recovering in the hospital, which gave me plenty of time to think about what had got me there in the first place.

•

ON THE EVENING OF JULY 28, 2013, I was lying on my sofa watching television when I felt a burning sensation in my chest. It only lasted a few minutes, but I had never felt anything like it. I wondered if it was a minor heart attack. My mother died of a heart attack when she was my age; ever since, I feared the same thing would happen to me. Despite that worrying thought, I led a life of excess which, if I was genetically prone to having a heart attack, would surely hasten it. Was a burning chest a symptom of a heart attack? Should I call the medical emergency number?

That was the last thing I remembered—wondering whether I should ring 999. I woke up over a month later in intensive care at University College London Hospital, hooked up to a myriad of beeping machines with my face covered by an oxygen mask. I was having difficulty breathing; it felt like the mask was suffocating me instead of helping me to breathe. A doctor at a computer screen next to my bed asked me what I had been told about my condition. I couldn't talk so I shrugged my shoulders as best I could. He said he was sorry, but he had to tell me that my prognosis was "not good." Not good? What did that mean? It went in one ear and out the other. I fell back to sleep.

Apparently I did ring 999. An ambulance arrived, and I was rushed to the Heart Hospital in Marylebone. I didn't have just one heart attack, I had a series of them. An angioplasty was performed; stents were inserted but there was no blood reflow. During the procedure I had cardiac arrest and was dead for three minutes before being resuscitated. As my heart struggled to survive I went into cardiogenic shock—all my organs started to fail. Pneumonia and sepsis would follow. That was in addition to the illnesses I already had before the heart attacks—HIV, Hepatitis C, COPD, and osteoporosis. I was intubated and put into a medically induced coma. Machines took over the functioning of my body.

I didn't remember any of that when I later regained consciousness. One minute I was relaxing on my sofa, and the next minute I was lying in a hospital bed, being told by a stranger that my prognosis was "not good." My life had changed in an instant. A completely unexpected instant. I had no memory of the heart attacks, the ambulance, the month I spent in a coma at the Heart Hospital, or being transferred to UCLH.

•

IRONICALLY, EARLIER ON THE DAY I had my heart attacks, I had been writing about somebody else's death: an obituary of Andy Warhol's art assistant Ronnie Cutrone. The obituary was for a website on Warhol and his superstars that I had started more than a decade before—warholstars.org—which had become a considerable success. It was the only personal Warhol site on the web and sometimes got over a million hits in one month. It was mentioned in a considerable number of books on the artist and his work. *The New York Times* had referred to it in their obituary for Cutrone, and some of the *Times* readers would be going to my site. I wanted to have an obituary there.

I didn't know Cutrone, but I had recently received an email from somebody who did—a woman named Susan Pile who had worked at Andy Warhol's studio, the infamous Factory, in the 1960s. I met Susan through my website in 2002 and had kept in touch with her ever since. After her Warhol days she had moved to Los Angeles, eventually becoming MGM's executive vice president for worldwide publicity. By the time I met her she had left MGM and had her own PR company. Susan allowed me to publish excerpts on the site from the diaries and letters she kept during her Warhol days. She was a dependable source of information about Warhol's world. In her email alerting me to Cutrone's death, she wrote:

> I knew Ronnie back in the day when he went to School of Visual Arts. First saw him (and Eric Emerson among others) on my debut trip to Factory July 1966, when Andy was filming the color scenes in "The Chelsea Girls." Last time I saw him was mid-'70s on a swing through NYC. He was always really nice. He was the only member of Andy's flock who was younger than I was, except for Nico's Ari, who was four. He hung with the Velvet Underground and cool guys & gals born in 1942. I have read that he befriended Jim Morrison and Jimi Hendrix, both claims 100% plausible.

I thought I might quote her in the obituary, but just then my niece, Anne-Marie, arrived. She was visiting London for a few days on her way to Paris on a trip arranged by her university in Philadelphia. She wanted to drop her luggage off at my flat while she did some last-minute shopping before catching her flight later that afternoon. I put the computer into sleep mode and went with her. I could finish the obituary later.

While we were in one of the shops I felt a bit dizzy and had to stand outside, but other than that I felt fine. When we got back to the flat she called a cab and off she went to Heathrow. I was tired after shopping and just wanted to chill. I turned on the television, lit a joint, and lay back on the sofa.

It was then that I experienced the burning sensation in my chest and evidently rang for the ambulance. I don't remember the ambulance, but I have a faint memory of being in a hospital room and Anne-Marie ringing me on my mobile about returning to London for a few days at the end of her time in Paris. I whispered weakly that I had had a heart attack, and she rang her mother, my sister Carol, in Philadelphia to tell her what had happened.

Carol arrived a few days later, delayed because she didn't have a passport and had to get the hospital to fax the embassy a letter saying I was on life support so she could get an emergency one. I hadn't seen her for more than two decades, and I'm not even sure I saw her then. I had already been put "asleep" and was still "asleep" when she left two weeks later.

Much later, after I had regained consciousness, I thought I could remember seeing her then—but is it possible to remember something that happened in a coma? Some doctors called it a "false memory." And yet

I remembered it distinctly—a feeling of overwhelming sadness because I knew I was dying and I would die without seeing her a final time. Then, suddenly, there she was at the end of a long tunnel, everything outside the tunnel blurred except her face, calling my name: "Gary? Gary . . ."

I tried to reach up to touch her face, but my arm wouldn't move. It didn't matter—the important thing was that I had seen her. Sadness gave way to a feeling of joy, of contentment. I had seen my sister. I could die now . . .

But I didn't die. Somehow I managed to survive.

•

My closest friend in London, whom I will call Cleveland, was listed as my next of kin in my medical records. We had met through a boyfriend I had for a few months in the '90s; I dropped the boyfriend but kept Cleveland as a friend. We had a lot in common in the way of music (R&B) and films (*Paris Is Burning* and Almodóvar), but our strongest shared interest was spliff. He was mixed race; his father was a Rastafarian who came in handy sometimes.

I had been through a lot of dramas with Cleveland during our friendship—or rather I had witnessed a lot of his dramas. He arrived at the hospital before they put me under, and I remembered telling him I didn't think I was going to make it. Sensing a drama that could outdo any other drama he had previously been involved in, Cleveland appointed himself as my main carer and took possession of my phone. Carol later told me that when she arrived at the hospital, he "was on parade with the staff, the compassionate, supreme caregiver with his lotions for your dry skin and later with his shaving equipment . . . I guess the better you looked the more attention he got."

That was so like Cleveland, and so perceptive of Carol. Cleveland loved attention. My illness became as much about him as me. His treatment of my skin with moisturizing lotions would have been endearing—except I had eczema, which he knew, and the lotions were causing my dry skin, not helping it. He refused to believe that expensive skin products could actually be bad for you. Mind you, he hadn't actually shelled out cash for the lotions, he had just collected the free samples that came with the beauty products he bought for himself. When I regained consciousness, my bedside tray was full of small samplers. A nurse told me she had used the same brand of moisturizer at home until she spilled it on a chest of drawers and it took off some of the paint.

•

After I came out of the coma, it took time to adjust to the real world. I drifted in and out of consciousness as the hospital staff appeared above me like ghostly apparitions, asking questions I didn't have the strength to answer—or the ability. A tracheotomy made it impossible to talk. Nurses brought me a pad and paper, but I was too weak to write, or to think. When I tried to write an "A," one slanted line of it took up the whole page, and my hand dropped from exhaustion before I could finish it. They brought a chart to the side of the bed and told me to point at letters to make a word, but by the second letter I forgot what the word was.

At some stage a speech valve was added to my tracheal tube, and I was able to turn a knob and talk for a short period of time. This allowed me to answer questions, but often my answers didn't make sense. The staff were asking questions from the viewpoint of the rational world, and I wasn't in the rational world: I was in a delusional world that would not have made sense to them any more than their world did to me. It's called ICU delirium.

I believed I was in the hospital because I had jumped out of a Syrian airplane during the filming of a popular television talent show, which was being shot in a Syrian airplane because the Syrian government thought it would be good PR during the war. I was part of the audience. At the end of the filming, the host of the show came out and addressed us: "I'm sorry, but we're going to have to kill you now in order to make way for a younger audience." I saw from the airplane window that we were flying low over Heathrow so I opened it and jumped. Syria was not happy that I had managed to escape and started bombing London in retaliation. I asked one of my visitors to bring me a newspaper, thinking I must have made the headlines. I had spent much of my childhood craving fame—I wanted to be a Hollywood star. Fame was finally within my grasp, although not for the reasons I had imagined.

•

I GREW UP IN SIMI VALLEY, a suburb of a suburb an hour's drive from Hollywood. Movies were an important part of my childhood. Every Wednesday evening I sat glued to the television with the rest of my family watching the week's new "Million Dollar Movie," which we treated like a Hollywood premiere. Sometimes we drove down to Hollywood to see a double bill at one of the ornate cinemas. The lobby of the Egyptian was almost as glamorous as the films. As we approached the city on the Hollywood freeway I was mesmerized by the glimmering lights below us and wished I was part of that exciting world. "Fame" would be the answer to all my problems: movie stars didn't have problems.

Afterwards we might drive down to Sunset Boulevard to check out the hippies hanging out on the street. My parents made fun of them, but I wanted to be one. I hated growing up in Simi Valley and dreamed of running away from home when I got older and becoming a hippie. First I'd become a hippie and then a movie star.

One movie that had a big influence on me was *Funny Girl*. Barbra Streisand became my childhood hero: I could relate to the story of an ugly duckling who became a superstar. I was not exactly ugly as a child—with my clothes on I was a cute kid with blond hair and green eyes, though I was skinnier than the other kids and bullied because of it. Also, parts of my body had been badly burned in a childhood accident. My mother tripped over me carrying a percolator of hot coffee on her way to the kitchen table. The spilled coffee missed my face, but I was left with third-degree burn scars on my shoulder, upper chest, and legs. While other California kids were sunbathing on the beach and going to friends' pool parties, I kept myself covered up. I didn't look ugly, I just felt ugly. Someday I too would overcome my problems by becoming the "greatest star," like Streisand had. I remained a Streisand fan as I grew up, so it was no surprise that she got a starring role in one of my ICU delusions.

In my Streisand delusion, I had a new job as a salesperson in the Dwell furniture shop on Tottenham Court Road, not far from where I lived in the real world. The shop was sponsoring Barbra Streisand's UK tour.

Streisand posters were everywhere and her music was playing in the background. On my first day at work I had a stroke, and my supervisor laid me on a bed in a window display to recover. As I lay there, I noticed a metal light fixture with miniature people moving about in the metal surround. I made a note in my mind to get one like it when I got better; it was such a clever idea to have real people in a light fixture. At the moment, though, I didn't have the strength to get out of the bed. I was stuck in a Dwell window display. That was a recurring theme in my delusions—not being able to get off whatever bed, seat, or sofa I was on—just as I wasn't strong enough to get out of my hospital bed in the real world.

The next scene of my Streisand delusion was set in a hotel café in a seaside town that was part of her tour. Paul Rutherford, from the '80s band Frankie Goes to Hollywood, had managed to get me a ticket for her show. As I sat there drinking my coffee, I saw Streisand and a roadie peering out from the stairway from the rooms, presumably to make sure they weren't about to get deluged by fans. I heard the roadie tell Streisand I was Paul's friend and ask her if they should offer me a ride to the gig. Barbra mumbled quietly, "Better not. You know Paul and the type of friends he has. He'd give tickets to anyone. We don't know who that person is." They quickly passed me and went out the front door. I never made it to the concert. I couldn't get up from my seat.

I knew Paul Rutherford in real life. I had met him through Sam McKnight, a hair stylist from London I hung around with in the mid-1980s when I lived in New York. Sam was well-known in the fashion industry. He had worked with most of top designers in catwalk shows or in print. Later he started doing Princess Diana's hair and became even more famous. I had kept in touch with Sam and his group of friends after I moved to London in 1986, and several of them were now visiting me in the hospital. Lilli Anderson was a regular from the start. I remember a short conversation I had with Lilli before they put me into a coma. She was going to Ibiza with Sam for their yearly holiday. Holding my hand, she pleaded, "Please, please, don't die while I'm in Ibiza, Gary."

I always did what Lilli told me to do. I stayed alive.

•

A WEEK OR SO AFTER I WAS TRANSFERRED to UCLH. the tracheotomy tube was removed and I was able to have longer conversations. The procedure for removing the tube was so straightforward, it was almost archaic. While I was fully awake, a nurse slowly withdrew it from the hole in my neck and bandaged up the hole to protect it from infection as it healed.

I could finally have "normal" conversations with people—although normal might be stretching it a bit. The delusions continued. I would begin a conversation sounding completely sane, then start describing someone or something from my delusional world. Real people, like hospital staff or visitors, would often appear in my delusions. I had a delusion about the Dalai Lama, for instance, which included Sam and Lilli and an Andy Warhol painting. The presence of Sam and Lilli made sense because I actually knew them, and the Warhol painting made sense because of my website, but I'm not sure why the Dalai Lama was involved. I had read his autobiography in the 1990s, but why would that stick in my mind after all this time? Had my brain retained everything I had done in the past?

The Dalai Lama delusion began like an old Hollywood movie with a series of black and white newspaper headlines: "Art Thieves on the Loose!" "Art Thieves Strike Again!" Then the headlines became more ominous. The papers reported that the famous hair stylist Sam McKnight was dead. I was shocked. Sam dead? I didn't believe it. Neither did Lilli. She thought it had something to do with the art thieves—that they were trying to steal Sam's Warhol painting. (Real Sam did not own a Warhol painting and was far from dead.) Lilli told me to go to Sam's flat, where all would be revealed.

The door to the flat was opened by the Dalai Lama; it seemed perfectly normal that Sam would know him. He pinched my cheeks like a Polish grandmother and told me what a good person I was. Then he explained the plan. I would pretend to be asleep on Sam's bed. A photographer from the *Evening Standard* (arranged by Lilli, who did fashion PR) would be hiding behind the bedroom door, waiting for the thieves. When they arrived, he would jump out and shoot them using the flash on his old-fashioned press camera. The plan worked. The *Standard* got their photo, and the police came out of nowhere to handcuff the villains. Sam was found in a hidden drawer in the wall of his front room, drugged but alive.

I was convinced I had actually met the Dalai Lama and so persistent when I told the nurses how nice he was that I think some of them actually believed me. Others looked at me worryingly. Eventually a psychologist was brought in. She assured me that what I was going through was normal for intensive-care patients who had suffered major cardiac or respiratory events. I had had both. I wasn't going crazy. I had also had sepsis, which causes delusions. Her continued reassurance, and a slight adjustment to the drugs I was on, hastened my return to the real world. It wasn't long after her intervention that Cleveland returned my phone, which helped me to piece together the events of the previous month, which helped me to piece together my mind.

2. Death by social media

THE FIRST EMAIL I SENT WITH MY PHONE was to Bill Wilson in New York. Bill was an art writer who, under his formal name William S. Wilson, had written an oft-quoted article on Warhol in 1968 in *Art News*—"Prince of Boredom: The Repetitions and Passivities of Andy Warhol." I met him through my website in 2003. In early 2004, I republished his Warhol article with a new introduction by him. Our initial correspondence turned into a friendship; by the time I ended up in the hospital, we had been writing to each other daily for more than a decade.

Although he knew Warhol in the '60s, Bill was mostly associated with the artist Ray Johnson, the founder of the "New York Correspondance School," a collage artist who commonly sent his collages through the mail; recipients often added to them and returned them or sent them on to someone else. He was a friend of Warhol's—they had both worked as graphic artists—but unlike Andy, Ray rejected the commerciality of the art world. His work was increasingly sought after, particularly since his suicide in January 1995. Bill was the last person Ray spoke to before diving off the Sag Harbor bridge and swimming to his death. Although some art writers conjectured that Ray committed suicide because he had AIDS, there was no hard evidence of it. Even if he was HIV positive, combination retroviral therapy, introduced in 1994, gave HIV patients a lifeline. Some people, including myself, questioned whether he had committed suicide at all—there was no suicide note.

The message I sent to Bill from my hospital bed was

short, but all I was capable of at the time: "Hi Bill, just wanted to say hello. Lots of love, Gary." He responded immediately: "Just wanted to say hello! There's no 'just' in that HELLO. My heart stopped when I saw your name, a rather inappropriate expression but it felt that dramatic. I wanted to get to London more than 'just' to see a Cézanne . . ."

The mention of Cézanne was a reference to his visit to London in 2005, the first time we met each other in person. One of the things we did was to see "Les Grandes Baigneuses" at the National Gallery. Bill's mention of that visit made me realize how much I missed him. Bill was eighty-one years old when I had my heart attacks; I was fifty-seven. He had already had a stroke by the time we started corresponding. Despite the difference in our ages and locations, I felt closer to him than I did to my younger friends. Researching warholstars, I had become so absorbed in the New York art scene of the 1960s that the world of "now" had largely retreated into the distance.

After emailing with Bill I turned my attention to my Facebook page. Maybe something there would help me remember the events of the past month. When Cleveland took possession of my phone, it was already logged in to my account, and he was able to post directly to my page. Kate McIlwain, another friend I had met through Sam McKnight in the '80s, had also posted health updates. Looking at their postings, it seemed like Kate and Cleveland were in competition with each other about who was my closer friend and who knew more about my health situation. Cleveland thought he knew me best because of all the time we'd spent together after I moved to London; Kate thought she knew me best because we had lived together in

New York. It was largely because of Kate that I moved to London in the first place.

Kate didn't work in the fashion business like most of Sam's English friends. I knew her as the "crisp girl": she took samples of flavored potato chips to offices in Manhattan, hoping they would place a large order and she would get a commission. She hung around with Sam's group because she had been to school with one of the models he knew, Ana Drummond. Kate was a "fag hag"—a straight girl who liked to hang out with gay guys. When I met her in 1985, she still retained elements of the punk look from the previous decade—bleached white hair, lots of cheap makeup, and always dressed in black. If something wasn't black, she dyed it black. She was the life of the party even when there wasn't one. She got very loud when drunk.

Kate and Cleveland both tried to be as positive as possible when posting news about my health. That was partly my fault. When I handed Cleveland my phone before I was put to sleep, I weakly told him not to be too negative, recalling a scene in *Paris Is Burning* when Eileen Ford warns, "When people ask you how you feel, don't tell them if you're sick, 'cause they don't really care."

Cleveland took optimism to another level. My destiny seemed more dependent on how many "likes" his postings got than on what was actually happening; positive updates got more "likes" than negative ones. On August 3rd, for instance, two days after he announced that I was in a "critical state," he wrote: "He is still sedated but there has been nothing but good news from his nurses. Thank you and have a wonderful evening. Watch this space!" He sounded like the the host of a television show. Kate echoed Cleveland's comment:

"He's doing really well, folks. We are filled with hope." There was no mention of the sepsis, pneumonia, and general organ failure I was fighting at the time, or even that I was in a coma.

•

My main supporter from the world of Andy Warhol was Joe Dallesandro, who posted messages of support almost daily on his page or mine. I knew Joe through my website. We didn't correspond regularly, as I did with Bill, so I was surprised by the extent of his attention on social media. Joe had been a counter-culture hero of mine ever since I first saw him playing the long-haired junkie in *Trash* when I was a student at Berkeley in the 1970s. Although *Trash* was advertised as a Warhol film, the director was actually Paul Morrissey. Warhol was more like the producer; he financed it and lent it his name for publicity purposes. I fell in love with Joe when I saw the film. Who would have thought then that my underground hero would be sending messages of support to me in a hospital in London more than thirty years later? Who would have thought that the internet would even exist?

On September 14th, Joe wrote to his 20,000+ followers: "I need some help here. A friend in need, Gary Comenas, needs us to raise our collective thoughts and remind God that he still has much to do on this earth. Just 30 seconds is all I ask and then we leave it in God's hands." His posting was accompanied by a recording of Bettye LaVette singing "Wish You Were Here." Other posts by him included attachments of Joe Cocker singing "You Are So Beautiful," Aretha Franklin singing "I Say a Little Prayer," an old photograph of him with a cute kitten (I forgave him for thinking I liked cute kittens),

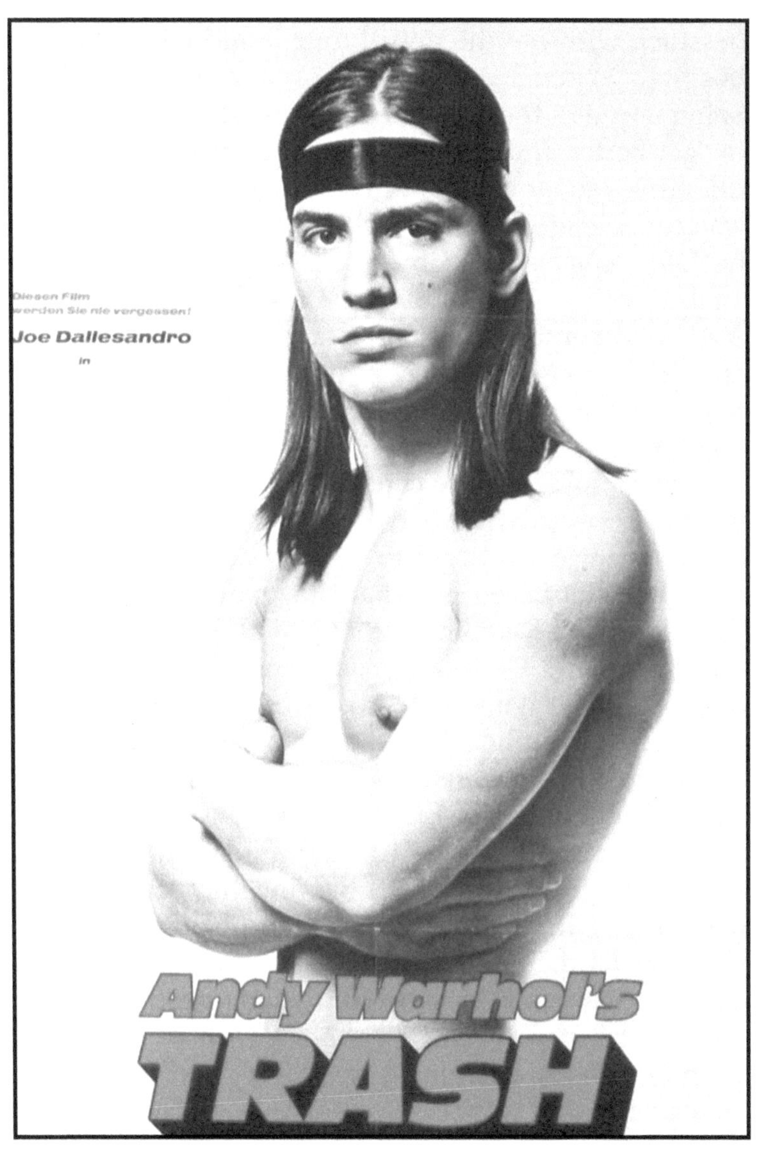

and a video of "I Will Survive" from *Priscilla, Queen of the Desert.*

I was in London and Joe was in Los Angeles, but

he stuck with me the entire four months I was in the hospital. When I complained on social media about being bored in the hospital, he encouraged me publicly to "get better and get up and get out of there," to "tell the nurses to let you go.". I was surprised he thought I was capable of going anywhere, but realized later that he had been seduced by Cleveland's overly positive analysis of my situation. After I finally got out, he told me, "I remember those messages Cleveland posted and how wrong or misleading some were . . . I did not realize you were still so sick. So it was kinda weird he'd do that."

Cleveland and Kate continued to update people on my health even when I had my phone and could be contacted directly. It got to where people were telling me how I felt based on what they were being told by Cleveland and Kate, instead of just asking me. I didn't mind Kate and Cleveland commenting on my health, but they did it with such authority that I felt that my illness had been hijacked. At one stage my own sister was telling me how I felt, based on updates Kate sent to a chat group that didn't include me.

Eventually I put a notice up on my Facebook page telling people that I was still alive and they could contact me directly if they had a question about my health. Kate was livid. She sent me a text: "If your post is about the fact that I talk to your family, you need to talk to me about it if you have a problem with it! . . . We're supposed to be friends so why don't you talk to me instead of passive-aggressive postings on Facebook???! Rather childish isn't it? . . ."

I thought it was a strange message to send to somebody who was bedridden in the hospital. I looked back at what I had posted. I hadn't named anyone—not

Kate or Cleveland or anyone else. I noticed that Sam had "liked" my comment and wondered if that fed into Kate's outrage. Sam didn't need Kate's updates—he relied on Lilli, who visited me almost every day. I don't know what I would have done without Lilli. But in regard to Kate and Cleveland, I wondered if they would have cared as much if social media hadn't existed.

I also wondered how much Kate's support had to do with Joe Dallesandro's. Before my illness she had noticed a poster in my flat advertising *Trash* with a shirtless Joe in all his long-hair glory. "Whoa! Who is that?" she asked. My heart attacks gave her an excuse to be in contact with him. She continued to write to him even after I got out. He liked Kate—he thought she was "wonderful" while I was in a coma; if he was ever sick, he'd want her in "his corner." As time wore on, he told me, "She never mentions you anymore. She only checks in to say hello . . ." Eventually he stopped responding to her messages. "Have you heard from Joe, lately?" she'd ask me sheepishly. "No," I lied.

The friendship with Joe I developed during my hospitalization enabled me to get answers to questions about his Warhol career that I had previously been too reticent to ask. For instance, I never understood why he hadn't pursued a career in mainstream Hollywood films, given how successful he was during his Warhol days. He told me that part of the reason was that Andy Warhol and Paul Morrissey were telling "any directors who would listen" that he "couldn't do a script and was a drug addict." According to Joe, when Francis Ford Coppola rang Warhol's offices trying to get in touch with him for the first *Godfather* film, he was told that Joe was a "drug addict" and "couldn't read." Although Joe did appear in *The Cotton Club*, he thought Warhol and Morrissey were preventing him from getting roles because "their cash cow had escaped and they were trying hard to derail my career and get me back."

Most of the films he made post-Warhol were in Europe, including a starring role in *Je t'aime moi non plus*, directed by Serge Gainsbourg. He was still friends with his co-star, Jane Birkin. I assumed he got royalties from those films, in addition to his Warhol films, but when I asked him about it, he told me:

> No, I don't [get] royalties from Euro films, none from Morrissey-Warhol films. I get small $10 or $20 checks occasionally. I still am trying to get Paul to honor the 5% he promised on all 5 films when they talked me into doing *Frankenstein* and *Dracula*. They had a deal with the money people that I had to star in the films or they'd take the money off the table. I'm still waiting for my percentage 40 years later. Which is why in Andy's diary he always talks about "Joe called asking for money" like I was some beggar, when in fact I was trying to get my percentage.

The five films were *Trash, Heat, Flesh, Dracula,* and *Frankenstein*. "Paul owns those," Joe said. "I had a film in Europe I put on hold to do *Frankenstein/Dracula*. Which is why we filmed them back to back really fast."

Instead of becoming a Hollywood star, Joe ended up as the manager of a residential hotel in Los Angeles that sounded like it mostly catered to senior citizens on welfare. He was also the handyman. During one of his repair jobs, he told me he "busted up" his elbow "trying to get up on the roof to clean out a gutter in the rain . . ." It didn't seem right that a Warhol superstar like Joe should end up having to do such things.

3. New York

A LOT OF THE COMMENTS ON SOCIAL MEDIA were by people who knew me from my Warhol website; the majority of my hospital visitors were English friends I had met through Sam in New York. Before I went into the hospital, the '80s friends had no idea about the website, and the Warhol friends had no idea of what I had been up to in the '80s. It wasn't until I became ill that the two worlds began to mix.

Most of Sam's group had moved back to England by the end of the decade, but one English friend, David Strettell, who meant more to me than any of the others, had stayed in New York. David had been a photographic assistant for Mario Testino and Pamela Hanson. After I left and made London my home, he worked for Magnum, then opened his own photography bookshop in Manhattan, Dashwood Books.

One morning a nurse arrived at my bedside with the hospital phone and said, "It's someone named David." She helped me hold the handset to my ear as I mumbled his name into the mouthpiece. He laughed. I probably sounded as out-of-it from all the hospital drugs I was on as I used to sound from the street drugs we took together in New York.

"How are you today?" he asked. "Can I come and visit?"

"Are you in London?" I replied, surprised.

There was a pause, then he said, "You do realize that I saw you yesterday, don't you? Don't you remember?" No, I didn't remember. That happened a lot. I forgot things, even visits from friends who meant as much to me as David. When I thanked Lilli for visiting me as if it was her first time, she reminded me that she'd been there at least nine times previously.

•

I HADN'T SEEN DAVID for quite a while before his hospital visit. I suppose he was there for the same reason so many of my friends from the past came out of the woodwork: they thought I was dying. The only person who was sure that I wasn't going to die was me. Given the state of my health, I'm not sure why I was so certain, but I was.

The doctors had managed to cure the pneumonia and sepsis, but I continued to have problems breathing and was still bedridden: I couldn't stand or walk. I had to be turned over in bed by a nurse so I didn't get bedsores, because I was too weak to roll from one side to the other by myself. I also still had to rely on the nurses to supply the dreaded bedpan as needed. Not only did they have to position the bedpan under me, they'd have to wipe my ass afterwards. I tried to make the situation better by telling myself that I was an animal and that all animals had bowel movements; people picked up their dog's shit so why shouldn't they deal with mine? But it didn't make it any better. I was still embarrassed.

I wondered why anybody would want a job that involved cleaning a stranger's ass. When I first came out of the coma, I thought about all the effort my nurses and doctors had put into my care. The gratitude I felt was stronger than any other feeling I'd had in my life—stronger than love, sadness, joy, or anger. I never felt unlucky for having had the heart attacks, I just felt lucky to have survived them.

When David arrived later in the day, a nurse propped me up on pillows because I was too weak do it myself. We had both aged considerably since the '80s, of course. David's beautiful thick hair was now grey, and he had developed a noticeable middle-age spread. It didn't matter. He was still the same David, despite the fact that he was married now and had a daughter. I don't remember what we talked about in the hospital. When I asked him later, he said I seemed pretty normal until the end of his visit, when I whispered to him, "All of the nurses are trying to give me blow jobs." My delusions hadn't quite ended by that point.

•

SEEING DAVID IN THE HOSPITAL took me back to a time I spent in New York that I can only describe as magical. It lasted less than two years, from spring 1985 to the end of 1986, but it would remain in my head and my heart as something special for the rest of my life. David was very much a part of it. Usually feelings are caused by events, but during that period the feelings came first. They were amplified by a new drug that had just appeared on the scene: ecstasy.

I thought I had given up drugs by the spring of '85. But soon after I came off a methadone maintenance program around that time, my ex-boyfriend, Jim Bresse, showed up at the welfare hotel I was staying in—the Hotel 17—and asked if I wanted to check out Steve Rubell's new club with him and a new friend, Sam McKnight. I had read about the opening of the club, the Palladium, in the *Times*. Jim was going to get some ecstasy, which I had never tried. I told him drugs didn't interest me anymore. Hadn't he heard? I was "clean." I was finally "normal." And I certainly had no desire to start clubbing again. Who was Sam McKnight, anyway? I'd never heard of him. Jim explained, he was English, an internationally famous high-fashion hair stylist: "He's worked with everybody, all the big designers. But he's not at all fashiony." I didn't want to meet any new people; I was still recovering from all the new people I had met before.

"You don't have to take drugs if you don't want to," Jim said. "You'll like Sam."

I wondered why he was being so persistent. Sometimes I felt sorry for Jim. Although he knew a lot of people on the club scene, he often seemed lonely. He was like a lot of people in New York who used nightclubbing as an antidote for loneliness. I felt guilty for refusing his invitation. Maybe a night out wasn't such a bad idea. Yes, I wanted to stay clean, but did I need to avoid life in order to avoid drugs? I didn't have to take ecstasy if I didn't want to, and meeting someone from London made the evening sound more palatable. So I went to Sam's with Jim. It changed my life. Ultimately, it was why I ended up in a hospital in London instead of New York.

•

SAM DIDN'T LIVE FAR FROM THE 17, so Jim and I walked to his apartment. When we got there, Sam introduced us to a friend of his who was visiting from London, a fashion editor named Kim Hunt who had worked for *Honey* magazine in the U.K. and the English version of *Elle*. Kim was beautiful. With her jet black hair and a slim figure accentuated by a jet black dress, she could have been a model if she hadn't been a fashion editor. Sam looked surprisingly average for an internationally known hair stylist. He was short, slightly balding, and casually dressed. You probably wouldn't have noticed him in a crowd, but his personality more than made up for his nondescript appearance. He exuded a natural charisma that drew people toward him. As I got to know him better, I realized he was like the Gatsby of the New York fashion scene. Every London model who came to work in Manhattan seemed to end up at his apartment. He would talk to anyone who talked to him, but he didn't suffer fools gladly: if he thought someone was a fake, he'd be the first to "take the piss" out of them. Jim was right. Although Sam worked in the fashion business, he wasn't at all "fashiony." I don't recall either him or Kim talking about fashion that night.

After a couple of drinks, the "E" was brought out. I was apprehensive and only took half a pill, just to see what it was like, completely forgetting Jim's earlier comment that I didn't have to take it if I didn't want to. Besides, ecstasy was hardly heroin.

It wasn't long before I was asking for the other half of the pill. Ecstasy was different back then. Purer. It wasn't like the speedy stuff that ravers would buy from dealers later on. It was more of a head trip—like acid but without the hallucinations or lack of control. There was a reason it was called ecstasy. We walked to the club from Sam's place; by the time we got there, the four of us felt like old friends.

There was a long line of people waiting to get into the Palladium, but that wasn't a problem. Nothing was. Obstacles ceased to exist. Events worked out automatically in our favor while we were high. Haoui Montaug was at the door, saw Jim, and waved us in. In those days New York's club scene was ruled by Haoui and Anita Sarko, the ex-Mudd Club DJ, who did the door at the Palladium's VIP space, the Mike Todd Room, once the office of Elizabeth Taylor's third husband. Haoui, who looked like a game show host or someone out of vaudeville, also hosted a cabaret show at Danceteria called No Entiendes. Anita looked like an old-fashioned showgirl—or a drag queen.

Jim showed us around as if he owned the place. New York had been mixing the club world with the art world, clubs becoming more like art galleries and galleries more like clubs. Kenny Scharf murals adorned the basement of the Palladium, and a large Basquiat painting dominated one wall of the Mike Todd Room.

"Watch this," Jim said as we entered the main floor, which was decorated like a scene from *Saturday Night Fever*, with booths like an old-fashioned diner and a tiny dance floor. As we looked, the "set" rose up into the rafters and the room was transformed into one giant dance floor. Not that we were on the dance floor for very long. After that first night, we'd go straight upstairs to the Mike Todd Room, where we were allowed to do just about anything we wanted without having to hide the fact that we were stoned out of our minds. It became our home away from home.

•

A COUPLE OF WEEKS LATER, Sam moved into a new flat with a large roof terrace that overlooked some of New York's most iconic buildings, including both the Chrysler Building and the Empire State Building. I described the scene there in my diary:

> July 5, 1985 — Yesterday was the Fourth of July. Jim and I went to a barbecue on Sam's terrace. Kim was there of course, and Ana, Amanda, Anita and Jacqui and eleven hits of E—as well as the gay neighbors. I talked to the Swedish one for half an hour without understanding a single word except for "Canada" and "foreign correspondent."

Kim was the loveliest one there. I liked the way she wrapped her arms around my waist and squeezed, saying how skinny I was. Dancing on the roof with fireworks and fairy lights in the background turned our feet black. Anita's rhinestones sparkled in every direction. She lives alone and wakes up generally happy but sometimes it's not enough, she told me . . . Her eyes are always as black as two tunnels.

We went to the Palladium (of course), and was it last night that we went to Area? Then back to the Palladium . . .

Amanda was a friend of model Ana Drummond. Jacqui Lefton, a stylist from England, lived with Helen Roberts, a fashion journalist. Other regulars at Sam's included English fashion models like Jo Kelley, Victoria Lockwood, Cecilia Chancellor, and Ana's roommate, Lindsey Thurlow. Some of the them were well-known in the fashion business; they all had their fifteen minutes of fame eventually. Victoria went on to marry Princess Diana's brother; Cecilia was the daughter of the journalist Alexander Chancellor and cousin of the actress Anna Chancellor; Ana Drummond would become famous as a Calvin Klein model; her brother, Miggy, was in the band Curiosity Killed the Cat. Lindsey's boyfriend was Gavin Rossdale, who later started the band Bush and, even later, married (and divorced) Gwen Stefani.

Jo Kelley eventually left the fashion business and raised a family in London with her husband, Bruce Carter. Jo and Bruce were regular visitors to the hospital after I became ill and two of the most charitable human beings I have ever met. As the models in our group got older, and particularly after they left New York, many

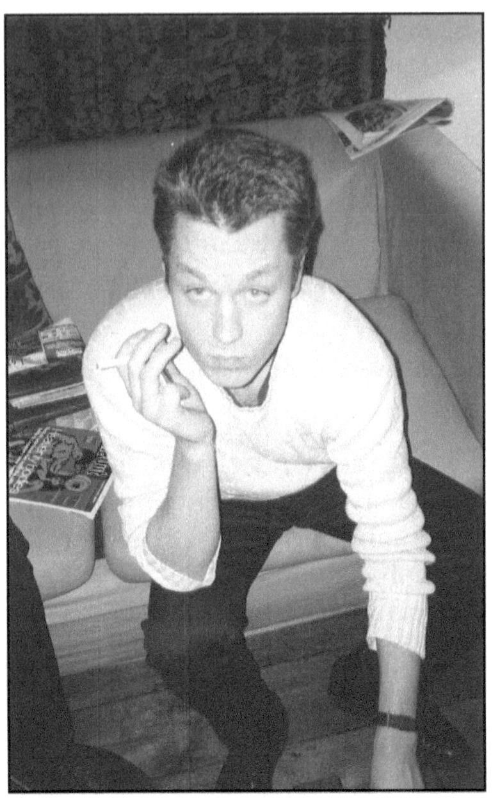

David Strettell

of their careers faltered, but in the '80s they were the next big thing.

When Sam's next door neighbors moved out, David Strettell's sister, a makeup artist named Jo Strettell, moved in, sharing the apartment with an English model, Jeny Howorth. Jo and Jeny combined their terrace with Sam's, giving us twice as much room for partying. It wasn't long afterwards that David arrived from England and moved in with his sister and Jeny.

I fell in love with David the minute I met him, but so did everyone else, male or female. He looked like he had just stepped out of public school and was on his way to Oxford or Cambridge. He was into books and art more than fashion; he turned me on to Joseph Conrad, and I turned him on to Jane Bowles. Many years later, we would get together sometimes when he was in London, and whenever we did, it was like the '80s again: we never lost the strong bond of friendship we developed back then.

•

Our nightly routine rarely changed. A core group of us would meet on Sam's terrace in the evening for drinks and then walk down to the Palladium. After a night out, it was back to Sam's to chill out in his upstairs bedroom. "Moments in Love" by the Art of Noise was our theme song and *Blade Runner* our favorite video—along with tapes of the British TV show *Coronation Street* that Sam brought back from England when he went there to work. As far as Sam was concerned, Bette Lynch was God.

I remember one morning, when we were all lying in bed together with the sun coming up, Sam put on "The Age of Aquarius" by the Fifth Dimension and opened the blinds exactly at the point where they were singing "Let the sunshine in." We were still so out of it that it seemed miraculous that the sun would be shining at the same time as the song. We all "oohed" and "aahed" until he finally closed the blinds. Paul Rutherford was there that night with his boyfriend, Joe Batty, and his press officer, Regine Moylett, who would reappear in my life years later.

We went out every night that year. Staying in was akin to death. There was so much going on and we didn't want to miss out on a single millisecond of it.

4. A dime a dance

A LOT OF THE BRITS stayed in New York for Christmas that year instead of visiting their families in London. They wanted to experience a real New York Christmas, like in the movies. I think they were expecting *Miracle on 34th Street,* but it was more like "Is That All There Is?" Christmas lasts about five minutes in New York; in London it lasts a couple of weeks.

On Christmas night we met up with our friends Jacqui and Helen at their place before going to a Japanese restaurant for dinner. I was surprised when the model Emma Woollard showed up at Jacqui's with Matt Dillon. I didn't think Emma was as good-looking as the other models we hung around with and not nearly as interesting, but Matt was. Like Lindsey's boyfriend, Gavin Rossdale, Matt was another adorable straight boy who was gay-friendly. He hadn't made *Drugstore Cowboy* yet, but he had been in *Rumble Fish* and *The Flamingo Kid* so he was already pretty famous. I think Emma got off on his fame, but to us he just seemed like a nice, friendly guy.

I wanted to give Sam and Jeny a Christmas present, but I didn't have much money. I had just started a new job at the New York office of the National Film Board of Canada, so I made them a tape of some of some of the films they distributed. One of the films was *The Big Snit,* an animated short featuring two characters arguing over a game of Scrabble as the world falls apart around them. One of the characters' tray of letters is all Es. The woman he is playing with, presumably his wife, takes her eyes out, like a lorgnette, and shakes them, making a rattling sound. When people got high on E, their eyes

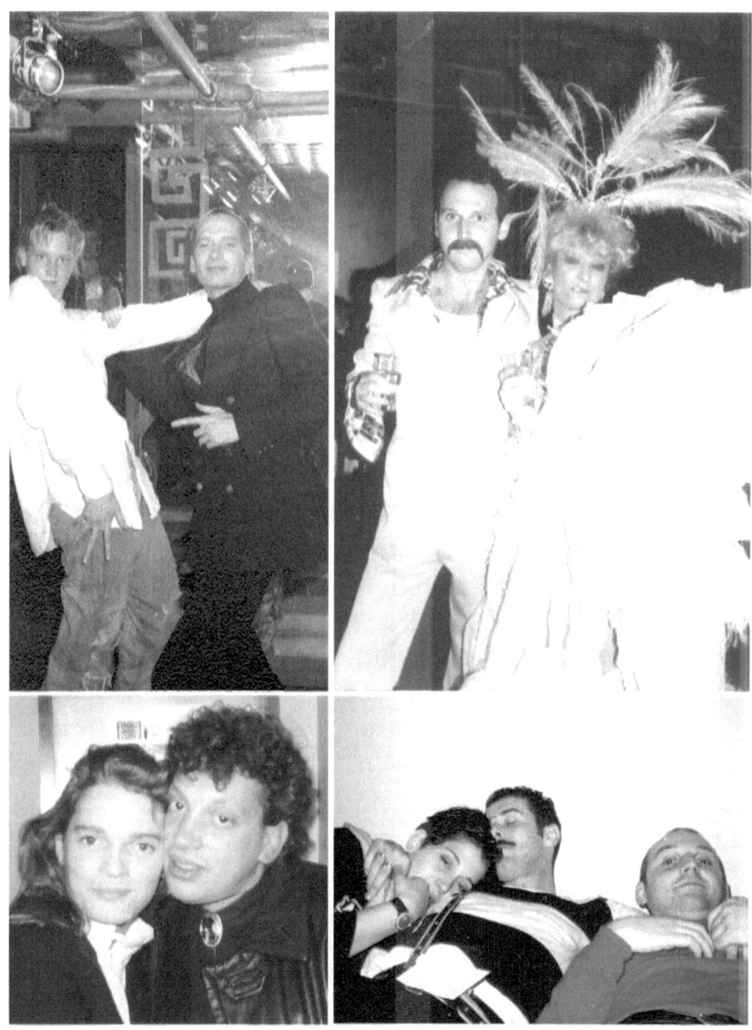

Palladium Nights. Top left: Jo Kelley and me downstairs in the Kenny Scharf-designed basement; top right: Sam McKnight and Anita Sarko at the Dime a Dance party in the Mike Todd Room; bottom left: Victoria Lockwood and Haoui Montaug; bottom right: Helen Roberts, Paul Rutherford, and Sam McKnight chilling on a futon on Sam's floor after a night out.

tended to roll upwards; "Stop shaking your eyes!," they'd yell, imitating the hand motions of the character from *The Big Snit*. The expression spread through the E crowd at the Palladium and beyond, later reemerging as the name of a club night in London.

•

IN ADDITION TO SAM'S FRIENDS, another group of Brits hung out in the Mike Todd Room when they were in town—usually referred to as the "Boy George crowd." Quite a few of them had lived in a squat on Warren Street in London that was often associated with George, although he never actually lived there. Most of them had been regulars at the Blitz club in the late '70s and Taboo in the '80s. The Wag was another popular club in London in the 1980s that a lot of the Blitz kids went to. When Anita Sarko decided to have a "Dime a Dance" party in the Mike Todd Room, she invited the Wag's DJ, Fat Tony, to do the music.

Tony had quite an entourage of friends from England when he DJ'd at the party—including three people from George's crowd who later on became friends of mine: Ray Allington, Paul Lonergan, and Lee Sheldrick. Like George, all three did heroin, which was becoming increasingly popular in the fashion business. There was a kind of reverse snobbery between the E users and the H users. The ecstasy crowd looked down on the heroin users, who thought they were superior to the ecstasy crowd.

Ray was a hair stylist. Paul and Lee called themselves fashion stylists, although I'm not sure how much styling Paul actually did. Lee sometimes assisted Kim Bowen during fashion shoots or music videos. He was a lot of fun when he wasn't nodding off. Sam and I had a great

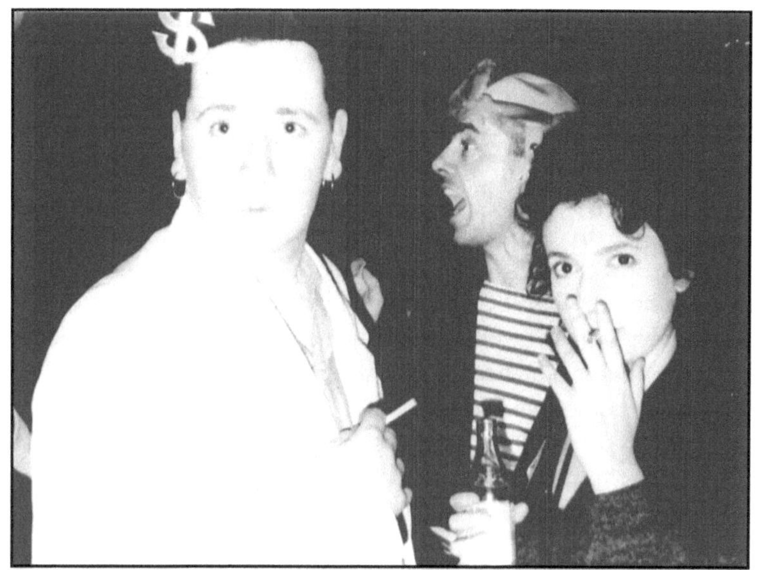

Fat Tony, Paul Lonergan, and Jacqui Lefton in the Mike Todd Room at the Palladium.

time with him one night in New York when he switched H for E. Most of Lee's attention was focused on Sam—I wasn't fashionable or famous enough. I think that's why Sam liked me: I wasn't "fashiony."

•

I STAYED FRIENDS WITH PAUL LONERGAN after I moved to London; he was one of my regular visitors in the hospital after my heart attacks. Boy George described Paul in his autobiography as "a sad-eyed queen with haggard film-star looks and a toxic tongue" who sometimes shared George's stash of heroin.[1] Paul was livid when he read that description. He didn't mind the bit about sharing

1 Boy George and Spencer Bright, *Take It Like a Man: The Autobiography of Boy George* (London: Sidgwick & Jackson, 1995), p. 392

George's stash, but hated the description of him looking "haggard" even if it was softened by "film-star." Paul did look a bit haggard for his age with his droopy eyes and lined face; but with his deep voice and Mancunian accent, he didn't have any problems getting trade on the gay scene in New York. My diary mentioned meeting him for the the first time:

> February 9, 1986: Thursday night (the night I wasn't going out) I stayed at the Palladium until 3:30 am . . . It was Dime a Dance night at the Palladium, Anita's party . . . I took some pictures with a camera I had got at a thrift store. The only person who objected was Teri Toye: "I mean really, Gary, it's like taking pictures of a drag queen at a nightclub."
>
> More drinks. Spliff. Paul Lonergan approached me on a rampage. He was wearing a red aviator's fur hat: "You're Jim's ex-boyfriend, you disgusting pig. I hate you and worst of all, you're ugly, ugly, ugly . . ."

Teri was a sex-change: hence the "drag queen" comment. She didn't hang around with Sam's crowd but was signed to the same agency, Click, as a lot of the English models he knew. Teri was more into H than E.

Paul's "I hate you" tirade presumably had to do with Jim Bresse, who after taking a break from heroin had started up again. God knows what Jim had told Paul about me. Having given up heroin, I had aligned myself with Sam's crowd, although I was beginning to wonder whether E was that much different than H. The effect was different, but I worried that I had simply substituted one addiction for another.

•

DRUGS HAD BROUGHT OUR GROUP TOGETHER but ultimately split us up as well. Jo Strettell was the first person to leave the group when she got involved with someone Sam nicknamed "Max Headroom" after the computer-enhanced host of a British television show. I never learned his real name. Jo and "Max" would stay at home, getting out of it on their own, while the rest of us went to the Palladium. Jo was married to a photographer in London so it was a bit disturbing to see her spending so much time with Max.

David became increasingly irritated by his sister's activities. Jo could get into Sam's apartment via the shared balcony. When she started bringing strangers back to Sam's when he wasn't there, David was outraged. In my diary I wrote, "Jo's let a massive amount of strangers around, messing up Sam's house for David to clean up today . . . the place is a mess with disgusting people."

David wanted to move. I had to move because my sublease was up. A Swiss friend, Walter Ramos, whom Sam dubbed "Swiss Miss," was also looking for a place to live. So was Paul Lonergan. Paul and Swiss had been an "item" at one point but were just friends now. In spite of his insults at our first meeting, Lonergan and I had become good friends. Kate McIlwain, the "crisps girl," also needed a place to live. The five of us—David, Swiss, Paul, Kate, and I—moved into a cockroach-infested ground-floor apartment on 12th Street and Avenue A. We carpeted the bedroom with wall-to-wall mattresses so everyone would have a place to sleep.

The area we lived in—"Alphabet City"—was overrun with Puerto Rican drug dealers and heroin addicts looking to score. Every afternoon the dealers began plying their trade across the street from our apartment. The dope was sold in small glassine envelopes with names like Big D, Liberty, and Green Tape, each controlled by a different gang. This meant that buyers knew more or less what they were getting—quality control for the heroin crowd. Paul was already addicted to heroin when he moved in, and it didn't take long for David and me to follow his example. All we had to do to score was to cross the street.

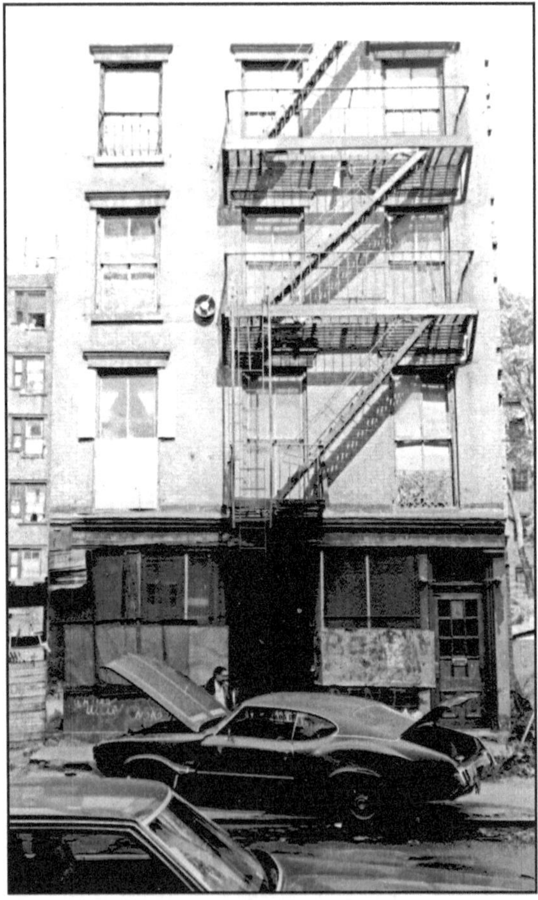

Our view across 12th Street

5. The funeral

Two weeks after Paul and the rest of us moved to 12th Street in 1986, I got a phone call from "Jim." I knew it wasn't Jim Bresse, who had gone home to Buffalo to try to clean up. It turned out to be my sister's husband, with worrying news:

> "Hi Gary, how are you?"
> "Fine. How are you?" (Pause) "Who are you?"
> "Jim."
> "Jim who?"
> "Oh, I'm sorry. It's Jim—Carol's husband. I'm at Carol's. She's pretty upset. Your mom is sick. She's had a heart attack."

I was shocked. My mother was only fifty-five. Jim gave me the number of the hospital my mother was in, and I spoke to a nurse who told me her condition was "stable." I thought that was good news; later, during my own hospitalization, I learned that "stable" could mean anything. The next time I rang, I was told that she had been taken off life support. Again, I imagined that meant she was getting better. But a few days later I got a call from Carol: "Gary, Mom is dead."

My brain struggled to grasp the news. How could she be dead? I thought she was "stable." The words "mother" and "death" went through my head but I couldn't link the one to the other. Death didn't exist in the '80s. We were too busy having fun to think about death. Nobody on the club scene talked about deaths in their families. Nobody talked about their families at all. Manhattan was where you went to escape from your family.

When I was lying in a London hospital bed recovering from my own heart attacks years later, I got a taste of what my mother must have gone through. My younger sister, Cathy, who still lived with my parents at the time, told me that some of the things she said in the hospital didn't made sense. I could understand that after having experienced ICU delirium myself. Who really knows what goes on in the minds of the dying? In a strange sort of way, I got solace later from the fact that my mother had probably left the world mentally before she left it physically.

I booked my flight home the next day. It wasn't the first time I'd been back since leaving Simi Valley, but it would be the first time my mother wouldn't be there. She had been my security blanket through most of my life. I could always depend on her when I got into trouble. Before I lived in New York, I lived in San Francisco—where I became addicted to heroin the first time. Whenever I needed money, my mother sent it by Western Union without asking too many questions. "Don't tell your father," she'd say. She must have known that most of it went to support my habit.

•

I WAS IN A DAZE during most of the flight. I had a hit before I left—I had only been using intermittently by that point and hoped that I wouldn't have withdrawals during the funeral. When we landed, I got a cab outside the terminal, and it wasn't long before we reached Simi Valley. I couldn't help noticing how similar most of the houses were, variations on the same fake-Spanish theme, like the average middle-class homes you'd see in TV shows about average middle-class families—except those were movie sets. Our house just looked like one. We lived in the Santa Susana section of Simi Valley, although most people just called the whole area Simi. A lot of cowboy films and TV shows were shot in the hills that surrounded the valley. Spahn's Ranch, the movie set that became the home of the Manson family, was located in those hills. When we were kids, we went horseback riding at Spahn's Ranch. My older brother John's Volkswagen was stolen by the Mansons. Before the Mansons, there was another cult in the area, the Fountain of the World religious cult, which had already been blown up by a disgruntled member by the time we moved to Simi. When our family drove past the ruins, I both dreaded and hoped that I'd see a ghost.

There was definitely something creepy about Simi Valley. The rural setting may have been the American dream for some families, but I felt threatened by it. Paranoia was almost encouraged when I was growing up. If a serial killer didn't get you, then the Russians would. At school there were regular drills in case of a nuclear attack; an alarm would go off and we'd crawl under our desks, as though a wooden desktop could protect us from radiation. I remember watching John F. Kennedy's speech about the Cuban Missile Crisis and being gripped with fear. I was six years old, too young to understand what was going on, except that it was the end of the world.

I dropped off my bags and walked to the mortuary by myself. Mom's coffin was in a private room so her friends and family could pay their last respects. A member of the staff went with me into the room. We stood in silence for a few minutes before it sunk in: I was looking at a box that contained a dead body, and that dead body was my mother. The coffin looked so small.

"Would you like me to open it?" the staff member asked. "We can open it for family members."

"Yes," I answered, without hesitation.

And there she was—my mother—lying in a padded box. Except that it wasn't my mother. It was a lifeless statue that resembled my mother but wasn't my mother. I stared and stared, trying to see the mother I knew as a child, but all I saw was a body that might as well have been a chunk of concrete. They had tried to create the illusion of life with makeup, which only made her look even more lifeless.

"They've done a good job with the makeup," the staff member commented.

"Yes," I said, automatically. That's all I said. Who cared about the makeup?

I didn't cry. There was nothing to cry about. I felt no emotions at all toward the meaningless statue I was presented with. So that's what really happens to all of us in the end, I thought, we end up like a meaningless block of concrete. How could anybody who had actually seen a dead body think there was an afterlife? One minute you're here, and the next minute you're gone. That's all life is. A small moment in time that disappears one day and is eventually forgotten forever. I realized that the same thing that happened to my mother would also happen to me. Someday I would also be dead. I asked the woman to close the coffin and walked home, feeling nothing.

The funeral service was as much of a disappointment as the viewing. The priest read from a standard script, never having known my mother when she was alive. He described her life in religious terms when she hadn't been religious at all. My father asked us who he was talking about. Afterwards people came back to our house, most of them strangers. I'd been away for such a long time, I had lost track of my mother's life and friends. A neighbor I remembered stopped by to contribute a cake she had baked. But she couldn't stay, she was too upset. She was sobbing as she left.

My father sat in an armchair, crying—more of a howl than a cry, like a wounded animal. My mother's friends looked at each other not knowing what to do. Someone asked me to take him into the bedroom. I helped him up and led him to the bedroom with his arm over my shoulder. We had never been particularly affectionate toward each other. I felt slightly disgusted by his touch. As I laid him on the bed, he started apologizing: "I'm so sorry, Gary, I'm so sorry." I thought he was apologizing for all the arguments we had while I was growing up, often about the Vietnam War. I grew up watching the war on television; my father defended America's actions by saying things like, "Orientals don't have the same respect for human life as we do." I was a pacifist, of course. Although our arguments about Vietnam had taken place two decades earlier, they were the first thing I thought about when he said he was sorry. "Don't worry, Dad, that's okay, I don't blame you about the war," I told him. He paused like he was trying to figure out what I meant. Then he said, "No, I don't mean that, I mean . . . everything. I'm so sorry about everything."

I was relieved when it was time to go home, to my real home in Manhattan. Back in New York, I kissed the ground outside the Port Authority terminal where the airport coach dropped me off.

•

A FEW DAYS LATER I CALLED CAROL to see how things were back in Simi Valley. She had stayed on with Dad.

"It's horrible, Gary. He just stands in front of Mom's dresses hanging in the closet and cries. We don't know what to do. We don't know whether to keep them or get rid of them." I had no idea what to suggest. What do you do with your dead mother's clothes?

6. 12th Street

I HAD PROMISED MYSELF that I would stay away from heroin once I got back to New York, but I had a hit the day I got back—and another one the next day and the day after that. A week after returning, I wrote in my diary, "How have I found my way back to this private hell? Three nights in a row of H. Death seems so much closer now. Why can't I change?" Using my mother's death as an excuse, I quit my job at the National Film Board of Canada. The real reason was that I had become so addicted to heroin that going to work was impossible.

Jeny Howorth disapproved of my habit, but she sensed that I was going through a difficult time and wanted to cheer me up. So one day she arrived at 12th Street and announced that she was going to teach me how to make a "dummy" to take my mind off things.

"I know you won't admit it, but you're really upset about your mother's death," she said. She was right.

By "dummy" she meant a Guy Fawkes dummy. She explained about Guy Fawkes Day in England, how kids would make a life-sized dummy representing Guy Fawkes out of discarded clothing and odds and ends found around the house, then prop their dummy up against a building and ask passersby for a "penny for the guy," which they'd spend on candy. Although Guy Fawkes Day is in November, and it was only late March, watching Jeny build the dummy did help to take my mind off things. I was very impressed by the end result. When she finished, we sat the dummy in a chair in the front window of 12th Street so the dealers would think there was somebody home and wouldn't break in when we weren't there.

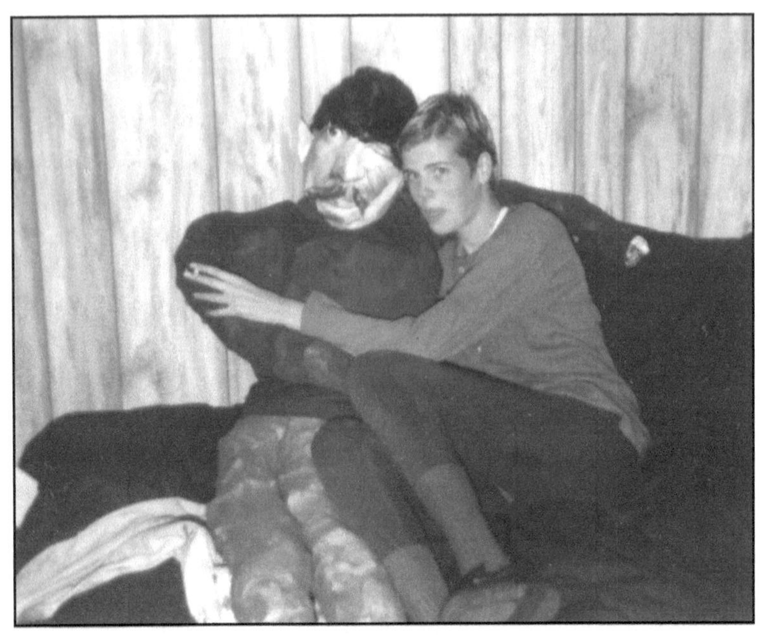

Jeny Howorth and her Guy Fawkes dummy in the 12th Street flat.

A couple of weeks later I turned thirty. I wasn't young anymore. My using escalated. I used heroin to forget that I was using heroin. Jim Bresse returned from Buffalo and also started using again. I saw him around the Lower East Side or at the Palladium or Danceteria.

Jim was living with Paul Gobel, also an addict, who had taken Jim under his wing and was training him to be a makeup artist. Gobel didn't like Sam and his group of friends—he referred to them as the "mob." He thought they were hypocritical for excommunicating Jim from their group because he was doing H when they were doing so much E. He was particularly vicious about Jo Strettell. Gobel claimed to be Sade's makeup artist, but Jo told people she did Sade's makeup.

Jim and Paul Gobel never visited our flat on 12th

Street, but I still kept in touch with them and wrote about it in my diary:

> Paul Gobel and Jim call . . . According to Gobel, Sade hates Jo. Jo never did her makeup. She asked her once as an unknown and Jo refused. Gobel's book begins with 40 *Vogue* covers. Jo fucked Bob Elms behind Richard's back. Jacqui and Helen think I'm fucking David. Jeny and Jo. Sam and Swiss. Max and Jo . . .
>
> Dinner at Theresa's restaurant with Paul and Jim. Paul tries to get me arrested by two cops who walk in, telling them I'm selling heroin to underage youths. "Look at his eyes!" Paul exclaims. I laugh nervously. My eyes were as pinned as pins. We'd just done some dope before we went to the restaurant. The cops didn't care. They just wanted to eat.
>
> Paul promises to tell the Mob I've been slagging them off unless I tell them. They go to Banditos for a drink. I go home.

Nothing Paul Gobel had told me was particularly surprising. Some of it was probably true. Jo was picking up people like Max Headroom, so it wasn't outside the realm of possibilities that she had also had sex with someone else. "Richard" was the fashion photographer Richard Law, who was married to Jo at the time. A lot of people thought David and I were having sex, but unfortunately we weren't. It probably was true that Paul Gobel's book had a lot of *Vogue* covers. He was a popular, talented makeup artist despite his heroin habit.

Sade had made her American debut at Danceteria in May 1982, billed as Sade Abu, with a quote from *The Face*: "Britain's first home-grown sex symbol!" I doubted if Sade hated Jo, as Gobel claimed. Three years later she was a major star and gave Jo tickets to her show at Radio City Music Hall for all of us. Sam and I spent considerable time getting out of it with her saxophone player, Stuart. One night we took him to a gay club in the meat-packing district, the Anvil, which featured drag performances on a stage with a runway into the audience. At one point during the evening he had to piss but didn't want to do it in the cruisy men's bathroom so he just pissed in a trash can near the stage. None of the performers batted a fake eyelash.

•

BECAUSE OF PAUL LONERGAN'S LINKS to the Boy George crowd, some of the English junkies who were friends with George would visit when they came to New York. Ray Allington was often at our apartment. Although some people in the industry gave Ray a hard time about his heroin habit, he was such a good hair stylist that he was never out of work for long. He used to say he didn't have a drug problem, he had access to the drugs and the money to pay for them, so what was the problem?

One night at 12th Street, we thought Ray had overdosed and weren't sure what to do. He was well-known in the fashion business at the time; calling an ambulance was the last thing he would have wanted, unless he really was on the verge of dying. We couldn't wake him up, but he wasn't turning blue, so we just kept on eye on him. He had just arrived from London and scored a "dime" bag, which was nothing for Ray, he had such a big habit. We warned him to test it first by taking a small amount, but he couldn't wait. He thought it would be safe because he was snorting instead of shooting it. He snorted up the whole bag and promptly blacked out. When we finally woke him up, the first thing he did was

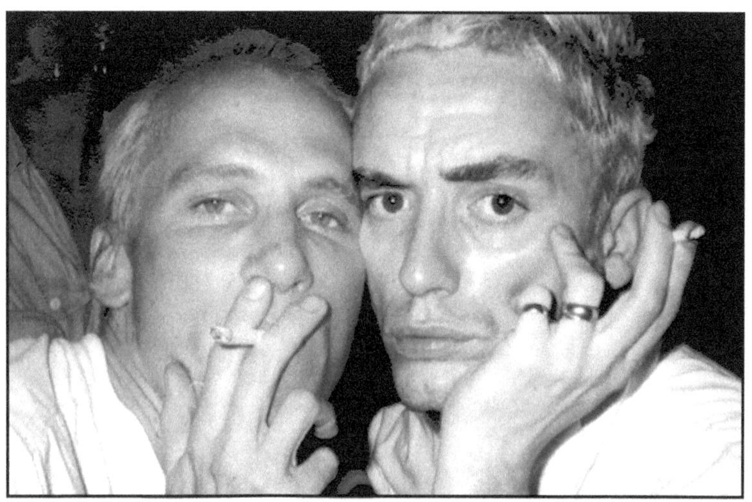

Me (left) with Ray Allington in the Mike Todd Room, 1986. (Photo: David Scharff.)

ask for more dope. As word got around, everybody else wanted the same brand of dope that had almost killed him. The stronger the better.

The English fashion designers John Flett and Stephen Linard also visited. In addition to designing clothes, Linard had hosted a club night in London called Total Fashion Victims. They were scared to death of our neighborhood but amazed at how easy it was to score. I don't think they had actually seen a Puerto Rican before they stayed with us. Flett was such a nice person and so talented. Stephen was (and still is) talented and hilarious—he reminded me of Kenneth Williams, once I found out who Kenneth Williams was. John Flett died about five years after that visit. He was only in his late twenties, and his career was really taking off. Officially it was a heart attack, but I wondered if drugs hadn't played a part.

It was around this time that I first met Boy George's

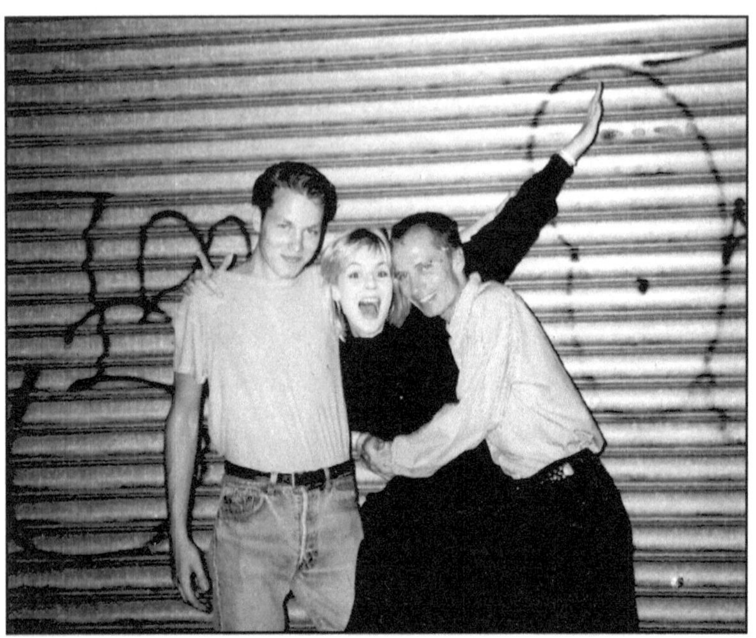

David Strettell, Kate McIlwain, and me. c. 1985.

dealer, Ginty, who had brought some brown heroin with her from London. The heroin in New York was white. New York junkies thought English brown was better, and the English thought New York white was better. George and Marilyn were in town, and Marilyn came over to our apartment one afternoon in a panic. He had passed a construction site and thought he had absorbed a stringy substance that was now coming out of his mouth. He sat at our kitchen table pulling imaginary strings out of his mouth, asking, "Did you see that? Did you see that?" I couldn't tell if he was serious or not. He just sat there at the table pulling imaginary strings from his mouth, one after another.

•

David began having an affair with Teri Toye while we were living at 12th Street. They'd get high together and fall asleep on one of the mattresses in the bedroom. Kate and I would be on the other mattresses, wondering if they were "doing it." When I asked David about it later, he said that sex was a problem with Teri. After she had the sex change she was supposed to stick something up her new vagina so that it wouldn't close, but she was so stoned all the time that she kept forgetting, and the hole closed up. So she didn't have a vagina or a cock. She had gone through all that trouble of having a sex change only to have her hole close up. She was so stoned, sex didn't interest her anyway. Later I heard that she left New York to go home to Des Moines. It was so strange to think of Teri living in Des Moines after having led such a glamorous life modeling in New York.

We lived at the 12th Street flat until our landlord kiucked us out toward the end of the summer for not paying the rent. By that time, Paul Lonergan had moved to Japan to try and earn some money—they were enamored of anyone who was English in the fashion business—and Swiss moved out shortly afterwards. David, Kate, and I stuck together. Kate was in love with me, and I was in love with David. One night, when I was particularly high, Kate and I were joking about getting married, and after that she started telling people that I was going to marry her; I'm not sure if she realized it was a joke. Dean Johnson, the lead singer of Dean and the Weenies, promised to sing "You Make Me Feel Brand New" at the wedding.

Years later, after I had moved to London, I heard that Dean was dead. He overdosed on the opioid oxycodone in 2007. I was surprised by the news. Dean wasn't into heavy drugs when I knew him. Suspicions about his death were were raised by *The Village Voice* after it was discovered that the person he had been with (apparently a john) had been involved in the overdose of another individual just four days previously from the same drug. There was a police investigation, but no charges were brought. Dean was a downtown celebrity in the '80s, but to the New York police in 2007, he was just another junkie.[2]

I don't think oxycodone —or "hillbilly heroin," as it came to be known—even existed in the '80s; the main "highs" then were ecstasy and cocaine. Heroin was off-limits for a lot a people, but it was so off-limits that it eventually became irresistible, even to people in Sam's group who had previously looked down upon us for using.

•

AFTER LEAVING 12TH STREET, Kate and David and I moved to a sublease off 14th Street, not that far from our old place. By this time Kate was working at the front desk of an art gallery and David was working as Mario Testino's photography assistant. I took the occasional temporary job—thank god I could type—and spent most of the money on dope. My habit increased daily. Although David was also using, he wasn't using as much as me and wasn't aware of how bad my habit was.

One night, when Kate and I were at the apartment watching television, I went to the bathroom and never came out. It wasn't unusual for me to have a secret hit in the bathroom, but this time I had overdosed. Kate found me collapsed on the bathroom floor, turning

2 Author uncredited, "Dean Johnson's E-Mails Shed New Light on His Strange Death," *Village Voice*, 5 February 2008.

blue, and called an ambulance. The paramedics arrived and injected me with the drug that every junkie hated, Naloxon, which counteracted the effects of heroin. Your pupils went from pinned to dilated in seconds. It felt like bad speed. As soon as I came to, I pleaded with the paramedics to stop, but they continued with the injection to make sure I wouldn't overdose. Then they took me to the hospital. I didn't stay. After about an hour lying on a trolley in a hallway, I got bored and left. It wasn't the first time I overdosed in my life. To me, it didn't seem like that big of a thing; it just went with the territory. But it was a big thing to Kate.

As the paramedics took me out of the flat, I told Kate not to tell anyone what had happened, but no sooner had I left for the hospital than she was on the phone to Jacqui and Helen telling them about what I had done to her "this time." Most of Sam's mob felt sorry for her. Except for David. He was on my side. I continued to use the next day, of course, and I wasn't any more careful than the day before. It got to the stage where all I could do was use and nod out. Work was out of the question. My habit was worse than ever.

I was becoming an increasing burden to Kate and David and really had no other choice but to clean up. I knew I wouldn't be able to clean up in New York—it was too easy to score. I'd have to go back home to California to do it. It wouldn't be the first time I went home to clean up, but it was the first time since my mother's funeral. I hated going back to Simi Valley and planned to return to New York when I got clean. It would be easier not to start again in New York than it would be to quit there. I forgot that I had left San Francisco for the same reason.

One evening when there was a small group of friends at our apartment getting ready to go out for the night, I called my father and awkwardly explained the situation I was in. I asked for a plane ticket home. His answer was "no."

No? What did he mean? He said he didn't want me coming home because I would do what I did the previous times I had come home to clean up. I took drugs with people I knew in L.A. The same father who had apologized for "everything" when my mother died was now telling me I couldn't come home to clean up. I imagine he thought he was practicing "tough love," but when had he shown me any type of love in the past? Still, he was my father, and being rejected by your father, particularly in a roomful of people getting ready to go clubbing, was like being punched in the stomach. I pretended to be having a completely normal conversation with him, but after I hung up, I turned my head to the wall so nobody would notice the clenching of my jaw as I tried not to cry.

As people started to leave, I pulled David aside: "David. I'm not going. I need to talk to you about something. Could you stay behind for just a bit?"

He answered immediately: "Yes, of course I can." He could tell something was up.

I told him what had happened. I told him how strung out I was, and how even my father didn't want me back. He put his arm around me as I started crying.

"I can't go out," I said.

"Don't worry, we don't have to go out," he said. "I'll stay here with you." He made the ultimate sacrifice that a person could make in '80s New York. He stayed in.

We talked honestly about my situation—the extent of my habit and how I couldn't cope. "I didn't realize it was that bad," he said. We sat in silence with his arm across my shoulders. "What are you going to do?" he asked. I didn't know. I didn't even have money to score. It was going to be a horrible night. David came to my rescue—it didn't take long before we were both stoned, nodding off together on the couch. We didn't bother to put on music; we just listened to the sounds of the traffic and the fragmented conversations of strangers outside.

After a couple of hours, our reverie was interrupted by the noise of someone coming up the stairs and a key turning in the lock. Kate was home. She looked at us lying on the sofa together and asked suspiciously, "What are you two up to?" David stood up, like a naughty child who had been caught doing something he shouldn't be doing, and went into his bedroom. Kate went into her room, and I fell asleep in my usual place—the living room sofa.

David must have told Kate about my conversation with my father, because the next day she came up with the idea of my moving to London with her. Her father had left her some money a couple of years ago; we could use it to tour Europe together.

"Gary, you're killing yourself here," she said. "Come to England." Her Canadian friend Jeannie lived in a squat on a Council estate in Elephant and Castle; we could stay with her until we left for our European tour. "But don't tell anyone that we'll be living on a Council estate," she warned. "If you give anyone the address, just give the street address. Leave off the 'Estate' bit." She was embarrassed that we'd be staying in a Council flat, but I thought it was great. When struggling designers like John Flett visited New York from London, they all seemed to live in Council flats. It sounded so exotic, like Council flats were where all the creative people lived. They didn't have Council flats in New York.

Later that day, Carol called to say that my father had changed his mind—I could go back to the family home in California after all. But by that time my head was full of dreams of Europe. I told Carol I was going to England, and that Kate and I were going to tour Europe together. Carol sounded so sad when I told her. I think she was afraid that once I left, she'd never see me again. And it did almost turn out that way: the next time she saw me was more than twenty years later, and I was in a coma.

7. Ciao Manhattan

ALTHOUGH I NEVER GOT TO SEE MY SISTER during her visit to the hospital, at least not consciously, my illness did bring us closer. It brought me closer to my other siblings as well— my older brother, John, and my younger sister, Cathy. Once I regained consciousness, we spoke on the hospital telephone more than we had spoken to each other since I first moved to London. Now when we ended our calls we always said, "Love you," instead of just, "Goodbye." Most of the time I was too weak to say much. The hospital started giving me physiotherapy while I was still in intensive care, and I often didn't have the strength to talk. A nurse would try to reassure them by saying I was "stable," but given the experience we had with our mother, it was hardly reassuring.

The first "exercise" I was given to do by the physiotherapist was to sit on a chair next to my bed. I laughed at the thought that sitting in a chair was an exercise, but when I tried to do it, I realized how difficult it was. I had lost thirty kilos in the hospital—that's sixty-seven pounds—and there were no muscles left in my arms and legs. I couldn't transfer myself to the chair, so a standing machine was brought in. If I could learn to stand for a few minutes, I should be able to get to the chair. The machine looked a bit like one of those upright units in a gym that are used for leg raises, except instead of facing outward, you faced the machine. I was positioned on the edge of the bed; my arms were placed on the forearm rests of the machine. When the physiotherapist pressed a button, the armrests rose and my body was supposed to follow. It rarely did. It was agonizing—like a modern version of the rack.

I asked if I could have a walker but was told that it was too dangerous: my legs were too weak to support my body, even with a frame to lean on. It wasn't just the lack of strength, it felt like my brain had forgotten how to send a command to my legs to "stand." I watched how my visitors moved when they got up from a chair or walked into the ward to see me. Oh, that's how you do it, I thought as I made a mental note of their movements.

During one of my attempts at standing, the feeding tube fell out of my nose, and the head physiotherapist decided to take advantage of the opportunity to see if I could eat through my mouth. Eating real food after two months of "nil by mouth" was one of the most pleasurable things that I have ever experienced. First they tried soft foods like plain, unflavored yogurt. My tastebuds exploded. That was followed by soft fruit like a banana. I never realized bananas tasted so good. Eventually I graduated to the hard stuff—like chocolate cake. The nutritionist watched my throat to check how I was swallowing the food; eventually she gave me the normal patients' menu and told me to order anything I wanted. When Lilli showed up for her daily visit, I couldn't stop talking about how great the food was in the hospital. She looked at my plate with scepticism. "I guess the baked potatoes are real," she said. She had a point. Once I got used to it, the food was pretty bad. The hot food was microwaved and not particularly tailored to the needs of patients. How could microwaved lasagna be good for a heart patient?

The head physiotherapist wanted me to try eating my meals sitting up in a chair. A portable hoisting machine was brought in, and I was put into a diaper-like seat. The nurse pressed a button on a remote control and up I went. She used the remote to guide me into position above the chair before lowering me down into it. Some staff had better aim than others; when I wasn't lined up correctly, I had to be re-hoisted for another attempt. For someone who suffered from vertigo even before my heart attacks, it was like scaling the Grand Canyon.

Sitting in the chair was even worse than being in the hoist. I wasn't used to sitting up. My brain had trouble adjusting to the new position, and I became nauseous and dizzy. My blood pressure plummeted; I felt like I was going to black out. The nurse would yell for help, and the staff would quickly hoist me back into bed. This happened again and again. Eventually I was able to sit for about ten minutes.

Having a urinary catheter made the hoist clumsier and more embarrassing than it would have been otherwise. They tried to remove the catheter tube a few times, but each time had to reinsert it. My kidneys had failed when I was in cardiogenic shock, and I continued to have problems. A doctor told me that I'd probably have to keep the catheter bag when I was discharged. "How does that work?" I asked. He explained that the bag would be strapped to my leg, and a community nurse would visit me at home to change it. At that stage, I was still looking forward to leaving the hospital and eventually returning to the type of life I led before my hospitalization, with the occasional visit to the gay scene on Old Compton Street to try my luck. That wouldn't be possible with a catheter tube inserted into the hole of my cock and a bag of urine taped to my leg.

I eventually gave up trying to eat and sit at the same time and continued to eat off a tray in bed. Appropriately, my view while I ate was the cabinet across from my bed where they kept the morphine. Though the cabinet was locked and two nurses had to sign for the drug, I doubt if it would have been as accessible in a New York hospital. It would have been too easy for addicts to break into it. I thought back on my junkie days and how, now that I was older and ill, I had access to all the drugs I couldn't legally get back then.

•

I CONTINUED TO USE HEROIN in New York even after I decided to move to London with Kate McIlwain. I tried to keep my habit in check but without much success. I kept working in temp jobs and then scoring with every cent I earned. Given the amount Kate complained about me during that period, I wondered why she had made the offer of a European trip in the first place. I overheard her talking to Ana one afternoon in the kitchen about what a loser I had become. She wished she had been around in the days when I gave Sam and Jeny the *Big Snit* video. Ana replied, "Yeah, back when he had something to offer . . ."

A typical conversation between Kate and me at the time, from my diary:

> "Gary!"
> I open my eyes.
> "What's wrong with you. You've been sleeping so much this weekend."
> "No I haven't."
> "Yes you have."
> "I didn't sleep at all last week."
> "Yes you did."
> "No I didn't."
> "You did."

And so on and so on. She suspected me of using, and of course she was right.

•

Paul Lonergan telephoned from London, back from Japan. I heard Kate tell him I was moving to London with her. "I think they're going to eat him for breakfast," she said. That became her favorite expression when she told anyone about my going to London with her—that the English were going to eat me for breakfast. I heard her say the same thing to Sam. I wasn't worried about being eaten for breakfast. I was more worried about something Sam had said when we told him about our plans: "They don't have coffee shops in London, Gary." No coffee shops? I spent a lot of time in coffee shops, reading books or writing in my diary. There must be an English version. How could they not have coffee shops?

As the day of our departure got closer, I continued to try to stop using so I wouldn't arrive in London with a habit. I stopped, I started, I cut down, I increased. I just couldn't take the depression that came with withdrawal. Heroin wiped out any resilience a human being had to depression. If you could take a pill and all your problems would disappear, wouldn't you take that pill? That's what heroin did—except that I injected it. I'd have a hit and the depression would disappear, at least temporarily. Each time I took it, I was convinced it would be the last time. But then it would wear off and the depression would start again and I'd think, "One more time won't hurt." And it went on from there. I had to get out of New York. It was just too easy to score. I don't know why I thought things would be different in London. I already knew about the heroin scene there from Boy George's crowd.

I still had a habit when Kate and I left New York, and I needed to have a hit before I got on the flight. When our cab to the airport got stuck in traffic, I knelt down on the floor and took out a spoon and a small bottle of water from my bag, along with a small packet of white powder. Kate saw what I was doing and screamed, "Gary, what are you doing?" I told her not to talk so loud. "Gary, I can't believe you're doing this!" she shouted.

What was the big deal? It wasn't the first time I'd shot up in a cab. In New York you could do almost anything you wanted in a cab. Surely she must have realized that I would need a hit before the long flight. Where did she expect me to do it? In the airport? After the injection, the rest of the cab ride was peaceful and calm, except when Kate's tearful voice interrupted my dreams: "How could you do this? How could you do this to me? Now you're going to be stoned when you meet my mother!" I ignored her and nodded off. By the time we landed in London, we weren't speaking to each other.

Part II

1. London

THE CAB RIDE FROM HEATHROW to Kate's mother's house in Fulham was ominously silent. As soon as we got off the main motorway and into the city, I realized I had made the wrong decision. London was no New York. It was raining and looked cold and dreary from the cab window. The buildings were tiny. Where were all the skyscrapers? It seemed more like a suburb than a city, particularly when we got to Fulham.

Once again I had ended up in a residential suburb. Fulham might not seem like a suburb to an English person, but it did to an American arriving from Manhattan. At one point we came upon a large homeless woman standing in the middle of the road waving at us as though she needed help. She was wearing an old pair of flip-flops in the rain, and it looked like she had slept in her clothes. To my surprise, Kate asked the cabdriver to stop. I sat mesmerized as she approached the woman as if to hug her. "Kate!" the woman screamed with outstretched arms. Oh my god, they know each other, I thought. Then I realized it was her mother! She had seen the cab approaching and decided to stop it in the middle of the street. We were home.

Once inside, we were treated to a dinner of hot soup and wine—mostly wine. Kate's father, the science fiction writer Charles Eric Maine, had died a few years before, and her mother was clearly drunk. The place was a mess, more like a charity shop than a home. I was exhausted, and the effects of the dope had started to wear off. We went to bed early, sharing a single bed in a small bedroom upstairs—if I hadn't been a skinny drug addict, I probably would have fallen off.

The next day we moved to Kate's friend Jeannie's squat—the Council flat in Elephant and Castle that Kate didn't want anybody to know was a Council flat. We lasted about a week there before Jeannie kicked us out, accusing Kate of rearranging her sweaters—"jumpers" to the English. Jeannie kept her jumpers arranged in meticulous rows on shelves in the bedroom; apparently Kate had been wearing them without folding them back up as neatly as she had found them, and not in the same order.

We went back to the single bed at Kate's family home. I drew an imaginary line to divide the mattress up into Kate's side and my side, but she kept sliding over to my side. Fortunately, the lodger in the attic moved out, and I got it. My first winter in London was spent in a freezing attic room with a meter that gave you heat at 50 pence a shot—which lasted about fifteen minutes. It was like living in a World War II movie.

•

On one of our first nights in London, Kate and I were invited to a party at Paul Rutherford's flat with some of the English people I knew from Sam's circle in New York. It took ages to get there. London was far too spread out to be a real city. Unlike downtown Manhattan, where you could walk to almost anywhere worth going, in London you had to depend on public transport or cabs. It took so long to get from A to B that by the time you got to B you wished you hadn't left A. Downtown New York was a community. You could walk down St. Mark's Place at almost any time of day or night and meet people you knew. There was no equivalent street in London. There was no sense of community. And, worst of all, Sam was right. There were no coffee shops. It would be quite a few years before the arrival of the cappuccino bars that later dominated London.

Finally arriving at Paul's, I expected a warm welcome in an urbane flat, like the welcome we gave to English visitors at Sam's apartment in New York. But the furniture was more Laura Ashley than Philippe Starck, and the welcome wasn't exactly welcoming. Sam was still in New York, but Lilli was there. It was the first time I met her. Although she had never been to New York, Sam had told me so much about her and how much I would love her that I was taken aback by her reaction when I met her at the party. "You know," she said, "you don't have to be my friend just because I'm Sam's friend."

Another problem was that they had ordered E but nobody had thought to order any for Kate and me. In London you had to order your drugs in advance, and it wasn't that easy to get more. In New York you just phoned someone, and they'd be delivered by bike within the hour. Coming to London was a big step for me, and I expected a friendlier reception. It was, after all, my ex-boyfriend, Jim Bresse, who introduced Sam to the Palladium in the first place and everything that went with it.

Kate and I were outsiders, the only ones not high, therefore on a different wavelength than everyone else. This had its advantages, though. We watched them all make fools of themselves as they tried to imitate some of the outrageous things they had heard the ecstasy crowd got up to in New York. It seemed a bit labored. In New York we didn't have to try to be outrageous—it just came naturally.

•

A FEW DAYS AFTER PAUL'S PARTY, I got in touch with Ray Allington. Hopefully, the H scene in London would be a bit more interesting than the E scene. It started out good—Ray was happy to hear from me and invited me over. He was staying with the fashion designers John Galliano and John Flett, who were boyfriends at the time. Their flat was more like the apartments in Manhattan I was used to, with minimal furniture. As soon as I got there, Ray and I left to find a phone box to score.

It wasn't easy. In New York, you just went to a phone booth and used it; in England, once you found a pay phone that worked, you had to get into a queue. Ray and I waited an hour before we finally made it to the head of the queue. An hour in junkie time is an eternity. I stood outside as Ray made his call, looking forward to the brown smack. He had to make a few calls; I could see some of the people in the queue getting angry. Apparently you were only allowed one call. If you needed to make more, you had to join the queue again.

Ray didn't look happy when he came out of the phone box. He couldn't score. The Boy George case was working its way through the courts (and newspapers) at the time, and dealers had stopped dealing. London was dry. I was dumbfounded. Whatever happened to Ray's claim that he didn't have a problem with drugs because he had the money to buy them and always knew where to get them?

The only London dealer I knew was Ginty. With George in trouble, she wasn't the best option, but she was the only option. Ray thought we'd have a better chance of getting something if I rang her instead of him. We joined the queue again. When it was my turn to use the phone, we squeezed ourselves into the phone box, and Ray listened in.

Ginty was as lovely as she had been in New York. She remembered me and invited me over. When I mentioned Ray, her mood changed; Ray had been friends with George and Marilyn, and she didn't know if he could be trusted. I assured her that he was okay. She said she didn't have any smack but I could come over to see her scrapbooks if I wanted to. I assumed that was a code word for smack. "Scrap" sounded like "smack"—the "scrapbooks" must be "smackbooks." Why would I want to see scrapbooks?

Ginty's flat was a bit like Paul's—uncomfortably cozy. Open planning took a long time to get to London. Ray and I waited on the understuffed floral sofa in the front room while Ginty made tea in the kitchen. Afraid that she would hear us, we tried to communicate with silent hand gestures about what to do next. Eventually I went into the kitchen on my own—maybe I would have more luck without Ray. Before I had a chance to say anything, she said, "I'm sorry I don't have anything, but let me get the scrapbooks."

She opened up a cabinet and there they were: scrapbooks. As she turned the pages I hoped that hidden among them might be something more interesting—but no, there was just page after page of newspaper clippings about Boy George's case. Then she brought out copies of the court depositions. According to Ginty, George and Marilyn were hoping to avoid a jail sentence by cooperating with the police, who were trying to get her on a conspiracy-to-supply charge. She was livid. She thought George was her friend. She had made the same mistake a lot of dealers make, confusing "customer" with "friend."

When it became apparent that we weren't going to get anything, Ray and I went back to the flat he was staying in and fell asleep on the futon in the front room, completely sober. John Flett was already asleep in the bedroom. We were woken up in the middle of the night by a drunken John Galliano screaming to be let in. Apparently they'd had a fight and Flett had locked him out. Eventually John let John in, and I went back to sleep.

We had to get up early the next morning because Ray was expected at a fashion shoot. I had never seen him take public transport in New York, where he traveled by taxi, or his client sent a car. As we went down the escalator to catch the train, Ray admired the boys on the up escalator, turned to me, and said, "Aren't English boys gorgeous?" Yes, English boys were gorgeous—but mostly straight. It seemed like things were reversed in London. In New York most of the good-looking guys were gay. In London they were straight; they just looked gay.

Ray and I eventually went separate ways. I was still clean, even if it wasn't entirely by choice. Kate could rest assured that I wouldn't be turning her mother's house into a shooting gallery. Although I was still living in her attic, I didn't spend much time with Kate. Needless to say, the promised tour of Europe never materialized. Sam came back to London, and I went out with him and his friends occasionally, but even that wore thin after a while. In London quite a few of Sam's friends acted like the sycophants that Paul Gobel had described them as. Many of the English models only hung around with Sam's "mob" when they were in New York.

•

ONE ADVANTAGE TO LIVING IN KATE'S ATTIC was that I became friends with Paul Rutherford's press agent, Regine Moylett, who lived nearby, just on the other side of Parsons Green. I often traipsed across the green to hang out with Regine after she got off work, amazed that you could walk across what would be called a park in Manhattan at night without getting mugged. London was a lot safer than New York—and they didn't have cockroaches. Maybe moving to London wasn't such a bad idea after all.

As a press officer for Island Records, Regine went to a lot of gigs, and I often went with her. Before long I was going out more with her and her friends than I did with the crowd I had met in New York. She eventually offered me some temporary work in the press office, and thus began my almost accidental career at Island Records.

2. Island Records

REGINE ARRIVED AT THE OFFICE every morning with a pile of newspapers and magazines from the local newsstand. She and her colleague, Debbie Walker, went through them, cutting out the articles about Island artists and filing them in the appropriate binder. When they wanted to interest a journalist in a band, they photocopied articles from their binder and sent a package off with a bio (usually written by the press director, Rob Partridge) and an album. The internet didn't yet exist; they couldn't refer a journalist to a website or a YouTube video—they had to send hard copies of everything. They had fallen behind with the clipping; there were stacks of newspapers and magazines on the floor waiting to be cut up and filed. That was my job. I finished it pretty quickly, and before long started answering the phones as well. After a few weeks I became a full-fledged press officer.

U2 was the most important band on Island at the time. Whenever we got a call from their office, it was handed straight to Rob. If he was on another call, he'd end it and take the U2 call. I wasn't that interested in their music—it sounded too much like American rock, the type of stuff Bruce Springsteen would do—but the band members were friendly. They often dropped in to the press office for a chat when they had meetings in other parts of the building. Soon after I started working there, U2 released what was probably the most successful album of their career, *The Joshua Tree*. After an expensive prerelease publicity campaign it went straight into the charts at number one. The newspapers were desperate for a comment or an interview with the the band.

The press's desperation became clear in a very real way one afternoon when I was on my own in the office. An Irish newspaper rang and wanted a comment about the band having a number one album and single in the charts at the same time. I told the journalist I'd get Rob to ring her back; as I was taking down her details we casually chatted. She had never been to the States and wondered what it was like. After I hung up the phone I didn't think twice about the call. I gave Rob the message when he came back to the office.

The next morning, I was shocked to find myself quoted on the front page of the newspaper. During our social chit-chat the journalist had mentioned U2's chart position, and I commented that they cared more about their music than things like chart position. It sounded humble to me, but the newspaper reported—quoting an Island representative (me)—that U2 didn't care about their fans. You could have heard a pin drop in the press office when Regine read out the article. The record company's massive publicity campaign for the album had been sabotaged in one fell swoop by an employee who had only recently graduated from the floor to a seat at the desk.

Rob and Regine rushed in and out of the office as they attended emergency meetings. Finally somebody asked me what I had actually said. I told them and managed to keep my job, but the incident showed how important the band was to the record company. Whenever a call came from their manager, Paul McGuinness, you could feel the tension in the room.

•

IN ADDITION TO ARRANGING individual interviews for Island artists, sometimes we had press conferences.

The first one I organized was for Anthrax, an American thrash band. I was a nervous wreck about it, figuring a heavy metal band probably hated gays. I made sure the conference room was amply supplied with food and alcohol, hoping that if I got everyone drunk enough, the afternoon would be a success. The band and their manager were already there when I arrived. Their manager, Johnny Z, looked like a Hell's Angel. I approached cautiously; he shouted out, "Island Records!" and gave me a bear hug. We sat down and he talked about how much he loved London. His favorite singer was Barbra Streisand. I couldn't believe my luck. From that point on, we were best friends. We discussed Streisand records as we waited for the journalists to arrive.

The guys in the band were completely different than I thought they would be. Instead of beer-guzzling party animals, they were teetotaling vegetarians. I had never met such polite kids. Since they didn't drink, it meant there was more alcohol for the journalists—and for me. We all got smashed and had a great time, the band got good press, and Anthrax went straight to the top of the UK heavy metal charts. My first press conference was a success.

After that, Rob assigned American artists to me. I suppose he thought Americans would be better able to relate to another American, but I wasn't so sure some of the rap artists, like the duo Eric B. and Rakim, would relate to a gay American. When they came to London, I sensed there would be trouble, and I was right. But it wasn't because I was gay.

Each journalist was given a scheduled time to interview them. Someone, I think from *No. 1* magazine, had the audacity to say that he preferred their previous single to their current one. Eric and Rakim didn't appreciate that. "Who are you to judge us?" they asked. "You're here to interview us." They stood up threateningly and told him to leave or they were going to throw him out the window—one of them had a knife. The journalist left immediately, apologizing to me profusely and blaming himself. I apologized as he apologized and promised him interviews with anyone from the label in the future. Back in the room with the artists, I pretended to agree with them. Being a press officer meant trying to make everyone happy. It was one of the reasons I would eventually become disillusioned with the job. I felt like a fake.

•

INITIALLY, WORKING AT ISLAND was like being part of a family. When Debbie's boyfriend needed a flatmate, I took up the offer. Hugh was in a local band, and most of his friends were musicians. We had some wild nights at that flat. One night, when Hugh and I were extremely drunk, we had sex. It wasn't anything serious. I wasn't particularly attracted to him, but when we were out of it, we'd go down on each other sometimes. You can imagine my surprise when, two decades later, Debbie Walker became one of my regular visitors in the hospital. She knew what Hugh and I were up to when it was going on, but she never brought it up in the hospital or even after I continued to see her once I returned home. I wondered if she actually remembered.

I didn't spend a lot of time at the squat because there were so many record company events to go to. My life revolved around work. My workload increased dramatically when Regine went on tour with U2. Before she left, she represented Rob at board meetings when he couldn't make it; now I was given that responsibility as well. As I became more aware of the business side of things and the internal politics that went on behind the scenes, my attitude toward the company began to change. Island wasn't as much of a family as I thought. Like any other record company, commercial considerations came first. When they bankrolled a new band, most of the expenses were recoupable from the band's eventual royalties. The cost of producing and promoting an album was largely paid for by the band.

Despite our bumpy beginning at Paul Rutherford's party, Lilli Anderson and I had become friends. When the U2 tour reached London, Regine, Lilli, and I hung out with Adam Clayton, the bass guitarist, in his suite at the Mayfair, which was the size of a large flat. One night, after getting stoned in the suite, we decided to go to the Limelight club, despite Paul McGuinness having told the band that places like that were off-limits because of the paparazzi. As our cab approached the club, we saw McGuinness going in. Slumping down in our seats, we asked the driver to take us back to the hotel. In the safety of Adam's suite, we could get as out of it as we wanted. Lilli and I ended up spending the night there—or was it the whole weekend?

•

THE JOSHUA TREE TOUR seemed to go on forever, and I looked after some of Regine's clients while she was away. Her most successful band after U2 was The Christians. The Christians weren't Christian—anything but. They were a soul band from Liverpool; three of the members were brothers with the surname of Christian. After a string of successful singles, their debut album reached no. 2 in the charts. The music papers loved them. Garry

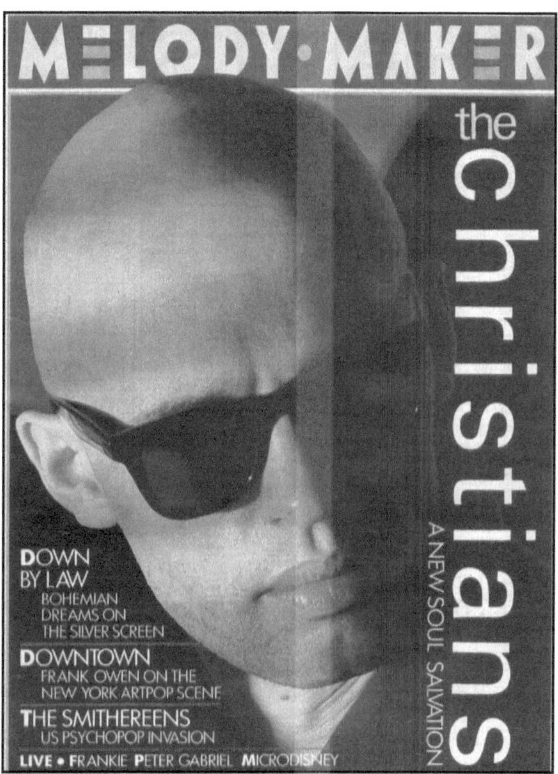

Garry Christian on the cover of *Melody Maker*, January 17, 1987.

Christian, the lead vocalist, a good-looking, six-foot-four- inch, mixed-race guy with a shaved head, got most of the attention. When *Melody Maker* put the band on the front cover, they only included a picture of Garry.

I loved doing The Christians' press because it meant visiting Liverpool. We stayed at the Adelphi, which, in those days, was as posh as it got in that city. We did press during the day, and I had the evenings free. After dinner I'd plop myself down at the hotel bar and discuss life with the barmaid, who always remembered me from the last time I was there. Both of us would proceed to get considerably drunk on my Island expense account. Back then, you didn't give the bar staff tips, you bought them a drink.

After a few drinks (or more), I'd head down to Sadie's, a gay bar not far from the hotel. You wouldn't know it was a bar, let alone a gay one, unless you already knew it was. An Irishman stood outside an unmarked door, charging fifty pence to enter. Inside, a dimly lit staircase led up to a small room with disco lights reflected on the mirrored walls. A few drag queens slumped over their drinks at the bar. Young, nervous-looking guys leaned against the walls, drinking their pints as slowly as they could, not knowing where the next one was coming from. I remember asking one of the regulars what he would wish for if he could have one wish. He answered that just once he'd like to be able to buy as many drinks as he wanted for himself and his friends. It was probably a subtle hint, but he seemed surprisingly sincere. The clubs I missed most after my heart attacks were places like Sadie's. The same people would be there the next night and the night after that. Sadie's was their home away from home. One part of me felt sorry for them, the other part envious.

I went on a lot of press trips with The Christians. The European tour promised by Kate never materialized, but I got to see a lot of Europe as part of my job. A performance in a foreign country was always a good angle for an article and an enticing lure for a journalist. Music journalists didn't make a lot of money and appreciated any hospitality that was offered, especially if it involved a free trip and lots of alcohol. The best way to a journalist's pen was through a free drink—usually quite a few free drinks. Getting a journalist drunk had the additional benefit of getting myself drunk as well.

•

I WENT ALONG WHEN THE CHRISTIANS played at the Rocksommer Festival in East Berlin. The Berlin wall was still up, and Rob thought the trip would make a good front cover. *Sounds* was interested. They couldn't promise a cover—that would be too much like bribery—but the editor thought it sounded like a good idea. The travel arrangements were easy, but Westerners were required to stay at a hotel designated by the East German government, which was full of American businessmen. It felt more like a trade conference in the midwestern U.S. than East Germany.

You also had to change your money at the hotel, and the exchange rate wasn't good. They accepted sterling and U.S dollars, but you received your change in East German currency, which was only good in East Germany. You had to take your main meals at the hotel restaurant and pay in cash; I brought a large cash float. On the plane the band and I joked about whether or not there would be East German spies following us during the visit, but we weren't even assigned an escort while we were there; nor was there censorship of the band's songs. There didn't need to be. A lot of their lyrics could be interpreted as anguished cries against capitalist alienation.

On our way back to the hotel after the concert, we noticed a group of punk rockers waiting to get into a club, so we stopped our coach and joined them. The last thing we expected to see in East Berlin in the late 1980s was a punk club. The doorman waved us in; he knew who we were because of all the publicity for the band's appearance. We were ushered to a private, roped-off table guarded by the club's security people and given as much Soviet "champagne" as we could drink. Somehow one of the club-goers, a young punk with spiked, bleached hair who looked like Billy Idol, managed to join us at our table. Afterwards he came back to the the hotel with us and spent the night in my room. When I got up the next morning he was still in bed. I told him I was going downstairs to change some money. He told me the exchange rates at the hotel were a rip-off; he had a friend who gave better rates. Without thinking—I was nursing a Soviet champagne hangover—I handed him nearly all the cash Island had given me for the trip, keeping some I needed for a photo shoot later that day. He left to see his friend, and I left to meet the band and the *Sounds* journalist and photographer in the hotel lobby. I had booked cabs to take us around the city for the photos.

I was not in a good mood when we got back. I had failed to get a single photograph with all the band members in it. Roger Christian refused to have his picture taken with the rest of the band. He thought he was the best singer and resented the attention Garry got as the most photogenic member of the group. It was the first time I wasn't able to convince an artist to do something they didn't want to do.

To make matters worse, the punk had not returned from his his money-changing expedition. I expected to find him waiting in the lobby. It was almost dinnertime; I needed the cash to pay for dinner. I hadn't told the band or their manager what I had done, of course. Now that I was sober, I couldn't believe how stupid I had been. The guy may have been beautiful, but he was, after all, a complete stranger. I had no way of contacting him. I waited in my room until the last minute, and finally there was a knock on the door. It was him.

"Thank god you're here!" I said as I quickly pulled him into the room. He looked puzzled. What was the big deal? He had told me he'd be back with the money, and here he was. Why wouldn't he keep his word? I assumed this was Communism in action—one comrade helping another—except that I was American and, therefore, his enemy. The amount of cash he brought back was outrageous. As a gesture of thanks, I bought him a watch in one of the shops in the hotel lobby and hired him to be our official guide. When he showed Garry Christian his new watch at dinner, Garry turned to me and asked loudly in his heavy Liverpudlian accent, "And what did you get from him?" The rest of the band laughed, and we ordered some more Soviet champagne on my expenses.

The punk shared my room the rest of the time we were there. He even saw us off at the airport. It felt like saying goodbye to an old friend. I was already missing him by the time I got on the flight; I realized that we hadn't even exchanged contact details.

I didn't have any alcohol on the plane to London, and as my mind cleared, I begun to wonder whether he had, in fact, been the East German spy we were expecting before the trip. I tried to remember exactly how we met and which one of us had made the first approach. He seemed to appear out of nowhere. Had he been helping us or spying on us?

It didn't matter. We were safely on our way home, and he was probably just a young music fan. When the Berlin wall came down a couple of years later, I wondered what happened to him. Berlin might be a better place without the wall, but East Berlin wasn't so bad with the wall. It was like entering another world—like a black and white film where you expected to see a dangerous Communist agent lurking around the next corner—and ended up with a Billy Idol look-alike.

When I got back to the press office and told Rob that I hadn't brought back a single picture of the band together, I was surprised by his reaction. "Fantastic!" he said. Roger had quit the band when they got back to London; the pictures would have been unusable if he had been in them. I had accidentally given Island exactly what they needed.

The trip was headlined in big letters on the front cover of *Sounds*. I was surprised to see my name mentioned twice in the article: once when the journalist reported that I was overjoyed when we finally got Roger into a cab for a photo session that never happened, and again when an interviewer for a radio station mistook me for Garry Christian because we had the same first name. We laughed when it happened; when Regine saw it, she reminded me of the unwritten rule that press officers shouldn't become part of the story. I had already been in trouble over U2.

•

A FEW WEEKS AFTER THE EAST BERLIN TRIP, Rob sent me to New York to do Anthrax again along with the B52s. I had done press with the B52s in London earlier in the year and looked forward to seeing them again. Sam would be in New York so I'd be able to visit him.

The session with Anthrax went fairly quickly. The photographer wanted to get a picture of the band skateboarding down the steps of the Metropolitan Museum of Art. We didn't have their permission, so I told the boys to do it quickly and the photographer to continue shooting even if security showed up. When two guards arrived, I apologized profusely and asked what the procedure was for getting permission. By the end of the explanation, we had our pictures and jumped into a waiting cab.

The next day we did the B52s. When I'd had lunch with her in London earlier in the year, Cindy Wilson was still really upset about the death of her brother, Ricky, co-founder of the band, from AIDS two years before, which he had kept a secret from her. Cindy's depression went beyond tears—it was difficult for her to be happy or excited about anything. AIDS was a horror story. Not long after that I learned that Paul Rutherford's boyfriend, Joe Batty, was HIV positive.

Cindy was in better spirits when I saw them in New York. Doing press for the B52s was a nice break from the usual Island artists. Usually I felt stressed out as I tried to make everyone happy, but the B52s couldn't have have more hospitable. It was fun watching them get ready for the shoot. They loved trying out different looks so much that I wondered whether they were ever going to be ready. The photographer wanted to shoot them on the hotel roof, and we were starting to lose the light. There were people in the elevator when it stopped at our floor, but they didn't seem to mind moving out of the way for all the big hair and wide skirts. We got the shots. Island regretted losing the B52s, because the album turned out to be one of their most successful. They were embraced by a whole new generation of fans. It was a pity that Ricky wasn't there to experience their comeback.

After the photo session with the B52s, I visited Sam. He had given up the apartment with the huge rooftop terrace that had been the site of so many wonderful nights. His new place didn't have a terrace. E was over. Alcohol and cocaine had replaced ecstasy, and Nell's club had replaced the Mike Todd Room. A friend of Sam's, the makeup artist Mary Greenwell, was staying with him, and we all went to Nell's and got extremely drunk. I ended up sleeping on his floor and woke up to Mary standing above me, screaming about how I had ruined her £500 shoes: "You fucking pissed in my shoes, you wanker!" Apparently I had got up in the night and mistook her shoes for a urinal. I apologized profusely and got out as quickly as I could.

Later that day she saw me out the window and started yelling again: "There's that man who pissed in my shoes!" Some people looked up, but most of them just thought she was a nutcase and kept on walking. I smiled and waved and walked a little faster.

•

WHEN I GOT BACK TO ISLAND after my trip to New York, Rob was playing the demo tape of Mica Paris, a new soul singer the label had just signed. He could see that I was enjoying her music so he asked if I'd like to do her press. Of course I said yes—her music was the type of music I actually listened to at home, soulful jazz. I didn't have to pretend like I did with some of the rockier bands.

I loved being Mica's press officer most of the time. She could be very stubborn, but I didn't mind that. As far as I was concerned, she had so much talent that she could be as stubborn as she wanted. Other staff members thought she was too bossy. If the sales people, secretaries, and envelope-stuffers didn't like an artist, they wouldn't go out of their way for them. The staff could forgive alcoholics and drug addicts, but not egomaniacs.

One of my first tasks was to supervise the photo session for the front cover of Mica's first single, "My

One Temptation." I had hired a stylist who brought along a selection of designer gear, but Mica didn't like any of it. She wanted shoulder pads and the high street fashion she normally wore. I begged her to try on a Moschino biker jacket that looked like an American flag, and she refused. Finally I tried it on, standing in front of a mirror and saying how great it looked. Not to be outdone, she grabbed the jacket, put it on for a few shots, and handed it back. One of the shots became the front cover of the single, which went into the top ten. The image of her in the jacket became associated with her early success. Soon she was being touted as the next Whitney Houston, even before the full album came out.

One of Mica's early gigs was playing at the Paris Jazz Festival. Rob envisioned a "Paris in Paris" cover story. *Record Mirror* was interested, and I took along a photographer and journalist. I loved Paris, having been there a few times before to check out the gay scene. I took the *Record Mirror* people to a mixed club the night we arrived, but they seemed uncomfortable. Neither of them spoke French, but I had studied French at Berkeley and didn't have a problem communicating with the locals. The drunker I got, the gayer I got. The journalist and photographer escaped to their hotel, saying they would meet me in the lobby the next morning for the photo session with Mica. By the time they left, I had met a fascinating bleached blond transvestite who looked like Candy Darling in *Women in Revolt*. When it got near to closing time, we went back to my room to continue our drinking.

I'm not sure what time I finally fell asleep, but when I woke up the next morning, the room was a mess. The transvestite was gone, and so was an expensive Issey Miyake shirt a friend had given me. I had a dim memory of throwing an empty champagne bottle out the window—not in a fit of anger, just in a fit of drama. The phone rang loudly, echoing in my head. I answered it carefully as though it was as fragile as I felt. I was in severe hangover mode. The call was from Mica's manager, Tracy—her third manager since she'd been signed. Mica wasn't feeling well and wouldn't be able to do the photos. Couldn't we do them in London? I couldn't believe what I was hearing. How could we do a "Paris in Paris" feature with photographs taken in London? If Mica was really ill, I wouldn't force her—I considered her a friend as much as a client by that time—but Tracy wasn't asking for a doctor, she was asking for a day off. I heard someone else in her room and assumed it was Mica. I asked to speak to her. Tracy refused. That was unusual—Mica and I normally spoke directly to each other instead of through a manager or other intermediary. Tracy and I began arguing—I called her a "fucking amateur" for demanding that we do the photos in London—and she hung up on me.

A few minutes later the phone rang again. It was Regine, calling from the press office in London: "What the fuck is going on out there! We got a call from the hotel. Who threw a bottle out the window? Mica's manager is on the phone to Clive Banks. She said you called her a fucking amateur and she can't work with you!"

Clive Banks was the managing director of Island. While Regine was away with U2, I had come to know him a bit better. Most of the staff, including Regine and Rob, didn't particularly like him, but I always got on fine with him. I told Regine that I called Tracy a fucking amateur because she was one. The stunned silence of Regine's response was interrupted by a loud knock on the door. "Hold on," I said and hung up the phone.

It was the cleaning staff. They took one look at the room and left, shouting to each other in French. I sat on the edge of the bed, head in hands, trying to convince myself that my hangover wasn't as bad as it was. The phone rang again. It was Regine: "The cleaning staff have told the manager that they refuse to clean your room. They are threatening to go on strike." I laughed—the French were always threatening to go on strike—and told her not to worry, I would sort everything out. "You'd better," she said, "your job is on the line!"

I was surprised by her threat—Rob was my boss, not Regine. I had such a severe hangover I don't think I cared if my job was on the line; even without the hangover, I'd lost my enthusiasm for it. I finally managed to talk to Mica, and she agreed to do the photos. We took a cab to the Eiffel Tower and got a shot of Mica in front of it; then we headed to the Champs-Élysées and got the Arc de Triomphe as well. Mica seemed to forget that she was supposed to be ill. When we got back to the hotel, my room had been cleaned and the staff hadn't gone on strike. Disaster averted.

When I got back to London I told Clive and Rob what had happened. It wasn't a major issue. On the morning that *Record Mirror* was due to come out, Regine warned me that the article "better be a front cover." It was. Mica's diva attitude hadn't gone unnoticed by the journalist, however. Describing her manner as "no-nonsense" in his article, he wrote, "It's enough to make you wonder whether she isn't just a little bit of a precocious monster."

Mica never made it as big as she should have. None of her other songs were as successful as "My One Temptation." Eventually she was dropped from the label, but I no longer worked for them by then. Years later, in 2007, she came out with a book, *Beautiful Within: Finding Happiness and Confidence in Your Own Skin*. I ran into her soon after it was published. Cleveland and I were walking down Oxford Street, and I noticed a poster advertising her book signing. I joked with Cleveland about whether we should go, then read the details on the poster and realized she was in the shop now. As we stood there trying to decide what to do, she nearly bumped into us. The book signing was over and she was leaving.

"Hi, Mica—it's Gary, your old press officer . . ."

"Oh my god! Gary!" she boomed. She turned to the person she was with and introduced me: "This is the person who made me famous!" I laughed. "Really!" she said. "He made me wear that Moschino jacket. That was the start of it all."

She asked me what I was working on now, and Cleveland started to tell her about my Warhol website. I cut him off, embarrassed that I hadn't progressed to something more important in the music business. "It's nothing," I muttered.

That only made her more curious, like she was missing out on something: "What new website? Give me your card!" she commanded. I told her I didn't have one. She turned to her manager: "Give him your card." He gave me his card, and I made a quick getaway, saying something like, "It's so great that you wrote a book." I never called.

3. The girl in the grocery store queue

I DIDN'T USE SMACK while I was working at Island, but I was drinking more, and my hangovers were fierce. One afternoon I felt so ill that I spent most of the day taking a long rest under the press office table. An ex-girlfriend of Island's founder, Chris Blackwell, was using a phone in the office at the time.

"Debbie, there's a man asleep under the table," she said.

"Oh, that's just Gary," Debbie responded as she reached for another binder. That's how used to my hangovers people were. I didn't drink more than most other employees, it just seemed to affect me more.

Some people in the industry only saw me drunk because they only saw me at record company parties. Once I got drunk with Fiona Russell Powell, a journalist for *The Face*, and we decided to switch shoes. She wore my Doc Marten loafers, and I wore her stilettos. It seemed funny at the time, but when it appeared in the gossip section of *City Limits*, Regine warned me again to stay out of the press.

Fiona knew some of the people I knew—mostly the addicts, like Ray Allington and Paul Lonergan. She started ringing me at the office asking if I knew where she could score. I wasn't using anymore, but I don't think she believed me. I finally got her off my back by giving her Paul's number, but I don't think her calls went unnoticed by the other people in the press office.

A few weeks later I actually did use, but not with Fiona. I was standing in a grocery store queue and noticed that the girl behind me had pinned eyes. She looked more like a student than an addict, but her eyes were definitely pinned. I waited for her after I paid for my groceries, and we got into a conversation which led to her scoring for me. She was suspicious at first, but scoring for me would mean a hit for her, and I've never known a junkie to say no to a free hit.

We shot up in a room she was renting. I made the mistake a lot of junkies make when they haven't used for a while. I thought I could handle more than I could. I blacked out. By the time I woke up, her boyfriend was there, both staring at me, intently. "Thank god," she said, "I thought you O.D.'d."

I laughed, reassuring them that I was okay, and acted more sober than I was. I was embarrassed and just wanted to get home. I didn't live far—a twenty-minute walk—but I had misjudged how stoned I was. I collapsed in a phone box trying to ring an ambulance. Fortunately for me, a car full of girls on their way home from a club noticed my legs sticking out of the booth and came to my rescue. On the way to the hospital I realized they weren't girls at all—they were drag queens. I felt instantly safe and told them everything. As they were dropping me off at the emergency room, I told them to ring me at work and I'd send them some free records.

I didn't stay long at the hospital. By the time the medical staff got to me, the emergency was over. I wasn't dying, I was just very stoned. I went home, slept it off, and even managed to get to work the next day. The press office was in full operation when I arrived—Rob and Regine were working the phones and Debbie was putting together packages for journalists. I apologized for my lateness but didn't get a response. Fortunately, another one of the phones rang, I picked it up, and things got back to normal.

Later, when Rob and Regine were out of the office,

Debbie turned to me and said, "Aren't you going to apologize?" I didn't understand what she meant. I thought I had apologized. "You don't even remember, do you?" I thought back to the previous night and tried to remember any part of it that would have involved Debbie. "You showed up at my flat after midnight and started screaming at my window to let you in. You knew I had to be up early." I must have passed her flat on my way home, before I collapsed. "Don't ever do that again," she warned as she slammed down the binder she was looking through and stalked out.

Toward the end of the day, Regine handed me a phone. "It's for you," she said. "Some man who says his name is Tabatha." It was one of the drag queens from the night before, telling me what records she wanted. I wrote down her address and put together a package. A few days later she called again asking for more records. I sent more records. By the third call she was asking if Island had a catalogue I could send her. I told her there wasn't a catalogue and stopped taking her calls. It was beginning to feel more like blackmail than a friendly conversation.

•

ONE OF THE CLUBS I FREQUENTED in those days was the 606 jazz club off King's Road. I first heard of it through the saxophonist Andy Sheppard. Rob had been put in charge of Island's jazz label, Antilles, and had me do press on Andy's first album. Most of the people at the 606 were musicians; they often brought their instruments with them and joined in on a jam session. Two players who impressed me were twin brothers, Paul and Jeremy Stacey. One night, over several bottles of wine charged to my Island expense account, I came up with the idea of putting them on at a club called Prohibition in the West End. One of their friends agreed to play the double bass to make it a trio.

I knew the manager of Prohibition because there was a regular gay night there, with Fat Tony as the DJ. The other nights were straight, and I thought it would be nice to have a jazz night featuring the Stacey brothers. I sorted out a deal with the manager where the venue would keep the bar takings and I would get the entry charge. I didn't expect to make much money on it—I just thought it would be more interesting than doing press.

I spent a lot of time in the press office organizing the event and didn't notice that Rob was getting upset. I was paid to be a press officer, not a club promoter. At the end of a Friday, when I had spent most of the day plugging my jazz night, Rob called me into an empty office next door and fired me: "I don't know what drugs you're on, but you've been rambling incoherently, and I can't take it anymore. I'm sorry, but I have to let you go."

I didn't know how to react. The reference to drugs threw me. I wasn't on drugs. Had he overheard my calls from Fiona or Tabatha? Had people been gossiping about me? A junkie's past tends to follow him like a shadow he can't get rid of. I wasn't particularly upset when he fired me—in fact I felt relieved. He forced me to accept a decision that I had already made for myself a while ago—I didn't want to work there anymore, but I was afraid to quit until I had another job lined up. It wasn't just Island, it was the music business in general. It all seemed a bit tacky—and it was very heterosexual. I was the only openly gay man working for Island at the time.

I wasn't too worried about my financial situation. Rob said he would give me a good reference and a month's severance pay. I was also due several months of expenses that were still being processed by the accounts department. They were behind in their reconciliations, and I was still due a considerable amount of money. Regine was surprised that I was only given a month's severance pay—I should have negotiated more. I didn't realize I could negotiate more. I didn't think I was that important.

A few weeks after I left the company, a clerk rang from Accounts to tell me they had finished their reconciliation—much to my relief. I had spent most of my severance pay on partying and hadn't even considered looking for a job. "You owe us £800," the clerk said. I laughed at his joke until I realized it wasn't a joke. He wasn't laughing back. He explained that they had gone through all my expenses, from when I first started working there, and disallowed a lot of the expenses they had already paid. "But don't worry," he assured me. "You won't have to pay us back. We'll just call it even."

I couldn't believe what I was hearing. How could they charge me retroactively for expenses they had already paid? Legally, they probably didn't have a leg to stand on. I should have sued them; instead, I scored some heroin. Hugh had a connection and we both got stoned—a "one-off." But then a couple of nights later, we decided to have another "one-off," and it just escalated from there.

I went through my money rapidly, and I still had the jazz night to organize at Prohibition. I had promised to pay the Stacey brothers with money from the door, but I became increasingly worried that there wouldn't be any money from the door. I hadn't spent much time promoting the gig after I left Island, but I had promised the Stacey brothers, and I had to go through with it.

When I got to Prohibition on the night of the gig, it was packed—but not by paying customers. Someone had booked the club for a wedding party earlier that day, and there were still people there from the wedding. I let them stay, of course. It made the club look full—but full of drunken louts. Regine arrived and looked around for anyone she knew from the music business. "Who are these people?" she asked. I smiled, hoping everyone would leave early so I could go home. The manager embarrassed me further by coming over to my table, saying that he was sorry that nobody showed up, but that he would treat me and my guests to a bottle of champagne. A friend who thought the crowd were paying customers started to argue. Then the truth came out. I quickly opened the champagne.

After the Stacey brothers played the two sets that were part of the deal, I paid them with cheques drawn on what was left of my overdraft. Then I went home and shot up.

•

It didn't take long for my habit to get to the point where I sold anything I could to support it. All those free albums I got while working at Island went straight down to the Record and Tape Exchange. Without the albums I didn't need my stereo so I sold that too. The last thing to go was my television.

David Strettell was in and out of London, and when he visited, he got stoned too. One night when we were out of it, we finally had sex. I wrote in my diary: "Last weekend was (another) blur. David spent the night Saturday and we sucked each other's cocks. To think that there was that period in New York when I was in love with him, when I would have died to have sex with him. And now? Now it was just something we did." Instead of bringing us closer, having sex caused us to drift further apart. He went back to New York, and I don't think I saw him again until after he was married.

When I couldn't score through people I knew, I scored at a rundown pub called The Boltons near Earl's Court, the main gay area before Soho took over in the early '90s. I had been to The Boltons when I was not using, and I couldn't understand why anyone went there. Nothing much seemed to happen. A few customers hung around aimlessly in the shadows, and you couldn't tell if they were gay or straight. Other pubs in the area, like The Coleherne, existed for a reason: they were all about getting drunk and picking people up. At the Boltons, people seemed to drift in and out without reason—at least until I started using again. Suddenly I noticed that there was a whole social scene going on that revolved around the buying and selling of smack.

I had never noticed Mary, for instance—a small Irish woman without teeth who always sat at the same table doing crosswords. When nobody else had any smack, Mary did, but she was usually the last resort as her stuff was so weak. When she ran out, she sold valium at inflated prices to addicts who hadn't been able to score and needed something to help them get through the night.

Another regular knew a doctor who gave him methadone that he would then trade for smack. He was thin, with long blond hair. Sometimes he dressed as a woman, supporting his habit by picking up men who wanted to have sex with a woman who had a cock. Other times he sold himself as a guy. His best friend also turned tricks, but never as a woman: his punters wanted sex with a real tattooed skinhead. I described him in my diary as "still very young and probably under the illusion that his current sentence of being trapped by the circumstances of life is temporary."

•

One morning Regine called to tell me that Joe Batty, Paul Rutherford's boyfriend, was in hospital with full-blown AIDS. When I visited, it was truly horrible seeing how ill he had become. He was so thin that his skin was practically transparent: you could see the veins pumping away. He spoke slowly, his eyelids drooping as though he didn't have the strength to keep them open.

"You should have seen me last week," he joked. "I was even worse." He started to laugh, but his laugh turned into a cough that wouldn't stop.

A nurse arrived and then a doctor. "Are you okay, Joe?" they asked. They stood above him, watching him carefully in case any action had to be taken.

His cough calmed down after a while, and we continued our conversation. He said he'd been crazy to do so many drugs in New York when he knew he was HIV positive. I hadn't known he was positive during that "magical" period in the '80s. I don't think many people did. I tried to find some reassuring words. What could I possibly say that would be of comfort to a dying man? AIDS was a death sentence regardless of what lifestyle you lived. Back home, in my diary I wrote, "I will never forget the look in his eyes peering out over the oxygen mask—a look of fear and confusion and shock, as though his eyes were asking why he had suddenly become so thin and ill and old. He looked like an old man. And me wondering why something so horrible happens to someone so nice. Chance. Pure chance. Thoughts of my mother's death."

Joe survived that stay in the hospital, but there were others. Then one night I got a call from Regine: "Gary, Joe is dying. If you want to see him, get down here right away." But I didn't want to see him. I was stoned. I didn't want to think about him. I didn't want to face his death. Or any other death. My life revolved around smack and The Boltons. I'm not sure who was with Joe when he died, besides Regine. She said it was difficult to reach anyone because they were all out clubbing.

Not long after Joe's death, The Boltons was busted, and the people who hung out there scattered. I would sometimes run into one of them on the street and be able to score from them, but eventually I had to find another source. An Italian dealer sold smack for a while from a bench in Brompton Cemetery, but it was risky: the cops periodically raided the cemetery to bust the gay guys having sex behind the gravestones. You were always taking a big chance buying from dealers you didn't know. It wasn't like New York, where the packets of dope were sealed and stamped. When things got really bad, there was a pharmacist in Shepherd's Bush who sold bottles of codeine that helped with some of the withdrawal symptoms, but they were no replacement for the real thing. I had left Hugh's squat a long time ago and had moved into a DSS hotel—the English equivalent of a welfare hotel—too embarrassed to tell anyone how low I had sunk.

4. Anonymous

Regine was one of the few people who kept in touch with me after I moved into the hotel. I didn't have a phone in my room, but she sometimes called me on the pay phone in the communal hallway. I never understood why she stuck by me. Maybe she remembered the good times we had before I started working at Island, when I used to hang out with her at her flat near Parsons Green. That seemed like such a long time ago.

One morning Regine phoned and said she had met someone who was the literature secretary at a gay meeting of Narcotics Anonymous. She encouraged me to go and gave me the details: it met on Tuesday evenings in a church hall in Notting Hill Gate. I went one night but didn't grasp much of what they were saying. It was like they were speaking in a foreign language. They looked too clean-cut to be addicts.

Ultimately, it was loneliness that caused me to return to the meeting. I couldn't take another night on my own in that desolate hotel room. There was no television or radio, of course—I spent all my money on dope. I wondered how a drug I had started taking to be part of a group could end up causing me to become so isolated.

The second meeting I went to wasn't much different from the first, but at least I knew the format now. I knew there would be a time set aside for newcomers to share, and I promised myself that I would at least introduce myself. I started with the required, "I'm Gary, and I'm an addict." As soon as I was finished saying it, I broke down and started crying. I never doubted I was an addict, but saying it in front of a group of people made it seem so real. Once I started talking I couldn't stop. I poured out my heart. At the end of the meeting I accepted a "one day" key ring from the secretary, although I had used that day; the other people in the group said it didn't matter, to take the ring anyway. A white plastic tag attached to the ring had the N.A. symbol and the phrase "Just for Today." If I stayed clean, I'd be given a different-colored key ring after a month. A cheap plastic key ring was one of the things that kept me clean.

There were quite a few N.A. meetings in London, day and night; it was suggested that you choose one as your "home" meeting. I chose the gay meeting. Every Tuesday evening I walked to a church hall on Portobello Road, made myself a coffee in the kitchen, and joined the other recovering addicts seated in a circle in the main room. I was surprised to see Elton John in the kitchen one night. Although I had noticed other celebrities at meetings, none were as famous as Elton John. The first thing I noticed was his hat—it was his Russian fur hat period—and only then realized who was under the hat. He wasn't making a coffee, he was just standing in the kitchen on his own, waiting for the meeting to start before he went into the main room. One of the tenets of N.A. was that nobody was "special" or "different" so I introduced myself, as I would to any newcomer, and extended my hand; he looked at it with horror, and I quickly withdrew it. Trying to make him feel more comfortable, I mentioned that I used to work in the music business, which was probably the last thing he wanted to hear. He looked petrified. I quickly escaped into the main room.

Elton shared in newcomers' time about how he had just come out of a treatment center in the States. He said he felt embarrassed about living a lie all this time by marrying a woman and pretending to be heterosexual. The other addicts in the group looked at each other. Did he really think anyone thought he was straight all that time? He was one of my teenage heroes. I always assumed he was gay. Now he seemed like a caricature of himself.

Another tenet of N.A. was, "Who you see here, what you hear here, let it stay here," but the next day just about everything he said at the meeting appeared in the tabloids. The following week, the room was packed with people who looked more like journalists than addicts. Elton never showed up again.

•

A lot of newcomers cleaned up at residential treatment centers, probably not quite as posh as the one Elton John went to. One of them came up to me after the meeting and said, "You're Gary, aren't you?" I had no idea who it was. He could see I was puzzled. "It's Lee," he said. "I met you in New York with Sam."

It was Lee Sheldrick, the guy Sam and I had gone out with one night when he traded H for E. Back then he had bleached blond hair and wore a long Commes des Garçons skirt for men. Now his hair was brown, and he was wearing Levis and Nike Cortez trainers. The only thing that made him seem a bit "fashiony" was that his shoes were green. I had never seen green Cortez trainers before.

After the meeting we went for a coffee to catch up. Soon after he got back to London, he told me, a close friend of his died of an overdose. Lee was with him at the time. Trojan was a Taboo regular and fairly well known on the London club scene. He was never in New York, but the regulars at the Mike Todd Room had heard

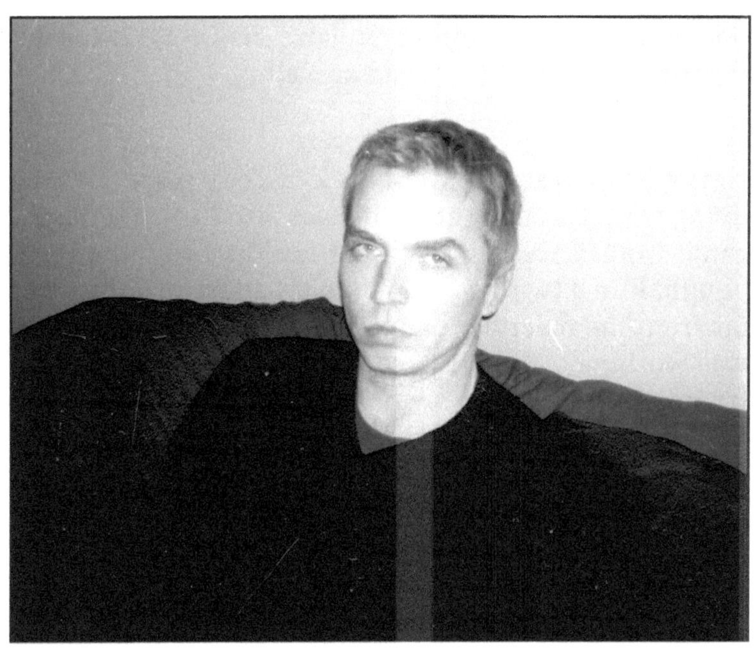

Lee Sheldrick

of him and even emulated him. He was only twenty-two when he died and was trying to make it into the art world. He overdosed at the flat of the film director John Maybury, who was his boyfriend at the time. Maybury, who would later direct an acclaimed film about the artist Francis Bacon, was not home when Trojan died: it was just Trojan and Lee. Press reports indicated that Trojan overdosed on pills, collapsing in the kitchen while Lee was in the front room, but I couldn't help wondering if heroin wasn't involved.

Lee and I became good friends after the N.A. meeting. Whenever I brought up the subject of Trojan, he would put his head in his hands and moan, "Don't," or "I killed him." Whatever had happened, Lee blamed himself for the death. The ICA in London put on a posthumous exhibition of Trojan's art in 2012, but by that time Lee would be dead as well.

•

AFTER OUR COFFEE we went back to Lee's place. He was living with a straight guy who was also in N.A. Edward came from a wealthy banking family. His father had bought him a two-bedroom flat in Ladbroke Grove, not far from the meeting; Lee rented one of the rooms. He was working as a part-time fashion consultant for two friends from Blitz days who owned a textile company. Style came naturally to Lee—he was often photographed at Blitz or Taboo—and he was still good at predicting colors and patterns that would be popular in the future. Paul Lonergan called himself a stylist and sometimes worked as one, but he didn't have Lee's natural talent—or the recognition by people in the industry.

I became a regular visitor to Lee at Edward's place. I liked Edward. He was going to university, working on his master's degree. During the day he worked on his dissertation about an African tribe he had visited—he showed us Polaroids from the trip that he planned on including in the paper, pictures of himself with members of the tribe.

Another of Lee's friends, the stylist Mitzi Lorenz, was also at the flat a lot. She had been one of the founders of the Buffalo fashion movement that Malcolm McLaren made famous in his song "Buffalo Gals." The Buffalo stylist Ray Petri had died a few years earlier of AIDS. Mitzi was still angry about how he had been deserted by his fashionable friends when he became ill. Her anger would take over when she was drunk, which was often. One night she started spitting and yelling at gay strangers on Old Compton Street, and I had to hide

Edward and Lee in a friend's flat. The next day she took me aside, drink in hand, slurring something about how she knew I was upset but that I shouldn't worry because I was part of "the family." In the nicest way possible, I told her that I was already part of the family before she arrived on the scene and that I could recognize an alcoholic when I saw one. I suggested she go to an A.A. meeting, but it was like talking to a brick wall.

•

I CONTINUED TO RUN INTO PAUL LONERGAN sometimes, but not at meetings. He was still using smack. I'd see him on Old Compton Street, usually with Fat Tony. When I told him about the gay N.A. meeting, he nearly choked with laughter: "Gay N.A.! I want to go!" He was laughing so hard that he started to spit. I doubted if either of them would ever clean up. Tony was more into coke than smack. Yet both of them did eventually stop using. Tony even stayed clean. Ray Allington was another person who surprised me by cleaning up. Like Jo Strettell, he was living in L.A.—I heard he was going to meetings there.

Lee and I often went to the "illness in recovery" meeting at the AIDS respite center, the London Lighthouse, which was not far from Edward's flat. The chair of the group was HIV positive, but not many of the people who went there were. Lee and I had been tested, and we were both negative; given the number of needles I shared in New York, it was miraculous that I didn't have AIDS. There were no needle exchanges back then. You had to buy a disposable needle from the dealer and reuse it. A sealed disposable syringe cost a dollar on the streets; a used one was 50 cents.

Soon after we started going to the Lighthouse

meeting, people began sharing about a new illness, chronic Hepatitis C. It seemed like everyone in the fellowship had it. I was tested and came out positive. I wondered if that was why I had such bad hangovers during my Island days. Not much was known about the virus. Some people progressed to serious liver disease and some didn't. I tried to find out as much as possible about it. At one talk I went to I met an infected girl in her twenties who'd already had a liver transplant. A gay guy at the same talk was infected with both HIV and Hep C. I couldn't imagine what that was like.

Having the illness helped me to become eligible for a Council flat. You had to be vulnerable to get a Council flat: my vulnerability was based on the fact that I was a recovering addict and had chronic Hepatitis C. It took over a year to get the flat, but when I did, the location was perfect, on a small street between Oxford Street and Tottenham Court Road in the West End—just a short walk to Old Compton Street, the hub of gay Soho.

5. Sex

In the late '80s the gay scene in London was centered in the Earls Court area, where The Boltons was. In the early '90s it moved to Old Compton Street with the opening of modern bars like The Village and The Yard, and really took off. Gay pubs had previously been hidden behind dark windows—or no windows at all; The Village had windows that brought the street into the brightly lit space. The proverbial closet had opened. The pink pound was born. Free newspapers like *Boyz* helped to spread the message that being gay meant having fun. Lee and I stopped going to N.A. meetings and started drinking again.

We usually started our nights at my flat before heading down to the bars on Old Compton Street. When those bars closed, we headed to late-night clubs like The London Apprentice in Shoreditch. You could smoke spliff openly on the top floor of the L.A. Although there were a few tables and chairs, most people sat on the floor passing a joint from one group to another, whether you knew them or not. After the L.A. closed, we went back to Old Compton Street. The best club in London wasn't a club, it was a twenty-four-hour café. In the middle of the night, the Old Compton café would be packed with gay people of every variety, from leather queens to drag queens, on their way home from clubbing. People were still high on the drugs they had taken earlier, and everyone was in a good mood, partying like it was their last day on earth. For some of them, it probably was.

By the '90s most of the back rooms in New York clubs had closed down because of AIDS, but in London they were just getting started. The larger gay clubs usually had a back room of some sort, even if it was just a bathroom adapted for the purpose like at The London Apprentice. There were also S&M clubs like The Block where on some nights the whole club became one big dark room. If you didn't have sex at a club, there were always the public cruising areas you could check out. The most popular were Hampstead Heath and Russell Square. You could easily spend an entire night at the Heath. Men searching for sex would gather around a campfire between visits to the bushes, and someone would usually bring along a portable music system. The pathway to sex began just behind the parking lot at Jack Straw's Castle pub, and the farther you went into the woodland the heavier the sex got. Older guys and people into "vanilla" sex would generally congregate near the beginning of the pathway. As you went further down the path, you might pass someone walking along in a jockstrap or bent over a tree trunk waiting to be spanked.

Russell Square was also accessible all night long but not quite as wild as the Heath. Men would either sit on the benches having sex or hide among the bushes as rats scurried at their feet. One regular in a business suit approached younger guys, offering them £20 to piss on him. Different types of sexual activities seemed to go in and out of style. "Watersports" was particularly popular for a time. There was a club in Kings Cross that had regular watersports parties in the basement, complete with an inflatable paddling pool and a man dressed head to toe in rubber who would clean up as best as he could with a mop and bucket as the evening progressed.

If you didn't find enough sex at the public cruising areas or the bars, you could always ring the chat lines.

Although there were no dating apps back then, there were plenty of telephone chat lines where you could have phone sex or invite someone over for real sex. One early morning, after being out all night, I came home drunk, got on a chat line, and made two dates for the afternoon. I usually only had oral sex with strangers, but this time I got fucked—by both guys. After the second guy, I noticed I was bleeding: it had been a long time since I had anal sex.

I didn't think about the experience again until a month or so later when a friend of mine, a woman I knew from N.A., rang and asked if I would go with her to have an HIV test. She had had unprotected sex with a newcomer in N.A. and was worried that he might have infected her. I went with her to the clinic and decided to have a test myself. In the early days of AIDS, being tested for it involved a lot of waiting. You first had to make an appointment to have the test, then you had to make another appointment to get the test result. You had to be given the result in person. Because I had been tested before and it was negative, I wasn't too worried until the day of the results as I remembered the chatline incident and the blood.

My friend and I went in for our results on the same day. We sat in the waiting room full of gloomy, nervous people and watched as they were called into a room and came out smiling. I had been told by one of my HIV friends that if they left you until the end, it meant you were positive. If there were two people in the room when you went in to hear the result, then it definitely meant you were positive; one of them would be a doctor and the other a counselor. People who weren't positive were told by a single person. There was no need for a doctor if your test result wasn't positive.

My friend was called in fairly early. I could see the relief on her face when she came back to the waiting room: she was negative. I asked how many people had been in the office when they told her. She said, "One." We then waited for my name to be called. I was the last person called. By then I already knew what the result would be.

I walked into the room, and just as I had been warned, there were two people behind a desk, a man and a woman. The man broke the news. He was the counselor. "I'm very sorry," he said, "but the test result has come back positive." He waited for a reaction, but there was no reaction. My brain had stopped working. I thought I had prepared myself for the possibility of a positive result, but how prepared can you ever be for a death sentence? I thought of Joe Batty and wondered how long it would be before I ended up like him. He only had HIV—I had both HIV and Hep C. I thought back to the guy I had met at the Hep C talk who had both illnesses and how sorry I felt for him. Now I was in the same situation.

After giving me the result, the counselor told me how they could help. They would provide counseling, he said, and help with benefits if I needed them, and they could also immediately offer me a microwave or a washing machine. Which would I prefer? I couldn't believe what I was hearing; it felt like a game show. I suppose the "prizes" were meant to soften the blow of the diagnosis, but it only made things worse. A microwave for when I became too weak to cook meals? A washing machine to wash my underwear when I lost control of my bowels? I had just been handed a death sentence. Did they honestly expect me to make a decision about an appliance?

Another blood test was taken to determine my CD4 count. Two weeks later I learned the results: it was 320. Once it got below 250 you were considered to have full-blown AIDS.

So many people I knew were positive that I didn't think the result would affect me as much as it did. Before my diagnosis, my HIV-positive friends didn't seem too concerned about the illness. They joked about being one of the "blessed." If anything, I had felt left out because I wasn't positive. After being diagnosed, it was a different story. It was as though a fog had lifted, exposing a secret world that had been previously hidden to me. It was like being unaware of the heroin scene at The Boltons until I became a junkie. Once I became one of the "blessed," HIV-positive friends opened up to me in a way they hadn't done before. Life, for the "blessed," meant waiting for the inevitable to happen. Waiting and watching. Was that a bruise on my arm or the beginning of Kaposi's sarcoma? Did I have a cold or was it the beginnings of PCP? Was I suffering from a sore throat or did I have thrush?

I dealt with the illness the way my HIV-positive friends did—drank a lot and did a lot of drugs. When having HIV was still a death sentence, doctors would prescribe just about anything to a patient because they knew what was coming. Of course it was difficult to sleep; I became addicted to "downers"—diazepam, Rohypnol, and temazepam, topped up with alcohol and spliff. I didn't drink at home, only when I went out, but I went out every night of the week. When I told Lee about my diagnosis, he didn't say much. He just went into the bathroom for a long time and came out with puffy eyes.

Lee and I continued our nightly drunken escapades

in Soho. One thing I hadn't thought about before taking the test was "disclosure." Was I meant to tell every potential sex partner that I was HIV positive before I took them home? The gay scene thrived on gossip, particularly in Soho, and telling one person your status usually meant that everyone would know. When I was HIV negative, I felt uncomfortable having sex, even "safe" sex, with someone I knew or suspected was positive. How could I now expect someone in a similar situation to have sex with me? And what exactly was safe sex? Nobody seemed to know. Kissing was safe, but was it still safe if you had bleeding gums? That was a "grey area," I was told at the clinic. There were so many grey areas that the only way to avoid infecting someone was not to have sex at all. Few people were willing to do that. In the real world, if someone positive had unsafe sex with someone else in the back room of a club, they assumed that the other person was positive as well.

•

OCCASIONALLY LEE AND I RAN INTO Sam McKnight on the gay scene, but I didn't have a lot of contact with him. I was surprised one day to see him mentioned on the front page of the *Times* at the newsstand I passed almost daily on Old Compton Street. When he cut Princess Diana's hair short, the new cut was called "iconic" in the *Times* and other major newspapers. He had crossed over from fashion into mainstream news, in print and on television.

With all the attention he was getting, Sam decided to turn one of his bedrooms into an office and asked if I would help him there. He asked Regine to be his press officer. She laughed: "What does he need a press officer for?" She had a point. His agency normally took care of his press. They also took care of his admin, so I wasn't sure what he needed me to do.

Things didn't get off to a very good start. Somehow I managed to lock myself out of his flat. Lilli Anderson, his sometime flatmate, had given me a set of keys, and I locked them inside. I was so embarrassed that instead of phoning Lilli and telling her what had happened, I tried to scale the security gate so I could get back in through the back window. The caretaker found me stuck at the top of the gate. After a few phone calls he confirmed who I was and let me back into the building. Later, when I saw Sam, he said, "Maybe it's time to stop doing drugs."

"I only smoke spliff," I responded.

"I know," he said.

I was afraid he thought I was doing harder stuff because I was hanging out with Lee. Sam had given up all drugs and alcohol, but he didn't judge other people by what they got up to. I would eventually get back into the harder stuff with Lee, but I was only smoking and drinking at that time.

Sam traveled a lot for work and was rarely at home. He would ring me before he left or leave a note as to what he needed me to do. Initially, I spent a lot of time dealing with photographs of him and the supermodels he worked with. It seemed like every time I went to his flat there were yet more photographs to take to the framing shop. He was decorating his flat with them. I thought back to Jim's original description of him as being "not very fashiony" and how much that had changed. If Sam had visited someone's apartment in New York during the '80s who had decorated their walls with pictures of supermodel clients, he would have been the first to mock them. Fortunately, the photos were a temporary diversion—when he moved to a bigger place, most of them disappeared. He had become bigger than a lot of the models.

Apart from odd errands and a bit of filing, Sam didn't have much for me to do. I was happy to help him out as a friend, but I didn't want to become an employee. After my HIV diagnosis I asked him to find somebody else to take over. He had a mutual friend, the singer Josie Jones, help out in my place. I didn't see a lot of him after that. I was closer to Lilli, who got her own flat in Notting Hill Gate, not far from Edward and Lee's place.

•

I SUPPOSE IT WAS INEVITABLE that Lee and I would start using again after we stopped going to N.A. meetings. It didn't seem like a big thing at the time—a "one-off" that became part of our nightly ritual. Edward also joined in. Mitzi stuck to booze and spliff. She didn't mind that Edward was using; in fact, she moved in with him, and they became lovers. Lee was not very happy about it. "I got there first," he joked to Mitzi, even though he really meant it. He had never been romantically involved with Edward, but he felt that his friend was being stolen from him—his rich friend.

Despite his addiction, Edward managed to finish his paper about the tribe he had visited. He asked if I would read it before he gave it to his professor. I expect he thought, in his upper-class way, that I would appreciate it because I had been to UC Berkeley. We arranged a time when we could be on our own so Lee and Mitzi wouldn't interrupt. He didn't want to give me the paper to read because he didn't want it to leave the flat. The Polaroids were originals, and he didn't want anything to happen to them.

The first thing we did when I arrived was to have a smoke of heroin—and then another and another. Then he brought out his masterpiece. Not wanting to influence my opinion of it, he retreated into the kitchen to do the washing up as I lit a cigarette and started reading. The next thing I remember was him shouting at me and fanning a dishcloth in my direction. "What the fuck have you done!" he yelled. I looked down at the paper. It was smouldering. I had nodded off and the cigarette ash had burned some of the irreplaceable Polaroids. He continued to shout insults at me in a manner that seemed increasingly flavored by class. I apologized and tried to ignore him—he was ruining my high. As far as I was concerned, a junkie was a junkie was a junkie, regardless of what sort of family they were born into. He wasn't any different than the other "trustafarians" I knew in the Notting Hill area—posh kids who supported their habits from trust funds.

Fortunately Lee and Mitzi came home soon after Edward's outburst. When I told them what happened, they laughed. Lee asked if there was any more smack. Edward handed him the tinfoil, Mitzi opened up a beer, and the nightly party began. After a few smokes, Edward calmed down, but I worried about what mood he would be in later. Lee and I left for Soho.

•

As Mitzi and Edward grew closer, the Ladbroke Grove flat became "their flat," leaving Lee feeling like a lodger. It didn't help his situation when someone he picked up at a bar stole Edward's laptop. Lee was asked to leave. He applied to the Council for housing and got a bedsit. He moved out, and Edward and Mitzi got married.

I didn't go to the wedding, but Lee did. When I saw him a few days later he mentioned that Rifat Ozbeck had designed the wedding dress and it made Mitzi look fat. People he knew from the '80s were there and told him how good it was to see him after all these years. Sam had asked how I was; Lee told him I was "coping."

At least that was what Lee told me had happened. I later learned from Lilli what actually took place. Lee got obnoxiously drunk at the reception and confronted Sam, saying, "Gary never wanted to work for you in the first place." I cringed. I wasn't working for Sam, I had just agreed to help him out as a friend. If I hadn't wanted to, I would never have volunteered.

I rang Sam about the incident. He was pretty laid-back about it. "We all get that way," he said, referring to Lee's behavior. I was already angry at Lee for other reasons, mostly financial. He had a habit of borrowing money and not paying it back. His latest excuse was that he was waiting for Kim Bowen to return to London so he could borrow money from her to pay me back the money he had borrowed from me. Lee had quit his job after he started using and was largely living off the kindness of friends. I didn't mind paying for the drinks or drugs when I could, but I saw how he took advantage of Kim financially and didn't want him to treat me the same way. I was supposed to be his friend, after all, not his bank account.

A few days after my conversation with Lilli, I saw Lee at Gay Pride with his brother. We talked about what had happened at the wedding, and he said, "I tried to tell you . . ." Tried? Who was stopping him from telling me the truth, apart from himself? He hadn't tried to tell me anything. The ease with which he could lie was astonishing. He asked for an "all is forgiven" hug. He said he knew how much I hated hugging people, but could he have a hug? I didn't want to seem like an ogre in front of his brother so I gave him a hug. As we embraced, he whispered into my ear, "I hate your fucking guts," and then he left. It was such a "Lee" thing to do.

•

One person I never expected to clean up was Paul Lonergan. But after I relapsed with Lee, Paul went into rehab. He had been busted for shoplifting, and one of his parole conditions was that he go into treatment. After rehab, he stayed away from London for a while. Once he got some clean time behind him, he visited one weekend. Lee and I were both still using. As Lee was shooting up, he decided to have a "heart-to-heart" with Paul, telling him to make sure he went to meetings and not to relapse. He said it with such sincerity that I thought the dope must be really good. Paul responded: "Lee, don't you think it's a bit hypocritical to tell me not to relapse when you're sitting there with a needle in your arm?"

Eventually Lee moved to L.A. with Ray Allington. I stopped using after he left. It wasn't easy, but I went back to N.A. for a while and that helped. The last time I saw Lee was when he was visiting from L.A. We spent a night together getting high for old time's sake. We talked about Ray; I had heard he too had HIV and Hep C. I asked Lee if he'd been sharing needles with him, and he responded, "Is the Pope Catholic?" Getting stoned with Lee that night was not the same as in the past. We were older and wiser and knew where addiction led. Still, I wish I had known then that it would be the last time I'd see him.

•

LEE WENT BACK TO L.A. after that visit and later moved to Japan. Paul came back to London and started working as a booker for Premier. He started drinking again and taking the drugs that were popular on the gay scene then—crystal meth, K, and GHB. He never went back to smack, though. I stayed away from heavy drugs and even limited my drinking. I started combination therapy at the end of the decade, which helped with the HIV but created havoc with the Hep C, causing a phenomenon known as "immune reconstitution." As the drugs boosted my immune system, my Hep C got worse. I had to stop drinking to limit the damage to my liver.

Combination therapy changed the gay scene. The "blessed," who had partied like there was no tomorrow, slowly came to realize that there was a tomorrow. A lot of them started working again, which meant an end to late nights. Getting used to the idea that we were going to live was almost as difficult as facing death had been. The camaraderie of the dying disappeared.

The advent of the internet at the end of the decade also brought a lot of changes to the gay scene. The first gay dating site started in 1999,and they proliferated in the early 2000s. While Paul and Cleveland used the net for dates, I used it to start a website. Instead of doing drugs I was writing about other people who did them—the "superstars" of Warhol's films. My online life replaced my "real" life. I became a recluse. I had the occasional visits by Paul and Cleveland and enjoyed hearing about their adventures on the gay scene, but for me, the '60s were much more interesting than "now." Thanks to the internet, I finally got to experience the decade that I had missed out on as a child.

Part III

1. Callie and Billy and Bibbe and Mark

I STARTED MY WEBSITE, warholstars.org, in 2001, when the use of the internet by the public was still in its infancy, bogged down by dial-up conections. Google had just released its search engine; Facebook was five years in the future. I heard about the World Wide Web and asked a net-savvy friend of Cleveland's how a page designed on a computer became a web "space" on the net. "Oh, that's really easy," he said, and proceeded to confuse me further by trying to explain "HTML." I decided the only way I was going to understand how the virtual world worked was to create my own website.

In those days most people didn't make websites about themselves, they created sites on a subject that interested them, such as an actor, an artist, or a period of history. I chose Andy Warhol's "superstars." I had seen Joe Dallesandro and Holly Woodlawn shooting up in *Trash*, watched Brigid Berlin and Ondine shoot up in *The Chelsea Girls*, listened to Lou Reed sing about heroin and the denizens of the Factory, and of course seen Billy Name's photographs of them all. They were everything I wanted to be when, as a child, my family used to drive into Hollywood to stare at the hippies—except Andy Warhol's hippies were more glamorous. I was too young to enjoy the '60s when it was happening, but I could be part of it in cyberspace. I retreated from the contemporary gay scene in London into the Warhol '60s of New York.

It was a good time to start an Andy Warhol website.

Unbeknown to me, Steven Watson was in the middle of writing the first important book about his circle[3], the scholar Callie Angell was writing the first volume of the Warhol film catalogue raisonné[4], and Craig Highberger was making a documentary on his transvestite friend Jackie Curtis[5], who had appeared in two of the films that Paul Morrissey directed for Warhol, *Flesh* and *Women in Revolt.*

Although I eventually would meet Craig and the others at different times in London, Callie was the person I was in contact with the most when I first started doing the site. There was a lot of inaccurate information out there about Warhol's films, and Callie was able to clear a lot of it up. As the adjunct curator of the Andy Warhol Film Project at the Whitney Museum of American Art, she had access to primary documentation, including developers' bills, Warhol's handwritten notes about the films, and raw 16mm footage. I didn't know much about her when we started corresponding, but I later learned that she was the daughter of Roger Angell, the fiction editor of *The New Yorker.* Her step-grandfather was E. B. White, the author of *Charlotte's Web* and co-author of *The Elements of Style,* a guide to grammar that was required reading when I was a high school student.

The first Warhol "superstar" who contacted me was Billy Name, the only person who had actually lived at Warhol's iconic silver studio on East 47th Street in Manhattan, the Factory. Although he appeared in some

3 Steven Watson, *Factory Made: Warhol and the Sixties* (Pantheon, 2003).

4 Callie Angell, *Andy Warhol Screen Tests: The Films of Andy Warhol Catalogue Raisonne (Vol. 1)* (NY: Abrams in association with the Whitney Museum of American Art, 2006).

5 *Superstar in a Housedress*, 2004.

of Warhol's earliest films, Billy was mostly known for his striking high-contrast photographs of the era, which have been widely reproduced in books about the artist. He was also a friend of Ray Johnson's and knew Bill Wilson; I got to know Billy before I met Bill.

It was largely due to Billy's support that my site took off. He recommended it to other Warhol scholars, who wrote to me with a respect I hardly deserved. A lot of the information on the site came from Callie and Billy.

•

NOT LONG AFTER Billy Name and I began corresponding, I was contacted by another "superstar," Bibbe Hansen. Bibbe is the mother of the recording artist Beck and was one of Andy Warhol's "Thirteen Most Beautiful Woman." I laughed at her husband Sean Carrillo's reaction when he heard I grew up in Simi Valley: "Simi Valley!!!!!!!! ARGHHHHH!!! My brother lives there. I'd rather drink bleach."

Attached to Sean's first email was an account of how Warhol got the inspiration for his film *Prison* from Bibbe's experiences as a juvenile delinquent. She met him the day after she was released from Spofford Street, a detention center for inner-city delinquents. Bibbe and her father, the artist Al Hansen, were gallery-crawling ("arting," she called it) and ended up at Stark's restaurant, where they joined a table that included Andy Warhol, his art assistant Gerard Malanga, and Edie Sedgwick's friend Chuck Wein. Bibbe ordered coffee and lit up a cigarette. She was only thirteen. Warhol was intrigued. "What do you do?" he asked. Her father answered for her: "She just got outta jail; I sprung her yesterday." Warhol asked what it was like "inside," and she told him some of her experiences. He asked her if she wanted to be in a movie, and the result was *Prison,* with Edie Sedgwick as her co-star.

Al Hansen died in the mid 1990s. Bibbe kept his memory alive by reenacting some of his performance-art pieces in Europe. After I got to know her and Sean through the website, I would see them in London on their way back to the States. One of the pieces she performed involved wrapping her head in duct tape.

"Are you mad?" I asked her when she told me about the performance during one of her visits. "What about your hair?"

"I know," she said. "Some of it came out. It wasn't too bad, but it really needs a cut."

Cleveland was having his hair cut on Charing Cross Road at the time—I was going to meet him later—so I rang him to see if he could get Bibbe an appointment. While Cleveland's hairdresser did her hair, Sean went next door and bought several copies of a discounted book about Warhol that had pictures of Bibbe in it. I showed them to the hairdresser and joked about how she was cutting the hair of a superstar. Bibbe now didn't look very different from Bibbe then. I was surprised when she took off her Ray-Ban Wayfarers for the wash by how beautiful her emerald green eyes were—and not a crow's foot in sight. She was the most youthful-looking person over fifty I had ever seen.

When Beck played the Royal Albert Hall in 2003, Sean was nice enough to get me a box. I took Lilli. There were already two students in the box; they had seen it was empty and decided to take advantage of it even though they didn't have the right tickets. Lilli and I were happy to have the company—I ordered a couple of bottles of champagne which we all shared.

•

Around the time I met Bibbe and Sean, I got an email from someone calling himself "imnot stopping" in response to an item I had posted on the site about Fred Hughes, Warhol's ex-business manager, who had died the previous year. *The Guardian* had published an interview with Duncan Roy, a film director who claimed he had been Hughes's lover. The journalist, Caroline Roux, quoted someone from the Warhol Foundation as saying, "Fred Hughes was a consummate liar, social climber, and a bespoke SOB who grew to total ghoulishness because of his connection . . . to Andy Warhol. Why is it, I wonder, that great people seem to love the presence of these reptile-like creatures?"[6]

That was strong language coming from the litigiously cautious Foundation, if it did come from the Foundation. The email from "imnot stopping" demanded to know who at the Warhol Foundation had made those "deeply offensive" remarks about Fred. I wrote back with the details of the article and asked why he wanted to know. He said he had known Fred for thirty years, adding, "Tell me more about yourself and your site and how you got into it, and I may then tell you more about my interest, OK?"

Who was this person? I told him I had lived in New York in the '80s and mentioned hanging out in the Mike Todd Room, thinking I might know him from there. He wrote back identifying himself as Mark Lancaster; he had been to the Mike Todd Room on opening night with "Andy and Co., I think Jean-Michel Basquiat, Julian Schnabel and Francesco Clemente, Keith Haring

6 Caroline Roux, "Film: Rake's Progress," *The Guardian* (London), 21 September 2002.

maybe . . . I was in and out of NY after 1964 until 1972," he told me, "when I moved there (from London) and stayed until 1985, seeing Andy and Fred frequently but just socially. Now I live in Rhode Island . . ."

I knew who Mark was from reading about him in *Popism*, the memoir of the '60s Andy Warhol dictated to Pat Hackett over the telephone, and wondered what had happened to him. He was an English art student, from Newcastle, who visited the Factory at the suggestion of one of his teachers, Richard Hamilton, while he was on holiday in New York in 1964. Warhol was shooting *Batman/Dracula* when he arrived at the Factory, and he ended up appearing in the film. Fascinated as I was by well-known "superstars" like Edie Sedgwick, I was even more curious about minor players like Mark who hadn't been heard from for a considerable time. The nice thing about having a website, instead of a published book, was that I was so accessible—I could be contacted with the click of a mouse—and I could keep adding to it forever!

Mark's random email began a correspondence that lasted more than a decade. I asked Mark what other films he was in at the Factory. He said that he gave one of Warhol's major superstars, Ondine, a blow job in *Couch* and was also in a *Kiss* film with Gerard Malanga. Gerard was straight; I wondered whether they had "french-kissed." Mark wrote back:

> Yes, Gerry and I did French-kiss. How else can you keep kissing somebody for three minutes, or was it six? I saw that movie right after it was processed, and I think I occupy most of the screen—it is all close-up head shots—probably because I was pushing against him harder than he was against me. He was sexy but not

my type. I spent a good deal of time that summer trying to figure that out and experiment with "types." I always assumed that Gerry was bisexual, most people seemed to think that. He had a crush on Gloria Wood, a friend from Newcastle I brought to the Factory a few times.

Kissing another man in a Warhol movie didn't necessarily mean Gerard was bisexual, it just meant he was part of the free-wheeling '60s. It was different with Fred Hughes. Mark confirmed Duncan Roy's claim that Hughes was bisexual.

Mark hadn't exactly disappeared after he appeared in the films. He subsequently moved to New York and designed costumes, lighting, and decor for the Merce Cunningham Dance Company. I was surprised to learn that during that first trip to New York in 1964, he had also met Jasper Johns, and they ended up in a twelve-year relationship.

It eventually emerged that Mark had known Ray Johnson and knew Bill Wilson. I was in touch with Bill by then and asked Mark if he would mind if I mentioned him to Bill. When I asked Bill about him, I got this as a response:

G.: About 1964, I allowed M. Lancaster to stay in my house for a summer, without rent or compensation for the inevitable expenses of a house. He left before I returned to NY, with no trace of "Thank You," but signs of ingratitude. When we returned, I found that two antique chairs were gone (the international phone bill can be set aside). The two chairs had intense emotional meanings for me. Also one was half of a pair, so that its twin has been deprived of symmetries.

I have no evidence of what happened. And I will not mention experiences of English sponges, the young men

> who as they cross the Atlantic raise themselves one or two social classes, graduate themselves from impressive educational institutions, and amplify twitteringly that they have once shaken hands with Harold Acton (Sir) into an abiding friendship and a month in his Villa, with such amusing people & superior wines . . . Because I have no interest in aesthetic hustlers, I have no desire to have Mark Lancaster's email address.
>
> He added pain to my pains during a painful period of my life. I regret even mentioning his name, which may pollute other Ray Johnson archives, but perhaps not mine, since one of my themes in art is aesthetic trustworthiness. Your offer to put me in touch with him is well-intended and is received as an appropriate gesture—your impulse to relay and network is correct. However, I want my chairs! Bill

When I relayed this to Mark, he responded: "I kind of knew to trust my instincts about what Bill Wilson would think of me. I knew I had not exactly behaved badly about his house, since I had not left it empty, because Nam Jun Paik was there, but I also had not stayed there until he got back. Of course there are English 'aesthetic hustlers' such as he describes (and I love the phrase), but I wasn't one." Grinding salt into the wound, he added that Bill probably "deeply regrets" that he doesn't have a brownstone anymore which would "now be worth $5 million." He ended his email with: "But I have nothing, absolutely nothing, bad to say about him."

Mark was wrong about the brownstone. Bill was still living in it. The situation with the chairs was eventually resolved, or at least repaired. A couple of months later, Bill wrote that his architect son, Andrew, fixed "the twin of one of the 'disappeared chairs,' so it is ready for my new 3rd floor, which is just begun . . ." I remained friends with both Mark and Bill but avoided mentioning the one to the other.

•

MARK WAS TELLING ME such interesting things about the art world of the 1960s that I asked if I could turn the emails into an interview and put it on the site. It was the first time I had the answers before the questions in an interview. We continued our correspondence for a decade, then suddenly he stopped writing. He didn't respond to my emails or to emails I forwarded to him from other people trying to contact him. The mystery of his disappearance went on for years. I searched for a death notice on the internet, but there was nothing. And then in 2017 I found out, completely by accident, what had happened to him from an unexpected source, Jo Kelley and Bruce Carter, her husband.

Jo and Bruce kept in touch after I got out of the hospital and occasionally would push me in my wheelchair to an art exhibition. During one of these outings they mentioned a neighbor who knew a lot about art, Richard Morphet. Mark referred to Morphet as his "oldest friend of all": he had known him since they were fourteen and kept in touch after Morphet became the keeper of the modern collection at the Tate Gallery and curated the first Warhol retrospective.

Jo and Bruce arranged a lunch with Richard at their house, and it was there I learned what happened. Richard told me that Mark was suffering from "inertia." As he put it later in an email, "Mark himself doesn't email anyone anymore, but David puts Mark in touch, via his email. David advises me to warn you that Mark, though healthy, has cognitive issues. I wish I could tell you what that means, but I have no idea." David was Mark's partner, the artist David Bolger.

Richard sent me another email the following day to clarify things:

> . . . just to avoid any confusion about Mark's situation healthwise. I don't know in detail what it is, but as far as I know he has not had a stroke. I think the change came when he had a horrible fall in the street in Miami Beach in late September 2010.
>
> As I understand it, he fell full length onto the back of his head. It was very serious at the time, but after a time he recovered his health, and from all I hear, he goes out and about normally, and he and David have a good circle of friends. His handwriting is as vigorous as it always was. One of my children had lunch with Mark and David in Florida in 2014 and found Mark as articulate and on-the-ball as ever.
>
> So I have no idea what the "cognitive issues" are. Maybe they concern memory about recent things (as my daughter said he was fully up to speed about the past)? I get the impression that he doesn't do much, proactively. I know he stopped painting quite some time ago, I think even before his fall.

•

I GOT A LOT OF MILEAGE from the the Mark Lancaster interview. It was cited in the Warhol catalogue raisonné, and David Strettell mentioned it in an email conversation we had in August 2004, although he was mainly writing to tell me that he had married. I was happy for him, but I would probably have been just as happy if he had ended up as a drug-addicted tramp living on the

Bowery. When we lived at 12th Street I joked about how he would become like everyone else when he got older and settle down with a family. I might have mentioned the word "bourgeois." He denied it vehemently, saying he would always be an outsider. I didn't remind him of this when he told me he was married, of course, I just congratulated him.

Toward the end of his email David mentioned something that was even more disturbing than his marriage, writing, "Sad about Ray—Jo was deeply involved and gave me a blow-by-blow account of the bitter end."

I hadn't been in touch with Ray Allington for a long time. I searched on the internet and found an obituary for him in *Women's Wear Daily*: he died on January 29, 2004 at the age of forty-six of liver failure.[7] David, surprised I didn't know, proceeded to go into a detailed account of how he died. The last time he saw Ray was at his sister Jo's house in Los Angeles. He hadn't changed much, according to David, "except that he had these huge horsy white teeth . . ."

Jo Strettell and Ray had become close friends. Living in Los Angeles, they were both in N.A. But then Ray relapsed and went back to England for Christmas 2003 to "sort out a few health issues." He landed at his sister's house in Manchester and "spent two weeks doing drugs in her back room." David wrote:

> Jo and her good friend Janine (wife of Anthony Edwards, Dr. Green on *ER*—in L.A. there's always a celeb thrown into the mix somewhere) had effectively ostracized him by this point, but they both became

7 Obituary: Hairstylist Ray Allington, 46, *Women's Wear Daily*, 4 February 2004.

> concerned when they heard he had not reappeared in L.A. and made a round of calls to track him down. An old friend of Ray's found out what he was up to, discovered him in a terrible state, and rushed him to hospital in London where friends could keep an eye on him. Jo flew over to be at his side and told me she got there on the day he died.

David added, "Just read your interview with Mark Lancaster—really interesting. A lot there. I particularly like the David Hockney gay coffee shop drive-by and value the information about Derek Jarman's cock." I laughed. Mark had referred to the the size of Jarman's cock during our interview: ". . . and by the way, I can't be the first person to tell you he had a really big dick."

•

NOT LONG AFTER I LEARNED that Ray Allington had died, I found out that Lee Sheldrick was also dead. The cause was similar to Ray's—cirrhosis of the liver. A memorial was held in London at Soho House. Lee's friends from the Warren Street days were there along with several of his past boyfriends; a few came up to me to complain that they still had "issues" with him. Issues? I still had issues with him, but for god's sake, he was dead. Who cared about "issues'? Mitzi was there, drink in hand, and Paul Lonergan put in a brief appearance. I ordered a bottle of champagne and drank it on my own at the bar. Kim Bowen, Jeffrey Hinton, and other people Lee had known in the '80s were dad-dancing to '80s music and hanging out together on a terrace outside the main room.

Lee would have hated it: a room full of ex-boyfriends with issues and a clique of dad-dancers from the past.

There was a microphone, and a few people got up and spoke, but not many, and they didn't say much. Nobody mentioned how great it was to get out of it with Lee. I didn't say anything, and I wish I had, armed with my bottle of champagne. Instead I left and went around the corner to Comptons. In the old days I would have probably run into Lee there. He hated memorials.

Lee's Japanese boyfriend was also at Soho House. I met him for lunch a few days later at Balans on Old Compton Street. He could barely speak English, and I couldn't speak Japanese, but I got the impression from the questions he asked that he hadn't known Lee for very long. I guessed that he probably took care of Lee financially in the same way that Kim Bowen had during their Warren Street days.

I asked the boyfriend whether Lee was using when he died. He said they had found some syringes in his flat, but they might have been from his interferon treatment for Hepatitis C. Hep C was now being treated with a long course of interferon. Lee had apparently tried it, but hadn't kept up with the shots because it made him too ill.

At one point during the lunch, the boyfriend reached into his bag and took out some photographs: "I made some copies if you want them," he said. They were pictures of Lee in his coffin, surrounded by flowers that friends had scattered around his body. The boyfriend explained that death was a time for celebration in Japan. "Happy time," he said, smiling. I looked at Lee lying in his coffin. Despite the flowers, he still looked like a soulless corpse, similar to how my mother had looked in her coffin. It was just another dead body. I told the boyfriend to put the pictures away; I didn't want them. We finished our meal in silence and went our separate ways.

Walking back to my flat, I thought about Lee, and about Ray. It felt strange outlasting them—I felt like ringing Lee and gloating about it. I had been closer to Lee than Ray. I had spent more time with him, both clean time and using time. In a way, I was glad both of them had died as they lived—as addicts. Maybe they would have lived longer if they had stopped using, but would they have been the same people? At least they were true to themselves. Part of me envied them.

So many people, including me, had cleaned up. Even Fat Tony was clean now. But were the recovered addicts as interesting as they had been when they were using? Was Tony as bitchy and funny? William Burroughs had remained a junkie for most of his life—he was taking methadone when he died in his eighties. Would he have been as interesting a writer without the dope? Drugs were an intrinsic part of Ray and Lee's souls. Instead of condemning them for their addiction, I recognized that they couldn't have lived any other way. I missed them for what they were, not for what they could have been.

2. The death of a New Jersey Comet

NOT LONG AFTER LEE'S MEMORIAL, my father died. I tried to remember something about him that I could attach to a feeling. I remembered lots of arguments about the Vietnam War. I remembered screaming because I was being attacked by mosquitos on a family trip to the Everglades and him yelling at me, "Really, Gary! When are they going to put you in a skirt!" I remembered him working a lot and falling asleep on the living room couch every night, smelling of grease from the machine shop he worked in. On weekends he'd work on his motorcycles in the garage. He made motorcycles for us kids out of the spare parts from his old motorcycles. I hated motorcycles. I was not very good at anything physical. I preferred to stay in my room and read about the exciting world outside of Simi Valley. I couldn't wait to leave.

Now that both my parents were dead, I regretted not having asked them about their lives before they became "parents." I regretted it even more, years later, when my own mortality was called into question. Their history was part of my history, and I didn't even know how they met. My sister Carol filled me in:

> So funny that you asked about Mom and Dad meeting. Just as I was about to respond and tell you that I'm surprised I don't know that, I remembered something Mom told me. As teens, they used to all hang out in the streets of Newark, New Jersey, porches, stoops, sidewalks. I just remembered that Mom told me that Dad was on his motorcycle and riding down her street. Mom was kind of a brassy teen and yelled, "Hey, give me a ride!" I don't think she thought he would stop, but he did, turning around, and Mom got

> on. And that's the story of little Gary Comenas. Really, I think their whole relationship was embedded in that motorcycle group, the New Jersey Comets.

I didn't mention my father's death to my London friends; the only person I told was Bill Wilson. He wrote:

> Gary: all my thoughts are with you at a time that is difficult at best. Freud wrote that the death of a father was the most poignant moment or event in a man's life. I doubt that any man can judge that he satisfied his father's expectations or hopes. But the onus then is on the father, who should have wanted what the son wanted for himself, and should have left him free to become himself on his own terms . . .

I learned about the circumstances of my father's death through emails from my sisters. It happened while he was returning to California with his girlfriend after visiting Carol in Philadelphia. It had taken him a while to get over my mother's death, but he had eventually found a new partner at a dance for widows and widowers. They had been together for a few years. Dad was in his early seventies. She was a few years younger but plagued with health problems; my father complained about how much she complained about her aches and pains. She became ill on the drive back from Philly, and they stopped at a hospital for tests. The hospital decided to keep her in overnight, and my father took a room at a nearby motel, promising to return the next day to visit her. He never showed up. They found him on the floor of his room, reaching for the phone. He had had a heart attack.

It seemed fitting, somehow, that my father died in an anonymous town in the anonymous Midwest. When we were children he would drive the family cross-country every summer to visit our Lithuanian relatives "back east" in New Jersey, where I was born. We had moved to the Sunshine State when I was four to pursue the American dream on the G.I. Bill. The thing I remember most from those trips is the migraines my mother had as we drove through the hot desert with sheets over the windows to block out the sunlight. I had read about families running out of gas in the desert and dying of dehydration in my mother's favorite magazine, the *Readers' Digest,* and I was sure we were going to be next.

Dad wasn't interested in seeing any of the sights; the trips were all about mileage: each day we had to achieve a certain number of miles toward our destination. Once we got to Jersey, we were allowed a certain amount of family sightseeing, but the thing I most remember about those visits is the deliveries of boxes of beer that

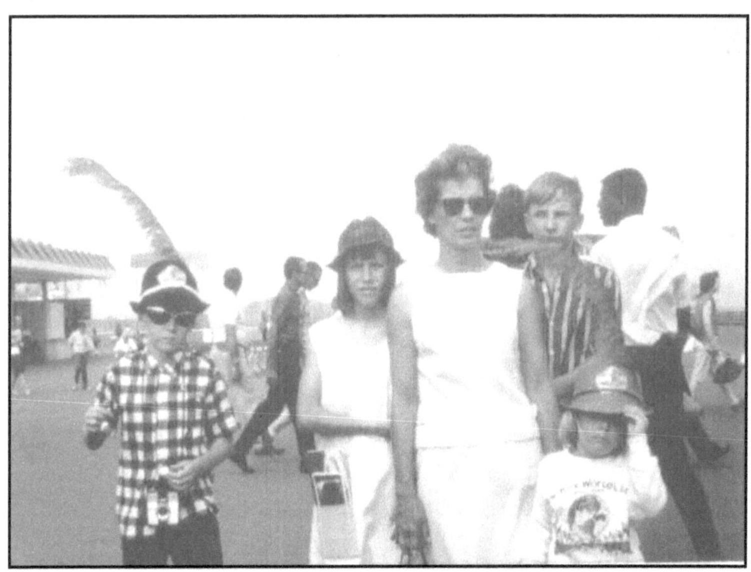

At the 1964 World's Fair: me, Carol, Mom, John, and Cathy.

my relatives seemed to be constantly receiving from the supermarket. We got to visit the 1964 World's Fair on one of the trips, but I was too young to remember much. Among ourselves we seemed to be constantly arguing. At parties, however, my parents were in their element. They worked off each other like a comedy team. They loved the television comedians, people like Moms Mabley, Phyllis Diller, and Jack Benny, and sometimes used their material.

Dad was still alive when they found him on the motel room floor; he died later in the hospital. Cathy and Carol flew out to get the body. I stayed in England. Carol described the funeral in an email:

> The funeral went well. Twenty-five members of Dad's Harley club showed up on their colossal motorcycles and processed behind the hearse to the cemetery. The service was nice. All the kids said a few words. We played Credence Clearwater.
>
> Everyone drove down to the gravesite, where Dad was given a military burial, complete with folding the flag and a bugle playing taps. Your wreath was placed next to the coffin during the ceremony. Your flowers were beautiful, the colors hopeful, the way Dad would have wanted it. Your card and quote brought most of us to tears at the viewing. We're all sort of decompressing right now.

The quote that I sent on the card was: "Everything that happens after I die continues the story of my life." It was the last line of a short story called "Men" from Bill Wilson's collection *Why I Don't Write Like Franz Kafka*.[8]

8 William S. Wilson, *Why I Don't Write Like Franz Kafka* (NY: Ecco Press, 1977)

I told Bill I used the quote and how it had brought my father's friends to tears. He wrote back: "So, now you can count amongst your fans, the Southern California Harley Riders Association! I am gratified that something of my voice could be heard at your father's funeral. You must be feeling eerie. Expect your father to return to you in dreams, if he hasn't already . . ."

My father did not return to me in dreams, but I got to know a little more about Bill's past as we discussed our fathers' lives. He told me his father had been a legislator for the State of Maryland and how relieved he had been when Bill was rejected for military service. I envied his relationship with his politically radical father. My conservative father would probably have been perfectly happy for me to join the army during the Vietnam War. Fortunately the draft had ended by the time I was eligible.

Bill's story about being rejected for military service led, as so often was the case, to a story about Ray Johnson. Ray was rejected by the draft board "because of a murmur of a heart," which Bill noted was "bureaucratic code for homosexual in those days." He added, "I have a friend who still thinks he has a heart murmur, but the doctor heard something in his voice and saw something in his demeanor, not in his heart."

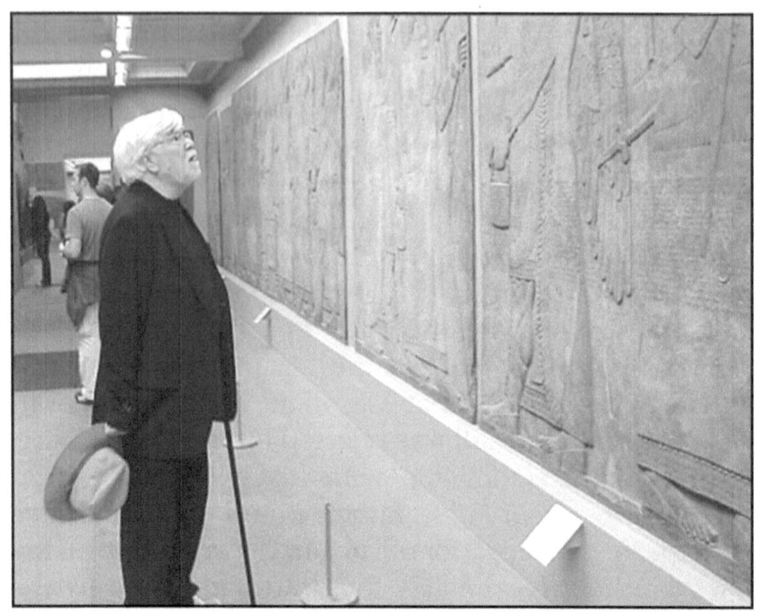

Bill Wilson at the British Museum, 2005

3. Bill Wilson

I HAD BEEN CORRESPONDING with Bill Wilson for two years before I finally got to meet him in person when he visited London in 2005. I arranged to meet him at Heathrow Airport and was so worried about missing him that I got there two hours early. As the passengers came out of the arrivals gate, I scrutinized each one carefully, trying to identify him from a photograph he had sent me with his first email. I had not realized there were so many men with white hair and beards in the world. As the thick curtain covering the gate was drawn shut, indicating that all the passengers had exited the plane, I panicked and ran to the Information Desk. The clerk put out a call that echoed through the lobby. I hurried back to the gate, and as I ran toward it, the curtain was suddenly pulled open and Bill made his entrance in a wheelchair wearing a fedora hat. He reached out in my direction, shouting, "There you are!" as though he had been looking for me for ages. "I've lost my cane!" I laughed, wondering how a person could lose a cane on an airplane. It was one of the best entrances at an airport that I'd seen. The fact that there were no other passengers by that time emphasized his importance: he wasn't *a* passenger, he was *the* passenger.

I took over the wheelchair duties from the grateful airline employee and wheeled Bill out to a black cab. As we got in, we nearly fell over each other. "No, no, you get in first," he said. I got in first. "Now pull," he shouted, reaching out his arms. I grabbed them and pulled him into the cab. Our Laurel and Hardy routine completed, he settled into his seat with a relaxed sigh. "There!" he said, as though it had been the easiest maneuver in the world.

I don't recall a single gap in our conversation as we headed toward central London. He had booked a room at St Margaret's, a bed and breakfast in Bloomsbury recommended by his friend Henry Martin, whom he would visit in Venice after London. Henry had cautioned him that he hadn't been to the B&B for some time, and the place had certainly seen better days. There was no lift, for one thing, just a rickety staircase. Bill held onto the stair rail with both hands while I followed behind to stave off a fall. He was still coping with the effects of the stroke he had had before I knew him. His room was tiny, just enough space for a single bed and a television set on an extension rail. It looked like it had barely survived World War II and not much had been done to it since.

"Do you really want to stay here?" I asked.

"It's got character," he replied. I left him to unpack and ran down to James Smith and Sons on New Oxford Street to buy him a new cane. Those were the days when I still could run. After my heart attacks seven years later, I'd be purchasing my own walking sticks from the same shop.

When I got back to Bill's room, he grabbed the cane and inspected it as if to find fault, but it suited him perfectly. Leaving his clothes in a heap on the bed, he said, "Let's go to the British Museum." As he sashayed down the stairs with his new cane, he kicked a leg in the air, Rockette-style, to show how agile he was. "There! You see!" he boasted. I laughed nervously as the leg he was balanced on started to shake precariously.

Once we got to the British Museum he walked straight to the Assyrian panels from Nimrud and carefully examined them. Then we left. That day it was the only exhibit he wanted to see.

•

As we walked back to his B&B, I noticed Bill was checking out some of the guys who passed us. I was reminded of Ray Allington's comment when I first arrived in London about how good-looking English guys are. I said the same to Bill; he responded with, "Yes, and they know it!" I laughed at his cynicism. It was one of the things I liked about him.

Speaking of boys, I asked him about his ex-wife, the artist Ann Wilson. Had he left her because he had come out as gay? He said it was the other way round: she had left him—for Gene Swenson. Swenson, an art writer and curator in the 1960s, was responsible for the interview that produced Andy Warhol's famous "I want to be a machine" quote. Exhibitions, essays, and even a lawsuit have been based on that quote, interpreted to mean that Warhol wanted to paint like a machine: to print his paintings rather than paint them. But when the original tapes of the interview were found, it turned out that Warhol had meant something completely different. On the tapes, he says he wishes everyone could be as non-judgmental as a machine, not that he or anyone else should paint like one.[9] Gene, like Bill, was primarily gay; Ann had left one gay man for another.

Bill had met Ann when she was living on Coenties Slip, a historic two-block street beside the East River in lower Manhattan. In the 1950s the old chandleries and warehouses became the studios and living spaces of artists who would later gain fame in the Pop world, including Ellsworth Kelley, Agnes Martin, Robert Indiana, Jack Youngerman (with his wife, Delphine Seyrig), and James Rosenquist. Bill told me about it in an email, saying, "Rolf Nelson lived at 3-5 Coenties Slip, in the same loft with my fiancée, whom I didn't marry, and with Anne Ubinger, whom I married." Bill continued:

> As you see, I wander away from Andy, not to confuse you, but to convey a sense of the whole huge field of the era, wherein Andy was one figure woven into an immense tapestry of people, many of them at that time aspiring to become successful artists, hence just like Andy at that time, that is, equal to Andy in the sense of having talent and potential to become significant.

9 See Gary Comenas, "Did Andy Warhol want to be a machine?" http://warholstars.org/Did-Andy-Warhol-want-to-be-a-machine.html and Jennifer Sichel, "Do you think Pop Art's queer? Gene Swenson and Andy Warhol," *Oxford Art Journal*, March 2018.

> Many horses were at the starting gate, and the race was only about to begin when I became intimate with Coenties Slip, where Agnes Martin blew up a telephone booth to get the money, she was so desperate. Robert Indiana did some sexual work for money. I don't quite know how to delineate Andy's splendid isolation—next to some other Pop artists, but never with them on the same plane socially. Ray was his friend, I guess, but each seemed to be in a world of his own, at least at a distance from other Pop artists of enduring significance . . .

Bill's recollections of Coenties Slip conjured up in my mind a romantic image of an academic falling in love with a young painter in an artist's loft in Manhattan. But as I found out more about Ann (whom he usually referred to as Anne), I realized that their marriage was plagued with problems. Jill Johnston's autobiography revealed something Bill hadn't told me—that Ann tried to kill herself in 1966. Jill wrote:

> Around that time [1968] I became acquainted with two people who bridged the worlds of art and politics and who would mean a great deal to me in the months to come. One of them had organized the demonstration outside MOMA the night of the Dada-surrealist opening; the other lived down the street from me, at the big, sprawling intersection of Canal Street and the Bowery where the Manhattan Bridge lies.
>
> Both had also been to Bellevue. Of the two, Ann Wilson, who lived down the street, had not gone crazy exactly but had tried to commit suicide by consuming quantities of pills. That was in late August '65, her stay at Bellevue preceding mine by several weeks . . .

> By the time I met Ann she was quite a well-known art-world character herself. With Bill she had twin daughters and a son, losing her standing with the artists by becoming a mother. She then lost her standing as a mother by falling in love with Gene Swenson ("a romantic escape," she has described it, "from the harshness and domestic responsibility of marriage") and running away from home. With Gene her standing was precarious because Gene was . . . an active homosexual, and during this period, he had a boyfriend called Harry . . . Sometime during '67 Gene cracked up and went to Bellevue.[10]

When I showed this quote to Bill, he responded:

> . . . if I read more of this quotation from Jill, going beyond the erroneous date, 1965 for 1966, I wouldn't have the composure to write the letter I am writing to you for you about Andy: a portrait of the young artist as a young blot . . . I need to compose myself in order to be composed enough to compose . . .

The "erroneous" date was the year of Ann's attempted suicide, which had taken place a year later than Jill indicated. By 1966 Bill was separated from his wife and mostly taking care of their kids himself while teaching at Queens College. He recalled:

> I had to go to bed early, get up and find three pairs of sneakers, get to Queens College to teach, wait around in the laundromat, shepherd three kids through the supermarket—so I didn't have the energy to drop acid or to party through the night. One morning, probably a little after 7, as I crossed Eighth Avenue toward the

10 Jill Johnston, *Autobiography in Search of a Father Volume II: Paper Daughter* (NY: Alfred A. Knopf, 1985).

subway entrance, I looked into a car that had stopped for the light, and there were Andy Warhol, Gerard Malanga, and a few other pale and forepined ghostly visages, on their way home as I was on my way to work. We lived in different life-worlds, committed to different world-designs, taking notes for different life-poems.

The most surprising thing Bill told me about his marriage was that he and Ann had never divorced. He wrote, "We are still married, she is entitled to a large percentage of my estate regardless of any legal will (I have the problem covered)." He explained why they hadn't divorced in another email:

> . . . in the 1960s, you couldn't divorce a person who had been in a mental hospital, and later her Catholic (albeit retired from practice) family had Nixon Mudge as their lawyers, who would have extracted the value of used Q-tips and taken the children away (an actual threat). We have made our marriage work by not seeing each other since 1966. I am slowly understanding what the two psychiatrists? psychoanalysts? said about Gene being attracted to a young father who was caring for his children . . .

Bill and I went to see the Cézanne that he later referred to in the email he sent me in the hospital after I came out of my coma. I remembered him at the National Gallery explaining "Les Grandes Baigneuses," balancing himself dangerously on the stick I had bought him while majestically waving his other hand over the painting. I was so worried he was going to fall that I didn't pay much attention to his analysis of color and form. Not wanting to seem inattentive, however, I asked him why the figure seated at the left of the painting appeared to be staring outside of the frame, presumably at the painter. He looked closely at it for a considerable time and proclaimed, "I have no idea. It's probably important. Let's have lunch."

When it was time for him to leave London, he insisted on taking the tube to the airport instead of a cab. "I never get to do things like this in New York," he explained. Since his stroke, he hadn't been able to take the subway in New York. He loved hearing the announcer tell passengers, "Mind the gap." It was full of philosophical ramifications.

I had grown quite attached to Bill by the time he left. Cleveland came over when I got home from the airport. Instead of asking me about the wonderful few days I had spent with Bill, he went into a blow-by-blow account of what his own life had been like. The words "bathhouse" and "drugs" were mentioned quite a lot, but I wasn't really listening. I was thinking about Bill.

•

BECAUSE OF MY INTEREST IN BILL and Bill's interest in Ray Johnson, I had to be careful that my site didn't become a Ray Johnson site. Although Ray Johnson knew Andy Warhol and referenced him in some of his collages, most of my site-users wanted to hear about "superstars" like Viva or Edie Sedgwick.

Bill told me one funny story about meeting Viva at a 1960s party. When he tried to engage her in conversation, she screeched, "Go find somebody else to fuck!" (If Bill was looking for someone to fuck, he probably would have been looking in the direction of the male guests.) After the put-down by Viva, Bill said Andy Warhol walked into the room and he and Bill "picked up with just ordinary talk." Warhol didn't talk in "that wispy way" when he was talking to Bill because they "knew the same people in Pittsburgh, and it would have been too fake."

4. Superstars

ANDY WARHOL'S most famous superstar, Edie Sedgwick, died of a barbiturate overdose in 1971. After a biopic about her, *Factory Girl*, opened at the end of 2006, Edie was again in the news. Not everyone was a fan, though. Ronald Tavel, Andy Warhol's scriptwriter, who was in his early seventies and living in Thailand when the film was released, wrote to me in March 2007: "[I] have no idea why the endless fuss over Edie, although it does give me the idea for a major satire on the whole period. But that's off in the future."

Tavel wrote many of Warhol's early full-length films, as well as quite a few Off-Off-Broadway plays, founding the Play-house of the Ridiculous and winning an Obie award for *Boy on the Straight-Back Chair* in 1969. His scripts for Warhol were "scenarios" that usually involved a considerable amount of improvisation. He'd lay out a scene, provide at least some of the dialogue, and the often stoned superstars would do the rest.

Edie wasn't the only person at the Factory that Ron was critical of. He called Gerard Malanga a "faux-poet," although Gerard had always considered himself more of a poet than an art assistant; his poetry continues to be published today. He really didn't like Chuck Wein, Edie's friend and de facto manager. When I told him the following year that Chuck had died, he responded, "Thanks for notice re Swine's death. You've made my day."

Edie's "replacement" at the Factory, Ingrid Superstar, also didn't escape his wrath. Ron wrote: "Ingrid was the worstest! Common is OK but she killed every scene she was in. Callie assumes it was suicide: the traditional leaving a pack of cigs on her workbench at some assembly line near a river—them rivers again! Ain't drown-ded bodies supposed to float up somewhere?" That wasn't exactly what Callie Angell said in the Warhol film catalogue raisonné, but it was the version of Ingrid's disappearance that was mentioned in quite a few other accounts.

Presumably Ron's comment about "them rivers again" was a reference to another Warhol death, that of Danny Williams, who was Andy Warhol's boyfriend briefly and did the lights for the Exploding Plastic Inevitable multimedia stage show featuring the Velvet Underground, which Warhol produced. Ron noted in the documentary *A Walk into the Sea: Danny Williams and the Warhol Factory*, "Gerard Malanga told me that he'd learned they found [Danny's] car by the water, he wasn't sure where, a river in Connecticut or the ocean off Cape Cod, with all his clothes piled neatly beside it. Danny had drowned himself."[11]

It was assumed that both Ingrid and Danny had committed suicide, but neither left a note behind. It was a bit like Ray Johnson jumping off Sag Harbor Bridge and swimming to his death. He didn't leave a note either.

•

THE FIRST EMAIL I RECEIVED from Ron Tavel was on February 21, 2007. He introduced himself and said that the Whitney had recommended my site, which I assumed meant Callie. Twenty minutes later, he sent me a follow-up:

11 Esther Robinson (director), *A Walk into the Sea: Danny Williams and the Warhol Factory* (Chicken and Egg Pictures and Thatgrl Media, 2007).

> Forgot to say that my website has a recent message from someone claiming to be Philip Fagan's nephew, who wants to do a book on his "mysterious" uncle. Again, I have not been able to reach this person. But I said most of what I remember about him on my site, and further information which I had was given to, and appears in, Callie Angell's (misnamed) Screen Tests book. Those 3-minute studies are Living Portraits. No one was being screen-tested.

Callie actually agreed with Ron in regard to the so-called screen tests being living portraits, and said as much in her book, the first volume of the Warhol film catalogue raisonné. She devoted an entire chapter to the elder Philip Fagan, who was one of Warhol's early boyfriends. Warhol planned to shoot at least one "living portrait" of him every day for a period of six months; unfortunately, the relationship only lasted about three months: 107 portraits were shot from November 6, 1964 to February 9, 1965.

Ron clearly became infatuated with Philip Fagan's nephew during their correspondence. Referring to him as "Philip III" in his next email, he wrote that the younger man had led "an adventurous life" and was "much too modest when he introduces himself merely as the late lovely's nephew." In another email, he noted with excitement that Philip III had "mucho contacts with Mexican theatre & film people!," adding, "Didn't I say, Romantic?????" The following month he wrote: "I'm eager to see that the new Philip Fagan not be discouraged. Ask for his website: he is not only a college teacher and filmmaker himself but a former police investigator. So we may have a live one here."

I got to see the original Philip in a Warhol film the following month. The British Film Institute presented a series of newly restored Warhol films at the National Theatre which included *Screen Test 1*. This was not one of the 107 short "living portraits" that Callie wrote about, it was a full-length film of Philip Fagan answering questions from an off-screen "interrogator" played by Ron Tavel. Philip looked in the direction of the interrogator most of the time, but occasionally his attention veered elsewhere. I asked Ron if he was looking at Andy Warhol, and he confirmed that was the case. When Ron asked Philip about his "girlfriend," I wondered if he was talking about Warhol, who was rumored to have a foot fetish. Philip went into considerable detail about kissing his girlfriend's feet in the film. When I made the point that "only someone with a foot fetish or who was involved with someone with a foot fetish could have been so specific," Ron responded:

> Glad you enjoyed SCREEN TEST I. Yes, AW had a foot fetish and SCREEN TEST I ain't the only flick in which I refer to that. Hedy Lamarr was arrested for shoplifting shoes! So there's the real inspiration for that opus. Well, I had to irk Drella in some way, no?

Hedy, another Warhol film that Ron wrote, was based on a real-life incident when the Hollywood actress was arrested for shoplifting. "Drella" was Warhol's nickname—a contraction of Cinderella—given to him by the Max's Kansas City door person, Dorothy Dean, who appeared in *My Hustler* and a few other Warhol films.[12]

12 Gary Comenas, "Notes on Dorothy Dean," https://warholstars.org/notes-dorothydean.html.

•

DURING THE FIRST WEEK of the Warhol film screenings, Callie came to London to introduce them, and I at last met her in person. Her lectures about the films drew small audiences; the series had been poorly publicized. She tended to speak in a monotone and approached the films from a scholarly perspective when most people were probably more interested in the gossip about the "superstars" who "acted" in them. I had started out wanting the gossip when I first put up my website. Now I wanted the scholarly stuff.

Callie had a busy schedule in London, but I managed to meet her and an underground actor, John Heys, at a restaurant on the South Bank one afternoon. Heys had made a name for himself by doing a "one-woman" show as Diana Vreeland at La Mama in the early '90s. The two of them had finished lunch by the time I got there, but I had a coffee with them and spent some time with Callie afterwards. I was struck by how grateful she was when I laid £2 on the table to pay for my coffee before we left the restaurant. She thanked me twice, making such a big deal out of it—"Really, thanks!"—that I wondered if she was joking. It left me wondering whether she felt taken advantage of by other people who expected her to pick up the tab because of her family's wealth. Maybe I was reading too much into it.

Callie had returned to New York by the time the BFI showed *Screen Test 1*. She wrote to me from New York about young Philip Fagan and the book he planned on writing about his uncle: "I'm not sure Philip Fagan is interesting enough to rate a whole book or movie—unless there's some great story behind his later life in Indonesia—but there does seem to be quite an archive of material, including a Warhol flowers painting."

I thought about Callie's comment later in the year when Ron Tavel finally got to meet Philip's nephew in person in New York. Ron went to New York once a year to visit his brother, Harvey. That year he was also participating in a "Coffeehouse Chronicles" panel discussion about Off-Off-Broadway at La Mama. When he returned home to Thailand, he wrote: "My public appearance went well . . . The Fagan family was touchy and trying, but I got through it and think they enjoyed meeting me and Malanga (who has aged drastically, walks very slowly after an accident 2 years ago, uses a cane, etc.)."

He referred to the Fagan family again in an email a few months later: "I found dealing with the latter's family a strain, quite tragic, but I got through it and hope I was of some help." By April, however, he had decided that the younger Philip was "not only talentless but a fool."

> From: Ronald Tavel
> Subject: Re: Straights! Like there WAS such a thing!
> Date: 17 April 2008
>
> Dear Gary:
>
> . . . Fagan III turns out to be the Poster Boy for Homophobic Revisionism. He INSISTS his "uncle" was straight. Mary, spare me!!!!

I didn't ask what happened, but it was clear that the infatuation had ended badly. The nephew's insistence that his uncle was straight didn't surprise me. As a "straight," Philip evidently found it difficult to admit that his uncle was gay; as far as Ron was concerned, Philip III was trying to rewrite history.

•

MY CORRESPONDENCE WITH RON continued and, as with Bill, we became friends. He wrote to me daily from Thailand about his life there, as well as keeping me abreast of Warhol events that other people wrote to him about. In one email he told me he had been contacted by a curator in Berlin, Marc Siegel, about appearing at a Jack Smith festival in Berlin to be called "Live Film! Jack Smith!" Smith was a radical gay artist and filmmaker whom Andy Warhol acknowledged as an influence on his own filmmaking. Some of the superstars who appeared in Smith's films also appeared in Warhol's films, including Smith himself.

I had been urging the Hayward Gallery in London to invite Ron to do a Q&A in conjunction with their "Andy Warhol: Other Voices Other Rooms" exhibition, which was due to take place from 7 October 2008 to 18 January 2009. The main focus of the show was on Warhol's film work, and I thought Ron would be perfect for a panel discussion. I went into press officer mode, put together a package about Ron Tavel, and sent it to Stephanie Rosenthal, the chief curator of the Hayward.

I mentioned what I was doing to Bill Wilson, who knew Stephanie. He wrote:

> On Stephanie Rosenthal, who has been in my house, where Daniel Wenk cooked dinner for us in the guest apartment upstairs: she was so ferociously in love with or in sexual desire of Daniel, who once was the most beautiful man in any world known to me, that she was indifferent and inattentive to me to the point of rudeness, and far beyond rudeness . . . She was dressed in ferocious black leather, with some metallic ornaments (belt?), so that my impression was of a

> tough, ambitious, intellectually fashionable curator, clawing her way to the middle. For me, I would have no interest in ever seeing her again, certainly not in my house . . .
>
> Stephanie, in my indictment, is intellectually chic and probably ruthless, but I gauge my harsh judgment according to her desire to capture Daniel Wenk and devour him—I really know nothing about her, but if her style "works for you"—if you can use her while she uses you—then go for it, but wear an iron jock-strap . . .

I wondered if Bill and I were talking about the same person. In a photo on the internet, she looked a bit plain, almost intellectual, certainly not the leather-clad seductress that Bill had described. I sent the photo to Bill and asked if it was the same Stephanie. He answered:

> Gary: I feel guilty that I wrote harshly about her because she was so intensely on the prowl for Daniel Wenk, who is a summit of male beauty—she is to be forgiven that she wanted me out of the picture—that she didn't just kill me shows her restraint.

As it turned out, Stephanie and her assistant, Raf, were not interested in a Ron Tavel evening. They wanted a night with Warhol's superstars similar to a panel discussion that took place on October 13, 2007 at the Lausanne Underground Film and Music Festival, which I had mentioned on my site. The panelists would include Holly Woodlawn, Bibbe Hansen. and Mary Woronov. I was disappointed about Ron, but he didn't seem to mind: "As for the Haywood [sic], think of it this way: I tire easily and quickly these days . . . I know once that adrenaline gets up, you can do much, but the years take their toll."

That was the first time I heard Ron, even indirectly, refer to his age. He was going ahead with the Jack Smith festival the following year, and I hoped that he'd be able to come to London then. In the meantime, I had my own panel discussion to worry about. I had agreed to moderate the Hayward event.

•

THE "NIGHT WITH ANDY WARHOL'S SUPERSTARS" took place on the evening of October 9, 2008. I arrived at the backstage door early and was surprised to run into Mary Woronov outside. She was instantly recognizable. Despite her grey hair, now cut short, she still looked much as she did in *The Chelsea Girls*. I am not sure what "star quality" is, but she had it. If I didn't already know who she was, I would have wondered. I introduced myself and asked her if she wanted a bite to eat before the others arrived.

The restaurant at the Southbank Centre was closed so we got a couple of shrink-wrapped sandwiches and coffee from a vending machine and sat at one of tables on the mostly empty concrete forecourt. I asked her the same question I had asked Joe Dallesandro: Why hadn't Hollywood snapped her up after her success in Warhol's films?

"Hollywood just didn't get me," she said. "They just didn't get it."

"Didn't get what?"

"It!" she repeated. "*It!*" I stopped asking. I was afraid she might think I didn't get it either, whatever it was. Instead I asked why she stopped making films for Andy Warhol. It seems her mother threatened to sue him because Mary had not signed a release for *The*

Chelsea Girls. They apparently settled out of court, but her career as a Warhol superstar was over. She appeared in many films after she left Warhol, but they weren't particularly mainstream. Her most famous roles were Mary Bland in *Eating Raoul* and Miss Togar in *Rock 'n' Roll High School,* which featured the Ramones.

In addition to being a superstar, Mary was a painter—she studied art at Cornell University, and a book of her paintings was published in 1994. I asked her what she thought about Warhol's art and Pop Art in general. "I hate it," she said. She equated Pop with Conceptualism and hated Conceptualism. Her work was Expressionistic. I had to admit that my interest in Pop was also waning. I had been doing the warholstars website for over seven years by then and had decided to explore Abstract Expressionism with a new chronology on the lives of the AbEx artists, similar to the one I had done on the superstars. The lives of the AbEx artists were every bit as wild as the denizens of Warhol's Factory, except that their drug of choice was alcohol rather than speed.

It wasn't long before my conversation with Mary veered from the death of art to the death of culture and ultimately of humanity. We were having such a cheerful conversation about the end of the world that we lost track of time. When we got back to the venue, Bibbe, Sean Carillo, Holly, and Holly's manager Robert Coddington were already there, waiting for us backstage.

Raf arrived with a bottle of champagne to lighten up the glum atmosphere. Mary screamed, "Don't open that! Holly will drink the whole bottle!" I laughed. "I'm not kidding," she said, and went to do her makeup. After saying hello to everyone I also retreated into my dressing room. I was exhausted. I didn't know it then,

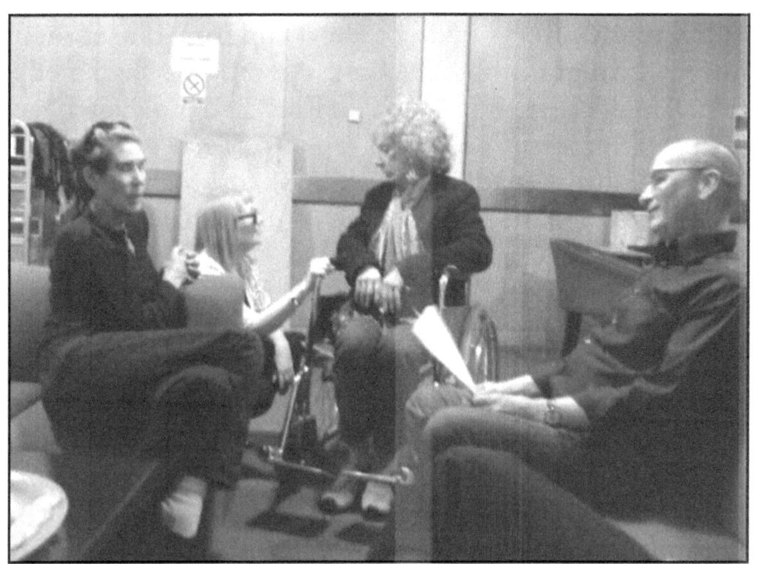

Backstage before the "Night with Andy Warhol's Superstars": Mary Woronov, Bibbe Hansen, Holly Woodlawn, and me.

but I was already suffering from the heart problems that would eventually lead to my hospitalization. Holly was nodding off in her wheelchair, and the others looked worried.

Eventually a panic-stricken woman came into my dressing room and told me it was time to go onstage. I weaved my way down a hallway, and suddenly there I was on stage in front of a sea of faces. Paul Lonergan was there with an ex-boyfriend I only knew as "the skinny one." Cleveland was sitting upright a few rows behind Paul, craning his neck and smiling so I would be sure to notice him. As my eyes scanned the rest of the audience, I thought, "My god, these people have actually paid to see this."

The set was minimal: four chairs in front of a large screen. The plan was to introduce each superstar individually after showing a short clip from one of their films. I brought Bibbe out first. We did not have a clip to show because her Warhol films had not yet been restored. Instead I projected a photo of her and played a recording she made when she was fourteen or so and sang with a band called The Whippets, which also included Jack Kerouac's daughter. I thought the song, "Go Go Go with Ringo," would be funny to an English audience, but they just looked puzzled. I wasn't sure they knew who Bibbe was; she arrived onstage to polite applause. I wasn't even sure they even knew who Jack Kerouac was, let alone his daughter.

I quickly introduced Mary after showing a clip from *Hedy*. I was going to show a clip from *The Chelsea Girls,* her most famous Warhol film, but Robert had insisted on *Hedy,* which he said was Mary's favorite. The film was unrestored and the clip so underexposed that even Mary was puzzled by it. Without seeing the rest of the film, it didn't make much sense. Mary had seen the clip from backstage. When she made her entrance, she looked at the screen as if to say, "What was *that*?"

Finally, it was Holly Woodlawn's turn to be introduced. She was the one most of the audience had come to see—she's the "Holly" Lou Reed sings about in "Walk on the Wild Side." Joe Dallesandro's co-star in *Trash,* she is often associated with Candy Darling and Jackie Curtis, her co-stars in *Women in Revolt.* All three drag queens were known as "Warhol stars."

Explaining that Holly had been part of the second Factory, when Paul Morrissey was directing the films, financed by Warhol, I showed one of my favorite scenes from *Trash,* where Holly tries to sell drugs to a student from Yonkers she has picked up in front of the Fillmore East. The boy was played by her real-life sixteen-year-old boyfriend. He gives her money to score drugs but says he doesn't want anything that requires an injection. "No needles," he says repeatedly. She reassures him—"Trust me, no needles"—before leaving to get the drugs. When she returns, she pulls down his jeans and injects him with a needle. He falls to the floor in a drugged stupor, and she begins kissing him wildly. The film is meant to be a comedy, but few people in the audience were laughing. Many shifted uncomfortably in their seats, probably wondering if they had just witnessed child abuse. Holly's boyfriend looked awfully young in his school uniform.

Holly came onstage quickly after the clip, and to my relief, the audience erupted in applause. She threw kisses to everyone and no one, whispering harshly in my direction, "Yes, I was part of the *second* Factory." Most people probably assumed that she was part of the original Factory with the likes of Edie Sedgwick, Billy Name, and Bibbe Hansen. She continued to blow kisses at her applauding fans, spreading her arms outward as if to hug them all. When she finally sat down, she promptly nodded off, and I turned my attention to Mary.

I had emailed Ron to ask for suggestions about what I should ask Mary. He knew her from the Factory days—he wrote the scenario for *Hedy*—and they were still occasionally in touch. He said he had dreamt about her "every other night" since meeting her and I should ask her "about how she imagines, when she's onstage, that she's telling stories to scare little children."

I read out Ron's email to Mary, and she gave me a confused look. "How strange," she said. "Stories to scare little children? I don't know what he's talking about." Neither did the audience, most of whom didn't know who Ron Tavel was. Trying to lighten things up, I said that Mary was "like a gay man trapped in a woman's body." The audience gasped, and her eyes narrowed. I recognized the look from *The Chelsea Girls*, just before she starts beating up Ingrid Superstar.

I turned to Bibbe and asked about her experiences in the detention center. She wasn't very forthcoming. "Oh, it was nothing really. Juvie. I was in Juvie." She wouldn't say much about Janet Kerouac or her son Beck, but when she started to talk about her father, Al Hansen, a leader of the Fluxus art movement in the '60s, Holly suddenly came to life, talking about herself and her other transvestite friends Candy Darling and Jackie Curtis, who had been in *Women in Revolt* with her: "They said said it was about feminism, and I thought they meant lesbianism. That's why my hands were all over Jackie."

I explained to Holly that we had been talking about Bibbe's father and the Fluxus movement. She looked at Bibbe, squinting as though she was trying to recognize her, and then back at me, saying, "The wha . . . ? The flux, the fuck—what did you say?"

For most of the evening the panel discussion became The Holly Woodlawn Show. I tried to talk to Bibbe or Mary, and Holly interrupted with stories about herself. At one point she dropped the mike on the floor. A stagehand handed it back to her, and she decided to approach the audience. I helped her to the edge of the stage as she started in on another monologue. She interrupted herself when she noticed that a section of seats in the front row were empty: "Whose seats are those?" she bellowed. I didn't know what to say so I told the truth: "They're your guest list, Holly." Before the show she had given Raf a guest list that included everyone from Vivienne Westwood to Boy George, none of whom showed up. She glared, the audience gasped, and I led her back to her seat the best I could. She fell back to sleep.

Eventually the hour and a half came to an end, I quickly said thanks to the superstars and the audience, and the stage lights went out. I had to get Holly off the stage to her wheelchair in the dark. It wasn't easy. In a gruff male voice, she commanded, "Just hold your arm straight and keep it solid." She held on to it as I tried to keep my legs from buckling beneath me. Fortunately Robert was in the wings and rushed to help. I told Mary and Bibbe there were fans at the edge of the stage, and they went back to sign autographs. Holly stayed backstage with the champagne. I made a quick getaway.

The next day Raf sent me a reassuring email: "Thank you very much for doing a fantastic job moderating the talk. I think it was the most entertaining talk I've ever produced. People I've spoken to enjoyed it enormously." I had to laugh—the audience got what they came for—to see the glamorous Holly Woodlawn completely out of it. The high point of the evening for me was the cheerfully dismal conversation I had with Mary earlier in the evening about the end of the world.

5. Raven Row

A FEW DAYS AFTER THE PANEL DISCUSSION, I wrote to Ron Tavel to let him know how it went. He wrote back from New York, where he was on his yearly visit to see his brother, Harvey: "Arrived safely in NYC in the midst of a mess of art-related activities and must hurry through my jet lag and catch up with everyone. The Berlin Fest is still on, apparently as yet unaffected by the financial crisis, and the subject matter involved is to be broadened." That was good news. If he came to Berlin, he would be able to visit London and I would finally get to meet him in the flesh.

Bill Wilson was also involved with a project that would bring him to London again. Alex Sainsbury was opening a gallery in the East End, and the inaugural show was to be an exhibition of works by Ray Johnson. The Feigen Gallery in New York controlled Ray's estate, but Bill owned a considerable amount of his work.

Bill had dropped a teasing hint about the show two years earlier in an email:

> From: William S. Wilson
> Subject: your ass will be lined with diamonds!
> Date: 2 July 2007
> To: Gary Comenas
>
> Gary: HUGE possible but so far secret SECRET developments pertaining to Ray Johnson in London call for exquisite tact and discretion. Maybe in mid-August I can tell you what is planned, if by then the plans are indeed formulated, signed, and sealed . . .
>
> I will share good news as it becomes share-able! People of great power to do good in relation to my work

are behaving modestly and correctly, encouragingly, constructively, so stick with me, and like Queen Elizabeth and the Duchess of Cornwall, we'll be farting through silk! I'm holding my breath between emails! Every delicate mention of Ray is a grace-note . . .

The developments didn't stay secret for long. A few weeks later Bill said he was cleaning his house for an "English visitor"; when I asked who, he responded:

> I thought I had been explicit. Fortunately Alex Sainsbury is flying to New York to meet me in order to discuss a Ray Johnson show which could open his new institute for contemporary arts. His emails are marvelous, modest and tactful, so I am eager to try to cooperate with him on a show. As I have said, stick with me and you'll be farting through silk. —B.

Raven Row, Alex Sainsbury's new gallery, was in a Grade 1 listed building in Spitalfields that had previously used by silk traders. Bill's "farting through silk" comment wasn't far off the mark. I was happy that Bill was involved with the inaugural exhibition, but I worried that his infatuation with Sainsbury would end up like the saga of Ronald Tavel and Philip Fagan III. Bill hadn't developed a romantic crush on Alex as Ron had on Philip, but his exaggerated expectations opened him up to disappointment.

I was confused about which member of the Sainsbury family he was talking about. There were so many of them. In the press, Alex was referred to as the son of Lord Sainsbury and other times as his grandson. But which Lord Sainsbury? What relation was he to the three brothers who funded the Sainsbury Wing of the National Gallery? Trying to figure out where Alex fit in was nearly impossible. But he was a "Sainsbury," and that was good enough for Bill.

A couple of weeks later Bill wrote wrote that Alex was visiting him again, along with two other Ray Johnson scholars: "Today Clive Phillpot and Alex Sainsbury, both in town from London, visit me, tomorrow Ina Blom from Norway, so the joint is jumpin' . . ."

Clive Phillpot, once the head of MoMA's library, had known Ray Johnson. Ina Blom had organized a Ray Johnson exhibition in Norway, Germany, and the Netherlands in 2003. The Raven Row show was going full steam ahead, which meant that Bill would be visiting London again. I looked forward to that visit as much as I had to his previous one.

•

As before, Bill combined his London trip with a trip to Venice. He arrived in London on December 27th, 2008, left for Venice on the 30th, and returned to London at the end of January, about a month before the opening of the new gallery. Bill stayed in one of the apartments on the top floor of the gallery building that Alex kept for visiting artists. They were only accessible by a long stairwell. I visited him the day he arrived, and even I was out of breath by the time we got to the top—that was four years before my heart attacks. Bill was not in a very good mood. He was disappointed with the apartment, which I thought was nice—a small, quaint studio apartment with a window that looked out on rooftops. I think he expected a lot more from a Sainsbury, perhaps a room in a stately home.

I visited Bill often in that studio and have fond memories of it. His neighbor Rebecca, a cockney woman in her nineties, was often there in the afternoon, filling him in on the history of the East End. She came with the building: she lived there when Alex bought it, and he agreed to provide her with accommodation as a condition of the sale.

When Rebecca wasn't around, Bill would usually be on his laptop. It was the first time I saw him typing. He typed with two fingers, and his hands shook as his fingers tried to find the appropriate keys. My heart sank. I thought of all the emails he had sent me over the years and how much time and effort he must have spent on them. I felt honored that he thought I was worth it. Physically, life wasn't easy for Bill, but he managed to plod on without becoming discouraged. He was as full of life as any of my younger friends.

Alex hired a group of young local artists to help get the gallery space ready for the inaugural show, and Bill spent a lot of time with them in the evening, sharing their hopes and dreams for the future over a bottle of wine—several bottles usually. Alex was often nowhere to be seen, and the exhibition increasingly seemed more like Bill's project than Alex's. Bill sent out personalized invitations and flew in his family and friends to see it. This included his assistant, Michael von Uchtrup, whom I met for the first time. I was surprised by how handsome Michael was. When I later commented on his good looks in an email, Bill responded: "A curator who came here once a week for research was actually coming for sex with my assistant while I was resting downstairs!!"

A private opening was scheduled for the night of February 27th, followed by a party at a local church that Alex had rented. I sat with Bill at a table near the entrance of the gallery, watching the guests as they came in; most of them looked like scruffy art students. "Is that the way people dress in London for an opening?" Bill asked. I laughed. Normally Bill looked a bit scruffy himself. I thought of an incident in the financial district of East London when we were waiting for the traffic light to change so we could cross. Bill tried to engage a businesswoman next to him in friendly conversation. She looked at his walking stick, at his disheveled white hair and the old pair of jeans he was wearing, and promptly walked away without saying anything. I think she was afraid he was going to ask for spare change.

Bill looked good at the opening. I had taken him shopping the day before, and he had bought a navy blue John Smedley polo neck jumper and a new pair of Levi 501s. The dark navy top contrasted nicely with his full head of white hair. He looked casually "artistic"—perfect for the opening of an exhibition by an artist who had revolted against the gallery system by sending his art through the post for free.

Frances Beatty from the Feigen Gallery was also there, dressed in a manner that was the complete opposite of Bill's. Dripping in gold jewelry and designer everything else, Frances was dressed to kill. It was nice to see a bit of New York glamor mingling with scruffy Londoners, although English reverse snobbery was quick to manifest itself in the looks she got from the other people at the gallery: she was too glitzy for an exhibition in a nonprofit gallery in the East End. Her son was with her, looking like a movie star. When they came to our table to pay their respects, Bill told Frances she had no right to have such a beautiful son. The son smiled. Frances laughed nervously. Sometimes it was difficult to know whether Bill was handing out a compliment or implying an insult.

After flirting openly with the son, Bill turned to

another woman from the Feigen Gallery and accused her of having an eating disorder—she was "too thin to be healthy." I nudged him, "Bill, you can't say that!" "But she is!" he exclaimed loudly as he told her he was only mentioning it for her own good. "You need to see a doctor," he said to the poor woman, who was looking thinner by the minute as she tried to disappear from embarrassment. And so the evening went, with Bill innocently insulting the bigwigs (at least it appeared to be innocent) while giving a warm welcome to his relatives and friends.

The writer Michael Bracewell was also there. I already knew him because of the Mark Lancaster interview on warholstars. Bracewell had written a book on Roxy Music and asked permission to drawn on my interview. Bryan Ferry, the lead singer of Roxy Music, had also studied art under Richard Hamilton at Newcastle University in the '60s. The first half of the book ended up being as much about Mark as about Bryan.

The reception at Raven Row was the first time I met Michael in person. He told me he had recently had a triple bypass, though he had never smoked a cigarette in his life and had kept to a healthy diet. "All those damned carrots," he angrily repeated, as we both started laughing. I knew how he felt when I had my own health emergency four years later. Laughter might not be the best medicine, but it does help.

•

A COUPLE OF NIGHTS AFTER THE OPENING, Alex took Frances Beatty out to dinner, while Bill took me and the artist-workers who had hung the show to a separate dinner at a different restaurant. When Michael heard there were two dinners, he looked puzzled and said, "I want to come to yours!" but he ended up going to Alex's. I'm sure ours was more fun. We had an absolute blast. We took up the entire upper floor of a local Thai restaurant, and Bill was in his element, entertaining and flirting with the young men who had put so much work into hanging the show. It was an unforgettable evening. The conversation never stopped flowing, and neither did the wine.

Bill flew back to New York the next day. A few weeks later he explained why there had been separate dinners:

> The whole staff of Raven Row was disappointed with and angry with Alex S., feeling deceived or at least misled about their roles in hanging the show, and soured by resentments of the guy Alex hired for the prestige of having a famous artist do the installation. My dinner-party was intended in part to get past the rancidities, to let the workers—reticent and muted in London, city of refusals of feelings, a town that doesn't encourage or allow for intimacies—put an experience of laughing together between themselves and Alex (who gave us the wine!). I also wanted Alex to wish that he had been at our party, rather than the party he was giving for people discolored by their evil, e.g., Frances Beatty.

His reference to Beatty, or any representative of the Feigen Gallery, in such a derogatory way was fairly common. As someone who knew Ray, had written extensively about Ray, and owned multiple works by Ray, he complained that ". . . the Feigen gallery does not refer scholars and curators to me, because they don't want people to see and to borrow my collages—they want the Estate Pictures to become saleable by being used in shows and catalogues . . ." Bill had "65 framed Ray Johnson collages," he said, because of which "Feigen regards me as a danger, should I sell collages. A posthumous auction of my collection would have the effect that they wouldn't sell another collage for a loooong time."

The gallery benefited from his scholarship to help maintain interest in Johnson's work; his essays provided "critical thoughts they can use in their salespersonship." Ultimately he and the gallery had a similar goal, but for different reasons. The gallery wanted to hype Ray's work in order to make money; Bill wanted to draw attention to it because he thought Ray was a great artist. As he put it, "Only a market will bring Ray's collages and mail-art, and sheer information, to the surface now, while I can still contemplate it and perhaps think with it. "

Bill ended his email with a personal note: "Alex did make it possible for us to see each other—I can't erase him from the events. I think of you when I wear a John Smedley shirt to bed because I can't bear to take it off . . ." I was grateful for that comment. It was rare for either of us to express affection toward each other. Our emails tended to be more cerebral than emotional.

•

WHILE I WAS FOCUSED ON BILL'S Ray Johnson show at Raven Row, Ron Tavel was involved with preparations for the "Live Film! Jack Smith!" festival in Berlin. In March he flew to Berlin for a weekend conference to help plan the full festival, which was due to take place in October. During the flight back to Thailand, Ron had a heart attack and died. Callie Angell notified Billy Name and me by email:

Hi, Gary and Billy:

I was getting ready to write you guys (and other people) today. Ron died on Monday, while flying home from Berlin to Bangkok. He was 71 years old. He had been attending a conference/festival of the Jack Smith films in Berlin over the weekend. I was there too, along with a number of other scholars, curators, artists, filmmakers, and colleagues of Jack's . . . The purpose of this Jack Smith conference was to plan a big festival (to be called "LIVE FILM: Jack Smith" or something like that) in Berlin in October. Ronnie was beginning work on a new play about Jack for the festival . . .

I think it was wonderful that Ronnie had attended the conference, where he received a lot of much-deserved attention and appreciation, and that he was already working on a new play when he died. I am very glad that I got to see him again.

I'll send out a more detailed email to everyone when I have more information . . .

Love,
Callie .

I searched the internet for news about the death, but the only thing I found was an anonymous report from a news site in India:

A German Airlines plane, with about 200 passengers, made an emergency landing at Netaji Subhash Chandra Bose International airport here today after a passenger died on board, airport officials said. The 73-year-old US citizen Ronald Tavel was flying from Muscat to Bangkok when he fell sick. Doctors at the airport declared him dead after examining him on landing

> here at about 0700 hours, the sources added. Since the passenger died on board, the airport authorities issued a certificate to the commander and allowed the airlines to take the body to Bangkok in the same aircraft.

There was no mention of Ron's work on films with Andy Warhol or his significance as a playwright. Marc Seigel sent me a statement from the Berlin festival organizers that I was happy to include on my website:

> We here are also thinking of Ron a lot . . . It's really so sad. Ron was the first person we contacted when it was clear that we got the funding for the festival, because we were all so eager to work with him again . . . There are so many of us with a great deal of respect for Ron's work and a great appreciation for his wry humor and delightful storytelling.
>
> I do think Ron's brother Harvey is devastated by his death. I've sent him a couple of notes and forwarded those from others, so that he can perhaps be comforted by the thought that although Ron did indeed die alone on the plane, he did at least leave Berlin hopeful and excited after a weekend with many friends and supporters . . .

Memorials eventually appeared in the press, including an obituary in the *New York Times*. I was glad that Ron got the recognition he deserved, but it didn't help how deflated I felt; there would be no more emails from him.

•

A WEEK AFTER RON DIED, Alex Sainsbury held a panel discussion on Ray Johnson at his gallery, with Michael

Bracewell. Bill had asked me to go as his "spy" and I had agreed, but now my heart wasn't into it. As I had promised, I went anyway. Bill wasn't particularly happy with his treatment by Alex. The exhibition was supposed to travel to Barcelona after Raven Row, and according to Bill, Alex wasn't being very helpful:

> [Alex] omits much information I need to have and should have. I do want the show to travel to Barcelona, so I must patiently co-operate, but am composing ground-rules for any further conversations between us—so that I understand the agenda rather than being astonished by what I haven't been told, and so that he is instructed to stop interrupting me (I feel like a screen onto which he has projected his father, or the whole clan of Sainsburys, so that he is addressing a phantom Sainsbury, using me in his family psycho-drama, not talking to me as a person) . . .

About the Raven Row show, Bill wrote: "I did watch this show become the production of Alex Sainsbury's Ray Johnson, even as I was earlier asked to write for the catalogue, and then the invitation was withdrawn." Bill took a final jab at Alex at the end of his email which, not unusually for Bill, began as a compliment but ended as an insult: "He acts modestly, but the show has become too much about him . . ." Alex had, in effect, stolen Ray Johnson from him. Given that Bill had been a close friend of Johnson and had written extensively about him, I found it curious that Alex did not want him to write an essay for the catalogue.

I took Cleveland with me to the panel discussion. He had absolutely no interest in Ray Johnson, but he was available. That was often the case with Cleveland. He had become my best friend largely because he was "there."

We arrived as the discussion was about to start. Alex and Michael sat at the front of a crowded room of expectant faces. I felt sorry for them after what I had been through with the superstar panel discussion. As Alex started speaking, Cleveland's lack of interest was evident. In fact he pretended to be asleep. That was typical of him. Whenever he wasn't the center of attention, he did something to make sure he was. At the end of his talk Alex thanked various people in the audience. He later told me he was going to thank me as well—"but your friend was asleep."

•

As preparations for the Barcelona show continued, Bill continued to express doubt about Alex:

> I want Alex to have suffered my absence. I am writing ground rules for him if, as he wants to, he visits me in NY with a curator from MACBA. He interrupts me constantly, making a point of his own, but then not stopping after he really has finished making his point. Once he has made his point, he continues talking to retain possession of the space for talk, and so he repeats a point long after he has explained it—then his words get emptier, and he finds himself dangling in air, with no ground to support his statements except his privileges, and so he bewilders himself somewhat (I think that he is back in childhood among siblings, trying to make himself heard in some self-defeating way) . . .

I had no idea during the Raven Row exhibition that Bill harbored so much ill will toward Alex. It wasn't until he got back to New York that he opened up about it. I remembered how happy Bill had been when he was first approached by Alex, but rather than "farting through silk," he had ended up feeling considerably marginalized. Bill's disappointments became my disappointments, but I was grateful that he shared them with me. I was still getting over Ron's death and looked forward to seeing Bill's emails in the morning even more than I had in the past, if that was possible.

6. Billy Name's missing negatives

TWO MONTHS AFTER THE PANEL DISCUSSION, I received an email from Billy Name with some alarming news. The negatives of his photographs—his life work—had gone missing. His former agent, Kevin Kushel, had left New York, and nobody seemed to know where the negatives were that Kevin had kept in storage for Billy. Billy's new agent was Steven Kasher—a good match given that he also represented other photographers from the '60s—but where were the missing negatives? On June 5th, Billy wrote:

> i don't know how much you've heard of the kevin kushel story going on, but steven kasher sent a private investigator to see him in san francisco yesterday.
>
> kevin left my negatives in a mini storage bin when he went to palm springs and subsequently the rent wasn't paid and the contents of the bin were sold, including my negatives and a bunch of prints. also some other photographic artists, as well.
>
> now, because he was so negligent, i fired him and have steven for my agent and dealer now. i've asked kevin for the scans of my negs on disks that he has, to replace the negatives so that i can continue to work, but he has ignored my several requests. steven says he may know who currently has my negatives, but they want a lot of money for them. so, that's pretty much where it stands now . . . kevin is acting like nothing is wrong, or whatever. i don't want to relate to him at all any more. only enough to recover my property . . .

Billy's concern about the negatives wasn't just about money, it was about legacy. Billy was almost seventy, suffered from diabetes, and complained about his lack of stamina. He wrote: "if I should die, Kevin would be trying to use the images all over the place."

I wished that he hadn't said "if I should die." I still hadn't got over Ron's death. I certainly didn't want Billy's death to be the next one.

•

DESPITE STEVEN KASHER'S BEST EFFORTS, he was unable to get access to the missing negatives. He managed to track Kevin down in Hawaii, but he wasn't very helpful. On September 25th, Billy wrote to tell me he had a new agent, whom I'll refer to as Cassandra Fleming. Cassandra didn't have much luck with the negatives either. On October 16th, I got an email from her saying that "the latest amount they want to get the negatives back is $200,000.00 plus 15% of future limited edition prints. Isn't that horrible? At least the price came down. There is not much they can do with all of the legal involvement. Now they are sitting on a box of useless negatives, because if the images show up anywhere, they will be traced . . ."

I wondered who "they" were. If "they" had made a specific offer, then Cassandra must know who "they" were. The price came down? What was the original price? If "they" wanted fifteen percent of future limited edition prints for the return of negatives that had been previously characterized as "stolen," then they weren't being too bright. They'd have to give their details to Cassandra and Billy to get their fifteen percent. I told Cassandra I would run an in-depth story, but she should try going to the press. She contacted the *New York Times*, who eventually ran a story about the negatives, but even they couldn't track them down. Kevin refused to answer their questions, citing advice from an unnamed lawyer. The article ended with a quote from Callie: "Billy told me one time when he was talking about Andy getting shot that Andy was always getting involved in these 'tacky tragedies' . . . And you might say it's happened again. This is a pretty tacky tragedy, but it's one I really hope has a happy outcome."[13]

Despite the *Times* article, the negatives remained missing. Billy wrote me a month later saying that Kevin had still not been it touch. Billy had received a folder that was supposed to contain scans of them, but you needed a password to open the folder. A clue to the password was provided—"your favorite person"—but not the password itself. The folder couldn't be opened, and there was no guarantee as to what it contained in any case. Billy finished his email with, "what a sad case kevin is, spending all his money on methamphetamine and crack and fucking people up."

Billy's reference to Kevin's meth and crack addiction added an additional tawdry element to the story. Methamphetamine or "Methedrine" was the drug of choice at the Factory in the '60s, and remained popular, particularly on the gay scene. Billy didn't do it anymore, of course, and even during the Factory days he had never injected it like Edie, Ondine, and some of the others. I had no idea that Kevin was into it, as Billy claimed in his email.

•

AT THE END OF OCTOBER the Jack Smith festival in Berlin at which Ron Tavel had originally been scheduled to

13 Randy Kennedy, "In Search of an Archive of Warhol's Era," *New York Times*, 8 January 2010.

appear finally took place, and Mario Montez, Warhol's first transvestite superstar, came out of hiding to do a tribute to Ron.

In December there was a memorial in New York for Ron. Callie Angell described it to me in an email soon afterwards:

> Lots of people showed up—most of them of course being older. (The procession of people with canes and walkers slowly climbing the two flights to the Anthology theatre was painful to see.) John Vaccaro came (no one expected him), Douglas Crimp, Randy Bourscheidt, Bob Heide, Danny Fields, Philip R. Fagan (the nephew of Philip Fagan), Penelope Palmer, Jeremiah Newton, even Lee Childers for some reason! And a lot of old theater people . . .
>
> The whole thing made me miss Ron a lot . . . I wish he could have been there (I kept hearing Ron's voice: "But don't I AT LEAST rate a SEMINAR?!?") . . .

Ron was now officially "gone." One thing I hadn't prepared myself for when I started my website was that I would become friends with the people I was writing about and have to experience their deaths. I wondered who would be next. The Warhol superstars weren't getting any younger.

7. Why?

After his appearance at the Jack Smith festival in Berlin, Mario Montez took part in a one-day event with Callie Angell at Columbia University on March 31, 2010. On May 18th Callie was due to give an illustrated lecture at Light Industry in Brooklyn about Warhol's unfinished film *Batman/Dracula*, which featured Mario in the cast, but she never made it. By May 18th, she was dead.

Callie's body was found on the floor of her apartment on May 5, 2010. I learned of her death while I was answering an email from Susan Pile—the same Susan Pile who would contact me a few years later about Ronnie Cutrone's death, just before my heart attacks.

On May 4th Susan wrote:

> I'm going to try to reach Callie Angell this week. Do you happen to have contact info on her? There are a couple of movies I was involved in that have not surfaced yet—*The Bob David Story* and *Ed Hood's Doctor's Office*, shot at Mass General (Ed receives electric penile stimulation . . . a comedy, of course). I think they should be mentioned in any filmography.

While I was answering that email, I received one from Bibbe Hansen's husband, Sean: "Did you hear the sad news about Callie?" I wrote back, "NO! What???" He told me she had died. More emails started coming through about her death, but nobody seemed to know the cause. It was attributed it to "natural causes." What natural causes, I wondered. She had never mentioned any illnesses to me.

Then I got the following from a complete stranger:

To: Warholstars
Subject: A death you might want to note
Date: 9 May 2010

Hello—

in case you hadn't been told, Callie Angell of the Whitney died last week, on Monday, I believe, apparently by suicide. She was found on Wednesday in her apartment. I barely knew her, though she was one of my neighbors, and as no newspaper has published an obituary, I thought I might pass the word. I don't know anything else about the circumstances.

Bruce Eder
New York, NY

Suicide? It didn't seem possible. Callie wasn't the type of person to commit suicide. She didn't seem particularly depressed, and it wasn't long ago that she had acquired a dachshund she was quite attached to; she even took him to work. She wouldn't have left him on his own.

I wrote back to Bruce and asked why he thought Callie had committed suicide. He said: "The doorman who informed me of it, and who was on duty at the time, said there was a note left, and described it as a suicide." He continued:

> I didn't know her well—in fact, in the last few years, I knew her dog slightly better than I knew her (a neighbor was taking care of the dog as of Friday).
>
> The last time Callie and I had a lengthy conversation was back in the 1990s, because our work almost overlapped, sort of—I was, in those days, a producer-narrator for The Criterion Collection on DVD . . .

> Basically, a friend and co-worker came to check on her on Wednesday, as she hadn't been heard from, knocked on the door, and heard the dog—no one had seen her, and the friend became nervous; the doorman sent the handyman up with the extra key to the apartment, and with her friend, and they opened the door and found her, and she apparently had been deceased for one or two days; the last time anyone remembered seeing her in the building was Monday of last week, which was the 3rd; the doorman told me, though, that there was a note, and he doesn't use the term suicide lightly—we have had deaths in our building, and not just of the elderly—drug overdoses and the like; he told me this was a suicide . . ."

I was shocked. Callie was such a dependable person that, as superficial as it might seem, I just could not believe that she would kill herself two weeks before she was due to give a lecture that had already been advertised. I contacted Matt Wrbican at the Andy Warhol Museum—I had been in touch with him many times over the years—thinking he might be able to confirm the cause of death. He replied:

> hi gary . . . i heard the news on thursday. it's so shocking! i've found it very hard to focus on my own work the past few days. it breaks my heart into a million shards. i've been so busy with all i'm doing that i hadn't talked with her for a few years, i just assumed she was plowing ahead with her writing. but i've heard some discussion that she actually didn't have much finished—could it be she had monumental writer's block? greg pierce, our asst curator of f + v, saw her a couple weeks ago in nyc, and she seemed fine to him.

The following day, the Whitney placed a paid

obituary notice in the *Times* which did not list the cause of death. I sent a copy to Matt and told him what Bruce had told me. He wrote back:

> what?! I was told that her assistant, Claire, found her, after she atypically fell out of contact for several days. Apparently Claire had a key to her apt (or maybe the doorman knew her, and let her in), and found her on the floor. I haven't heard anything about a cause, but that would certainly answer the questions i had. oh no, i really don't understand. this is just unbelievably awful news, so much worse.

He also brought up Ray Johnson's death and wondered whether Ray's suicide had anything to do with Callie's:

> i remember her often discussing ray johnson, and his suicide. i was a big fan of ray's work, and had the strange pleasure of talking with him on the phone (well, listening) maybe 3 times. she was also a fan, and grew a bit obsessed by the intricacies of how he set up his death. she recalled that they would often talk on the phone, and he was very interested in her name as related to hinduism (Callie = Kali) and various manifestations of angels. we went to ray's memorial together, at a quaker meeting hall near Gramercy Park.

Callie's full obituary appeared in the *New York Times* two days later, confirming suicide as the cause of death. Bruce Eder had been right.

Still trying to make sense of Callie's death, I wondered about the effect Ron Tavel's death might have had on her. It was clear from her email about Ron's memorial that his death still affected her. The event she had participated in at the end of March would also have reminded her of Ron. Marc Siegel, from the Jack Smith festival, was one of the panelists.

I thought back to when Callie was in London and so grateful when I paid for my own coffee. I wondered if she had felt generally used by people. So many people asked her about Andy Warhol; how many people asked her about herself? Callie was special because she wasn't special. As the author of the film catalogue raisonné, she wrote about "superstars," but she was fairly ordinary. Maybe that was part of the problem. She was overshadowed by her subject matter. She was the last person you would expect to commit suicide, and probably the last person you would think of who would be interested in Andy Warhol's superstars. Had she inadvertently become a casualty of Warhol's glamorous world? When I wondered who would be next after Ron died, I never expected that it would be Callie.

•

A MONTH AFTER CALLIE DIED, Billy Name had a stroke. He posted the following on his Facebook page at the end of June: "hello everyone. for those who are interested, i haven't written on my facebook page for two weeks, because, two weeks ago i had a stroke on june 12, new moon night . . . i'm having trouble with my right side, but it's all healing now. i will not be very active for the immediate future, taking a little break until i'm all better again. love, billy name"

Cassandra Fleming, his new "manager," wrote me a few days later to say that Billy had had a stroke but she didn't want it publicized. I wondered if she read her client's Facebook page. She warned, "Making a big thing about a stroke is not a good idea and will open the door to a lot of problems for him . . . the vultures will come back out of the woodwork."

Vultures? I queried, "Do you mean Kevin? But he's in Hawaii." (He was posting pictures from Hawaii on his Facebook page. If he had stolen the negatives, it would not have been difficult for the authorities to find him.)

Cassandra: "If you lived nearby and experienced all of this first-hand, you would have a very clear understanding of the word 'vultures.' Jayne County could explain it well . . ." If I had to rely on Jayne County to "explain it well," I doubted that I would ever get an explanation.

In addition to Billy, Cassandra was also representing Jayne. I'd had a few run-ins with Jayne over the years that hadn't exactly endeared her to me. She first sent me an email in 2005 complaining that the listing of Andy Warhol's play *Pork* on my website's timeline was "lazy." I had failed to mention that she was in the cast, although I had mentioned that David Bowie was in the audience. She wrote: "If you are going to do history, do it good! Gay history? David Bowie isn't even Gay, but a fake all the way round." I had never claimed that my site was "gay history." She continued to send me similar complaints over the years. The last email I got from her was in May 2006, again accusing me of "robbing Gay people of their history!" and referring to my site as "half baked rubbish." I wasn't impressed.

•

By October, Cassandra was no longer working for Billy. On October 21st, he wrote:

> hi guy. i feel as if we haven't been in touch for a while,

> but i guess that's because i've been really sick for all of october . . . i have an announcement for you, and it's about Cassandra artistic management. she is no longer representing me. i have terminated our relationship. i feel like i've been under a spell and i finally broke it. i'm free again . . . dagon james will begin inventorying my archives and we'll start a nice relationship . . . sorry i haven't written for a while, but like i said, i was under a spell. billy name xox

When Billy said "under a spell" he meant it. He had got into white magic while he was living at the Factory, and he still practiced it. It was reassuring to hear that Dagon James had taken over. I knew Dagon. He had been in touch when he was the editor of *Lid* magazine, which published a series of Warhol-related issues. I was impressed by his knowledge about the Warhol scene and the quality of the magazine.

•

THE FACT THAT BILLY COULD WRITE ME AT ALL was a good sign that he was recovering from his stroke. It wasn't Billy's health that I should have been worrying about, however, it was Bill's. On February 10, 2011, I received a worrying message:

> hi gary, you may remember me from london, michael, the assistant of bill wilson. i am writing you because bill is in the hospital. he had an obstruction removed from his colon—a couple other issues were addressed as well—but he is recovering and should be back in the saddle again before too long . . .

The news was upsetting. I hadn't had my own health crisis yet, but Bill was my Rock of Gibraltar. I was relieved when he wrote me the following upon returning home from the hospital:

> Gary: my constant distress has been not keeping you informed, but everything is rather difficult. I am recovering well but slowly from emergency surgery which caught cancer in the large colon by removing four feet of colon. I weigh 40 pounds less! I am doing physical therapy after 2 weeks in bed in hospital, & have lots of help . . . I hope to be able to write more soon—All my love—Bill

Given how ill he was, I was surprised that he had written at all. I wrote: "Am thinking of you daily if not hourly—or minute-ly." Ron had died and Callie had died and I really didn't want Bill to be next. I didn't think I'd be able to live without him, he had become so much a part of my daily life and thoughts.

•

AT THE END OF 2011, DAGON JAMES wrote that he was now officially Billy Name's "publisher and archivist." He had been helping Billy rebuild his archives since the theft of his original negatives and wanted to know if I had any good-quality images of his work. Unfortunately, I didn't. I sometimes got requests for Billy's work and assured him that I would forward the requests to him. He responded:

> Thanks for your reply. Over the years I've seen how mismanaged Billy was with Kevin and Cassandra with some worry. Thankfully things are normalized and a lot of good is being done with him and his work. Feel free to refer any requests to me and cc Billy of course so he knows what's going on.
>
> *The Silver Age* is turning out really great and I'll send

you copies when I get them from the printer . . .

Thanks again for everything.

Following several limited-edition monographs by Billy from Waverly Press, Dagon would bring out a large, comprehensive book of Billy's Factory photographs, *The Silver Age*—but by that time I was in the hospital.

•

BILLY'S NEGATIVES WERE STILL MISSING after my heart attacks. I received the following message from a complete stranger during my last days in intensive care:

> Hello . . . I have some Andy Warhol negatives. One is of him at the Factory with the Band Velvet Underground (Lou Reed, Maureen Ann Tucker, and the Famous Red Couch) and one is of Andy and a man I dont recognize. I would like to find out what they are worth. Pls call me at [number withheld]
>
> I would appreciate a reply as soon as possible. I'm looking to sell them. I know that the photographer Billy Name lost the 3000 negatives that he had.
>
> Thank You
> [Name withheld]

The figure of three thousand had been reported in the *Times*. I forwarded the email to Billy: "I'm in the hospital at the moment but I received this strange email. Not sure if he is talking about one of your missing negatives." Billy hadn't heard that I was in hospital; he was dealing with his own health problems. Still, he managed to respond: "thanks gary, i'll have my agent dagon james check it out. i hope you will be well, what's the story? love, billy." I answered, "Am glad that Dagon will check it out. I'm in hospital because I had a series of heart attacks. Been in intensive care for two months. Driving me nuts but am much better."

8. Physio

IT WASN'T LONG AFTER BILLY'S EMAIL that I was finally transferred from intensive care to the general ward. Patients were kept in the Intensive Care Unit until they could be taken off the machinery that kept them there. The last thing to go was my urinary catheter. The tube leading to the drainage bag had become so clogged with sediment from ongoing infections that I woke up one night in a pool of my own piss. The urine couldn't get through the tube so it was cascading down the outside of it onto my bed. I rang for a nurse, who rang for a doctor, which we both knew would entail a considerable wait, given how late it was. I was in so much pain that the nurse ended up pulling out the tube herself. I continued to have urinary infections, which were eventually controlled by a permanent prescription of antibiotics. I'm still on them, but at least I don't have a catheter bag taped to my leg.

As my transfer to the new ward was being processed, I thought back to all the visitors I had in intensive care, who had kept me alive. My physiotherapist told me that having so many visitors was zapping my strength, but I'm sure the opposite was the case. Knowing that people wanted me to live made me want to live.

All of the 12th Street flatmates had visited—Paul Lonergan, Kate McIlwain, David Strettell, even Swiss Miss. Kate and Paul lived in London and were at the hospital almost every day. David and Swiss had made the effort to fly to London to visit.

Paul hadn't been out of hospital very long himself. He had finished treatment for oesophageal cancer shortly before I went into hospital. I remembered congratulating him when he took his last pill. That type of cancer was particularly aggressive. I knew the rest of his life would be a waiting game. I didn't realize that mine was about to become one as well. Two weeks after Paul's last pill, I was in a coma.

Lilli had been a godsend. She visited daily and after I was no longer "nil by mouth" regularly brought me fresh food to help me gain weight. Cleveland had also visited regularly, at least at first, soaking up as much of the drama as he could. At one point he started bringing me "get well" cards from the people in the apartment building I lived in and insisted on reading them to me—accompanied by a liberal amount of crocodile tears. There were about thirty cards in total, which he read in small batches. Paul later told me that he had advised Cleveland to leave the cards with me so I could read them at my leisure, but no, Cleveland had to read them to me dramatically, as tears fell from his eyes. When I pointed out to him that he'd already read me some of them to me the day before, his tears quickly dried up, and he angrily left the remaining cards on my bedside tray as though I had deprived him of an acting job.

Later my sister described a visit to a pub with Kate, Cleveland, and Paul, while I was still in a coma, which pretty much summed up how Cleveland felt about Paul and Kate. My niece, Anne-Marie, refused to go to the pub because Cleveland was going to be there and she didn't like him—he was too self-centered. Carol described the pub visit in an email she sent me after I got out of the hospital:

> I think I was leaving the next day and we all decided to get something to eat after visiting you. Anne-Marie wasn't with us because Cleveland was. We walked

> around near the Heart Hospital and found this real old fashion (according to Kate and Paul) pub called Gunmakers Pub in Marylebone. Kate described the food as traditional pub food, heaped high and tasteless.
>
> Kate and Paul ordered a couple of bottles of wine, and when they screwed up our food order, they gave us another bottle of wine for free. Kate and Paul were drinking a lot, and they talked with their mouths full and food seemed to be flying everywhere. I remember Kate making sexual comments about a soccer team sitting next to us. The more she drank, the louder she got. I can just imagine if Anne-Marie was there.
>
> So, Cleveland was acting sort of pretentious, I think he felt left out because Kate and Paul seemed like such good friends and were sharing so much history. Kate was all over Paul, as if they had once been lovers, recounting things they did together and places they'd gone. When we left, they were very drunk and walked in front of us. Cleveland, his nose in the air, was walking next to me and in a tone of utter disdain, leaned over and said, "addicts."

Cleveland's claim that Kate and Paul were addicts wasn't quite true. Although Paul and I were heroin addicts when we lived together at 12th Street, Kate was never a user. She was a drinker; her drug of choice was alcohol. Cleveland did have a point in regard to Paul and myself; there's nothing that brings friends closer than the shared desperation of a heroin habit.

•

ALTHOUGH MY NURSES HAD TOLD ME that the move to the general ward was a good thing, I wasn't so sure. In intensive care there were two patients per nurse; in the general ward there were eight. I was wheeled in my bed to the new ward, and one environment was replaced by another in a matter of minutes. I had been in intensive care for such a long time that it felt like I was leaving home. "We'll miss you," one doctor said as I was being wheeled out. I would miss them as well. They had become more like family than carers.

The first medical professional to visit me in the general ward was a cardiac pharmacologist who would be in charge of my care now. He matter-of-factly told me that, given the damage to my heart, they would not attempt to resuscitate me if I had another heart attack as there was little chance I would survive. He wasn't asking whether I wanted to be resuscitated or not, he was informing me that they weren't going to do it. When I objected, he said there was less than a five percent chance that I would survive another attack. I pointed out that there was probably less than a five percent chance originally, and yet I had made it. I stressed that if I had another attack, I expected the hospital to make every possible attempt to resuscitate me. He answered, "I didn't know you felt so strongly about it. I'll make sure that it's noted in your file." He seemed surprised at my reaction, but I was surprised that he was surprised. How could anyone not feel strongly about their own life? I wondered how he would have felt if he had been the patient.

The beds had curtains between them, and it wasn't difficult to hear what was going on next door. One morning I heard the patient next to me complaining to his doctor that he might as well be dead. He never had visitors; nobody really cared whether he lived or died. The doctor, who sounded scarily like my own consultant, angrily asked him several times whether he wanted to die. At first the patient seemed shocked into silence by the doctor's manner, then repeated what he said before—that he might as well be dead. I heard the doctor ask one of the nurses to bring him form number such and such. Was there a form where a patient could give up the right to live? That's what it sounded like. He didn't really want to die, he was just lonely. He didn't need a form, he needed a friend. Another patient warned me: "Don't let them put DNR on your medical file. It means Do Not Resuscitate." I asked a nurse whether I had DNR on my file,; she reassured me that I didn't.

I tried to hold onto the gratitude I felt when my life was first saved, but as time went on, I became more aware of how dissatisfied some of the nurses were with their jobs and how easily their negativity spread to other nurses. There clearly weren't enough nurses in the general ward. It was true that they had a lot to do, but that didn't make it any less scary for the patients. At night the nurses seemed to disappear altogether. There were two occasions where I had to ring the main hospital switchboard to get someone to bring me a bedpan because they weren't answering my alarm. What if I had been having a heart attack? I wondered how many deaths had resulted from unanswered alarms during the night shift.

•

I NEEDED DAILY PHYSIOTHERAPY, but there weren't enough physiotherapists in the general ward either. By early November, the beginning of my fourth month in hospital, I still couldn't stand or walk. I was transferred to St. Pancras Hospital, where I was told I would get the physio I needed. With each transfer I seemed to move down a rung on the medical ladder. At St. Pancras they didn't even have an in-house doctor. A doctor visited the ward a few times a week, but if anything happened when he or she wasn't there, the hospital had to call a GP in the community. If I had another heart attack, there would be no doctor at hand.

On my arrival at St. Pancras, the ambulance staff transferred me to a bed using a plastic slider under the guidance of a hospital nurse, who then said she had to search me for contraband.

"Contraband?" I asked. "I've been bedridden for the past three months, and during one of those months I was in a coma. What sort of contraband were you expecting?"

"You'd be surprised," she replied as she proceeded to check the contents of a small bag I had with me. "Do you have any alcohol?" she asked.

"No, of course not," I answered. "I have a serious heart condition. A drink would kill me."

"You'd be surprised," she repeated.

After she finished ticking off boxes on a form, I was given my evening meds, including a sleeping pill. I stared out the window, waiting for the pill to take effect. My bed was next to a window with a view of a fire escape like the ones you'd see on the Lower East Side in New York. When I posted a photograph of my new surroundings on Facebook, Sam McKnight joked, "Well, at least you're not standing on top of a cloud playing a harp." I LOL'd and so did quite a few friends, followed by a wide assortment of emojis. I sent Bill Wilson an email:

> I've been transferred to St. Pancras Hospital for physio. It's like a welfare hotel . . . Everything is getting on my

nerves at the moment . . . Thank god for sleeping pills.
xg

The nursing staff at St. Pancras did their best to keep the patients' spirits up, treating us more like an audience than as patients, regaling us with stories about their lives in the outside world. Most of the patients were elderly, with varying stages of dementia, which made me wonder if that was what my doctors thought I had become. I still felt young in my mid-fifties, but I probably came across like someone in his eighties. I wondered if I had been moved to St. Pancras because they thought I, like most patients there, was at the end of my life.

Fortunately, I did get daily physio—none of the other patients wanted it. On the first day, I asked my physiotherapist if they had a standing machine. She laughed. There wasn't enough money for such things—I'd have to make do with an ordinary walking frame.

"Thank god for that," I said. "I hated that machine."

I felt more control over my limbs with the walker. I began by sitting up and hanging my legs over the side of the bed, with the walker in front of me, then used it to support me as I stood up. After standing and sitting for a few days, I was able to take a few steps with the walker. Eventually I made it all the way to the door—not far, but a big achievement. From the door I could see a long hallway, and that became my next goal. Each day I went a few steps further down the hallway with the encouragement of the staff who passed on the way. Their encouragement would probably have seemed corny to an outsider; for me it was like being cheered on during the Olympics.

After about a month, I could walk down the main

hallway and get to the bathroom using my frame and do shorter distances with a walking stick. I wondered if I would always need a frame or a stick, but it didn't really matter. I was alive and walking. I had beat the odds.

Part IV

I. Home

I WAS TAKEN HOME ON NOVEMBER 27TH in a wheelchair pushed by my physiotherapist. I phoned Cleveland the day before I was discharged to ask if he could tidy up the flat; I had given him a set of keys four months before, when I first went into the Heart Hospital. "Make sure there aren't any roaches in the ashtrays," I whispered.

The place was a mess when we arrived, but at least the ashtrays were clean. The physiotherapist had a quick look around to make sure the flat was safe. Workmen would be along later to make some alterations. She transferred me from the wheelchair to the sofa, we said our goodbyes—and suddenly I was on my own.

I sat in silence, waiting for something to happen. When I was in the hospital, I was desperate to get home; now that I was home, I was scared. There were no machines to monitor my blood pressure and heart rate, no nurses available in case of an emergency. I had grown so accustomed to the noisy machinery of the hospital that the silence made me uncomfortable. I knew how to be a patient but had forgotten how to be an ordinary human being.

A couple of hours later there was a flurry of activity. Couriers showed up with medicine that St. Pancras had forgotten to give me when I left; workers arrived to install handrails throughout the flat; an electrician installed an electric chair in the bathroom so I could lower myself into the bathwater with a remote control; a social worker arrived, then a community nurse.

I was exhausted by the time a "home help" person appeared at the end of the day. Her job was to help get me into bed. It was 6 p.m. I told her it was too early for bed. Could she make me something to eat? No, she wasn't allowed to make meals—but she could "prepare" them. Would she be able to tidy the flat for me? No, she wasn't allowed to do housework. Could she take me out in my wheelchair? No, it wasn't covered by her agency's insurance.

"Would you like a cup of tea?" she asked.

"No. I don't drink tea." She made me an instant coffee, I signed a piece of paper saying she had been there, and she left. I got the impression that the paperwork was more important than the help. I was alone for the rest of the evening. For the first time in four months I slept in my own bed. I made sure that the phone was next to it in case I had to ring for an ambulance in the middle of the night. I thought of how horrible it must have been for my father, who had collapsed on the floor trying to get to the phone when he had his heart attack.

•

THE NEXT MORNING I SAT DOWN at my computer for the first time in four months. It was still in sleep mode, and I hit the space bar to wake it up. Ronnie Cutrone's half-finished obituary was on the screen. It gave me an eerie feeling—as though the past four months had never happened.

I never expected I would still be working on the warholstars website more than a decade after starting it. When I first corresponded with Bill Wilson, I described the website as my "Winchester Mystery House," joking that I would die when I stopped building it, just like the woman who built the mystery house. I felt compelled to continue adding to the site once I got home—despite my illness, or because of it.

Bill had sent me an email overnight with "free at last?" on the subject line. I confirmed that I was indeed back home. He responded, "I am thankful for you in any condition . . . When you can, I am eager to hear where you are, how you are, and what can I write to you about which would help get you back in the groove? For Thanksgiving I am giving thanks for your presence in my life: Bill." With that, we returned to the routine we had established before my attacks, emailing each other on an almost daily basis.

Much of my time was spent resting on the sofa. I became a news junkie as I tried to get back in touch with the real world. The Syrian War was still going on, the refugee crisis in full force. Despite the "hugs," smiley faces, and heart emojis that proliferated in modern social media, the world wasn't any more compassionate now than it had been when I was growing up during the Vietnam War. Before my hospitalization I had listened to the statistics of people killed in Syria with a heartless nonchalance. Now I realized that behind the numbers were individuals with just as much right to live as me, whose lives had been cut short simply because they weren't the "right" nationality, religion, or class. It reminded me of a 1908 speech by Rudyard Kipling I had passed regularly in a glass display case at the hospital: "Gentlemen, It may not have escaped your professional observation that there are only two classes of mankind in the world—doctors and patients . . ."[14]

Although I had to go to the hospital for the Heart

14 Rudyard Kipling, *Doctors: An Address Delivered at Middlesex School of Medicine* (London: Macmillan & Co, 1908).

Failure Clinic, most of my other medical appointments took place at home. I was initially seen by two nurses, a community nurse and a cardiac nurse. One problem I had was that every night I was plagued by horrible, vivid nightmares, usually involving a threat of some kind. Sometimes I woke up screaming, and sometimes I continued to hallucinate briefly after waking up. The community nurse diagnosed Post-Traumatic Stress Disorder and referred me to a counselor, who rang me a couple of days later. When I told her my medical situation, she referred me to palliative care, and a palliative care team was added to my home visits for a couple of months. I continued to have PTSD, but any treatment for it fell by the wayside as most of the attention was focused on my medical needs. I was prescribed sleeping pills to deaden the nightmares.

A physiotherapist visited a couple of times each week, and with her help I was eventually able to walk to a nearby cafe. I still had to use a walking stick, and sometimes it felt like I wouldn't make it, but I thought it was important to establish a routine. Every morning I went to the same cafe. On some days my conversations with the staff were the only ones I had. On the days when I didn't speak to anyone else, I still had Bill Wilson at the end of my computer, and that made all the difference.

•

One of my first social outings was lunch with Sam and Lilli. Although Sam had sent messages of support through Lilli or social media while I was in the hospital, the last time I had seen him in person was at a barbecue at his house in North London two weeks before my heart attacks. Garden parties had replaced E parties.

Sam and Lilli picked me up at the flat, and we walked to a nearby restaurant. As we entered, I looked worryingly at the flight of stairs leading up to the toilets. Stairs were my enemy. If I had to go to the loo during

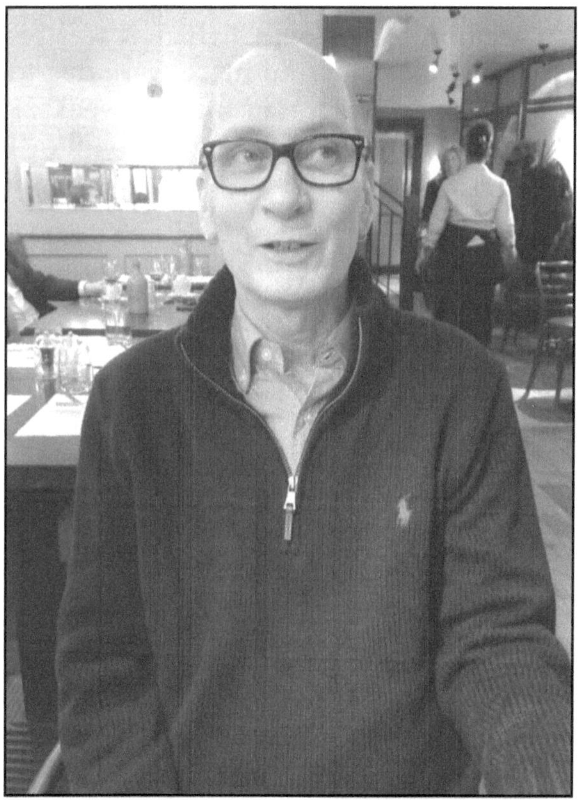

Me after hospital, late 2013

the meal, I wouldn't have the strength to get up them, but I felt too embarrassed to say anything.

At one point during the lunch, I started telling them about the Dalai Lama delusion I had in the hospital and the newspaper headlines announcing Sam's death. I meant to be funny but stopped when I saw their expression. It made me realize how accustomed I had become to talking about death, a subject other people found uncomfortable.

Much as I enjoyed getting out of the flat, I felt so dizzy when I got home that I spent the rest of the day in bed, watching television. Christmas was less than a month away. My sister and niece were due to arrive the day after Christmas for a couple of weeks. I hoped I would last that long. I hadn't seen Carol in more than twenty years, apart from a possible sighting down a long tunnel.

2. Magic Lessons

CHRISTMAS EVENTUALLY ARRIVED, and I finally got to see Carol and Anne-Marie. Carol and I spent a lot of time reminiscing about our childhood. I was closer to her than my other siblings. She was only a couple of years older than me, and as children we had shared the same interests. We both wanted to be entertainers when we grew up. She played the guitar and sang. I wanted to become a magician.

My father had bought me a magic kit when I was about ten years old; by the age of twelve I was putting on shows to local community groups, billed as Gary the Great. Magic was one of the few interests my father and I had in common. Every year he took me to see *It's Magic!*, an elaborate show of stage illusions, at a theatre in Hollywood. I subscribed to *Genii*, the official magazine of the the Academy of Magical Arts, which was based at the Magic Castle in the Hollywood Hills. Most of the tricks in the magazine were too complicated for a twelve-year-old kid, but I enjoyed reading the monthly column about the goings-on at the Castle. I wrote to the editor, Bill Larsen, Jr., him asking if there was any way that I could visit it, pleading, "I'd even be willing to perform in the parking lot." To my surprise, he rang me at home and said I could visit the club as long as I was with an adult. My father was as excited as I was. The Magic Castle was the most famous magicians' club in the world.

•

ONE SUNDAY EVENING MY FATHER drove me to the club; my mother didn't want to come so Carol came in her place. As we came in on the Hollywood Freeway, the twinkling lights of the city below us seemed to be beckoning me toward fame and fortune.

When we arrived at the actual "castle," it was almost a letdown. It looked a lot smaller in real life than it did in the pictures in *Genii* magazine. We were greeted in the foyer by Guy Thompson, the official host. I recognized him by his handlebar mustache from pictures I had seen in *Genii*. After greeting us, he bent closer and asked if I'd like to visit the secret members' library. I had read about it in the magazine. Only magicians were allowed in it because of all the books revealing the tricks of the trade. When Guy told my father and sister they'd have to wait in the lobby because the library was only open to magicians, I felt like I had been accepted into a secret society. I was a "real magician" now.

After we returned to the lobby, Guy gave us a quick tour of the rest of the club before leaving us on our own. We watched some of the shows, but the rooms were so small that it was difficult to see the acts. It was more like a nightclub than a magic club. Waitresses in skimpy costumes circulated among the tables serving drinks to a mostly male clientele—I had never been in such an adult atmosphere before. As we were leaving, Guy Thompson mentioned to my father that he gave magic lessons to kids on Saturday afternoons at his home and I would be welcome to join them. He wouldn't charge for the lessons. My father told him I would definitely be there.

I was thrilled when my visit to the Magic Castle was mentioned in Bill Larsen's column in the August 1968 issue of *Genii*: "So many out-of-town magicians in the Magic Castle that I'm sure I won't remember them all," and there was my name, "Gary Comenas of

Santa Susana," among a column of visitors. He hadn't identified me as a kid magician, just as an "out-of-town" one. I had finally hit the big time.

•

THE FOLLOWING SATURDAY my father drove me to Mr. Thompson's apartment for my first magic lesson; it was located in a building called the Nirvana Apartments. When it was first built in the 1920s, the building probably resembled an oriental paradise; now it looked more like the set of a horror film. I had never been in an apartment building before—I was used to suburban houses with front and back lawns. We walked down one musty deserted corridor after another before we finally found Mr. Thompson's door, which he opened with feigned surprise, theatrically waving us into his living room, where another kid sat nervously. The place reeked of stale cigar smoke.

You had to be a magician to attend the lessons so my father was asked to leave. He said he'd be back in a couple of hours. No other kids arrived. Mr. Thompson taught us some card tricks and said he'd teach us more complicated tricks in the future. Then my dad picked me up and promised I would be there the following Saturday.

It became a regular thing. Thompson sometimes answered the door in a dressing gown with a crown of thorns on his head. My dad laughed it off. It was part of the eccentric character he had adopted as a magician. It was part of his "act." Not that he had an act. I never heard of him performing as a magician—his act was being host of the Magic Castle.

It wasn't long before the second kid disappeared. What had started out as the suggestion of a group of kids was now only me. I didn't like being alone with Guy Thompson, but I didn't know why. Sometimes during a lesson he would start to play around with me, tickling my stomach. I hated it but laughed because I was ticklish. So he would tickle me some more. He asked me to keep my shirt unbuttoned—how could he tickle me if I kept buttoning up my shirt? He was an adult. I did what he told me to do.

Every Saturday I tried to think of an excuse to avoid returning to the Nirvana Apartments. Usually it was a stomachache, but I couldn't have a stomachache every Saturday afternoon. When my mother called him to say I wasn't coming, she repeated whatever excuse I had given and assured him that I would be there the following week. The lessons became more than magic lessons, they became lessons in life—in how to become an adult. He was doing me a favor, helping me grow up. At one point he brought out some (heterosexual) porn magazines. I moved away from him. I had never seen porn before. Rather than turning me on, it disgusted me.

Usually we were on our own, but one afternoon there was a blond teenager in the apartment. Guy introduced him as his foster son. He had an errand to run and asked the boy to make me a hot dog for lunch. He would be back soon. I thought the kid might be an ally—he looked about sixteen. I asked him if he thought Guy was weird. "What do you mean?" he responded. I didn't know what to say—I couldn't think of any examples. He answered almost angrily—no, he didn't think Guy was weird, in fact Guy had been really nice to him. He made me feel as though I was the weird one for asking the question. It wasn't long before Guy came back. I never saw the foster son again.

I don't recall a single magic trick from the afternoon

sessions. He was more interested in my personal life. He asked if I had a girlfriend. No, I didn't have a girlfriend. He asked if I had ever had sex. No, I hadn't had sex. He asked if I knew how a man got a woman pregnant. I told him I thought that he urinated inside of her. When he laughed, I felt embarrassed by my ignorance. He asked if I had ever masturbated. No, I hadn't done that either. I didn't know how. "Well, I can see that I have a lot to teach you," he said. He told me how to masturbate and said that I should try it out at home when I was on my own. "Does it hurt?" I asked. He laughed again and said no, it didn't hurt. He told me to try it at home and tell me how it went at the next lesson. It was all very casual. He didn't make a big thing out of it.

When I showed up the following Saturday, he asked if I had masturbated. I told him I had tried, but it hurt so much that I stopped, which was true. I really didn't know what I was doing, and I didn't feel right doing it at home. The door of the bathroom was locked, but what if my mother heard me or figured out what I was doing?

Guy laughed when I said it hurt and said it looked like it was up to him to show me how to do it. He said this matter of factly—there was nothing to be concerned about. He was teaching me how to do it for my own good. He took me into the bedroom and told me to lie down on the bed. Then he locked the door. I remember him locking the door so clearly. My eyes were like a camera lens that zoomed in on the lock. I knew I couldn't escape. He lay next to me and told me to close my eyes. I closed my eyes. He told me to unzip my jeans. I unzipped my jeans. And then he began to masturbate me. I kept my eyes closed. It felt like my mind had left my body—like it was floating above my body. I don't remember how long it went on. It seemed like a long time. And it hurt—it was not a pleasurable experience. I don't remember getting off the bed or my father arriving to pick me up or the drive home.

•

I DREADED HAVING TO GO BACK to Thompson's apartment the following Saturday and became increasingly anxious as the days went by. I finally opened up to Carol on Friday night. I didn't tell her the specifics, I just said I thought he was strange, that sometimes he answered the door wearing a robe and a crown of thorns. She immediately sensed that something was wrong: "Gary, you've got to tell Mom."

I didn't tell Mom, I was too embarrassed. But Carol did. The next morning my mother opened my bedroom door and said, "Carol told me about Guy Thompson. Do you want me to call the police?" I was so relieved that she didn't ask me for any details about what happened. It would be easier to talk to a stranger. I answered, "Yes," without hesitation. She called the police.

Everything happened in fast motion after that. A policeman arrived, and we sat down at the kitchen table. My mother left the room. The officer took out a small notebook and asked me what happened. Before I told him, I asked him not to tell my parents. He promised not to repeat anything to them. Afterwards, my mother came back into the room, and I heard the officer tell her that they definitely had a case. A crime had been committed. I realized then that Guy Thompson was in trouble, not me. I would never have to go back to the Nirvana Apartments again.

Despite his promise, the policeman did, of course, tell my parents what happened, but I didn't learn that until we were in the office of the L.A. County district attorney. My case had been transferred to L.A. because that was where the crime had occurred. Being interviewed in L.A. was a lot different than talking to a local policeman over the kitchen table. The D.A.'s office was like something you'd see on a television series—a cluttered desk and dozens of random notes pinned to a bulletin board. The detective was wearing a wrinkled grey suit instead of a uniform. When he asked, "Didn't your parents ever talk to you about sex?" I told him no, but my mother quickly interrupted: "Yes, of course we did," not wanting to seem like a bad parent. My father slumped down in his chair with embarrassment.

When it became clear that my parents had been told all about what happened, I got angry: "He said he wouldn't tell!"

"He had to," the D.A. snapped. The case could not have moved forward without the police telling my parents, but at the time I felt I had once again been betrayed by an adult.

At least the L.A. detective was honest. He asked me quite a few questions—he wanted to make sure I was telling the truth and I wouldn't back out before the case went to court. Once the information was out there, he told us, more kids would probably come forward. We drove back to Simi Valley and waited for a call telling us the court date.

We didn't talk much about the incident at home. My mother told me that when my father found out what had happened, he wanted to punch Guy Thompson. He didn't mention anything like that to me. Later I wondered whether, when he apologized for "everything" after my mother's funeral, dropping me off at the Nirvana Apartments was part of it.

My dad drove me to L.A. for the preliminary hearing

that had to take place before the full trial. We didn't talk much during the ride. There was nothing unusual in that. Whenever we did talk we got into an argument about the Vietnam War, which was in full force by then. And I had given up magic—we didn't have that in common anymore. I grew up fast after the incident with Guy Thompson. I didn't have the same respect for adults that I had before. I knew that adults often got things wrong—like the adults who were bombarding Vietnam. I felt closer to the hippies on Sunset Boulevard than I did to my family.

The hearing room was filled with people charged with minor offences like traffic violations. When my case came up, the room was cleared because I was a minor. People peered through a window in the door to see what was going on. I could see them straining to get a look at me. It was the closest I ever got to stardom.

From the witness stand I could see Guy Thompson and his lawyer seated at a table in front of me. I looked straight at Thompson, who avoided my glance. One of his arms was broken and in a sling. His attorney looked shabby, as if he had been up all night drinking and was still wearing the same polyester suit he'd had on all week. He phrased his questions carefully: "Did you unbutton your shirt, or did Mr. Thompson?" he asked. I answered just as carefully: "Mr. Thompson told me to unbutton it." When he asked, "Did you unzip your pants, or did Mr. Thompson?" I answered, "Mr. Thompson told me to unzip them." And so on. He was trying to make it seem like I had seduced Thompson, or at least that what happened had been consensual, that it was my fault as much as his. There was one fact that he couldn't avoid: I was only twelve years old.

At the end of my testimony, my attorney stood

up and asked that it be entered into the record that Thompson's broken arm was self-inflicted. Thompson's lawyer confirmed that it was true. The judge asked him if his client was going to make a statement. No, Guy Thompson didn't want to make a statement.

My father drove me back to Simi Valley in silence. We waited for a phone call to tell us when the full trial would be. As more and more time went by, my mother finally got fed up and phoned the D.A.'s office. They apologized for not getting back to us—the case had already been settled. Guy Thompson had pleaded guilty and was sentenced to six months in a psychiatric institution. That was the best sentence they could get, because no other victims had come forward. They had interviewed the foster son, and he had nothing but good things to say about Thompson; in fact he was angry at me for bringing the case. He said Thompson never touched him. And that was that. The case was closed.

•

BUT I COULD NEVER ENTIRELY FORGET Guy Thompson. Once the internet started up I would occasionally search for news of his existence—or, preferably, of his death. I found a few mentions of his name. The most disturbing was in an online game for children. Someone by the name of Guy Thompson had taken the role of a magician as an avatar. I also came across a couple of postings by him on a website about Cary Grant. Thompson said that Grant continued to say hello to him at the Magic Castle after he "reverted to" his "former status as a member." He had lost his job, as I suspected he would, but was still a member. Didn't they realize he was a child molester?

Why else had he lost his job?

When *Genii* put their archives online, I searched their back issues for his name. I was surprised to see that, although I had been molested in 1968, it wasn't until the November 1970 issue of the magazine that a short notice appeared announcing that Thompson had "left the Castle staff to devote full time to writing and the book business."[15] Even more surprisingly, he continued to contribute to *Genii*. He took a lot of the cover photographs during the '70s and co-authored a series of articles in the early '80s.

Then, during one random search, I came across a comment in the readers' forum section of the magazine's website:

> Guy Egbert Thompson, who used to post here under the name "Tonga," liked little boys and put himself in situations where he had access to them: junior magic clubs. He was a Lt. Commander in the Navy and hung around the Mystics Magic Club of Long Beach when I was a kid. Later, after he left the Navy, he held a position of authority at the Magic Castle.
>
> Thompson tried unsuccessfully to get to me and my younger brother when we were kids. Later, when I was an adult, I could do something about it and I did.
>
> After Thompson left the Magic Castle he moved to Tucson, Arizona. I'd heard through the grapevine that Thompson had been accused of molestation there. I called and spoke with the sergeant in charge of the investigation. Seems the parents of the child didn't believe their own kid, and the investigation was at a dead end.

15 "Late News," *Genii*, November 1970.

> I'd researched Thompson's behavior in L.A. and found that he'd already been arrested, tried, and convicted of misdemeanor child molestation in L.A. County, something that didn't come up on the Tucson cops' radar. I gave them the case number, disposition, etc. That was enough, and the flood gates opened. When the dust cleared Thompson was convicted of fifteen felony counts and served seven of a fifteen-year sentence in Arizona State Prison. I was told privately that he was guilty of much more, but this was what they could convict him on . . .

The comment was dated December 30, 2008. The case he mentioned in Los Angeles County was my case. I emailed the person who posted the comment: "I saw your entry on Guy Thompson in the *Genii* forum. I wanted to thank you for posting it. I believe that I am the person who was molested that you mentioned in regard to the L.A. County case . . ." I gave him the details of what had happened to me. He wrote back:

> I cannot tell you how heartened I was to receive your email... Even though you did not get justice you did absolutely the right thing in bringing the case and testifying, because your case—Thompson's conviction—laid the groundwork for the Tucson case. It was the keystone that everything else was built on. The kid that complained in Arizona was not believed by his parents. The L.A. conviction was ABSOLUTELY ESSENTIAL to getting the case up and running in Tucson and gave that victim credibility. That, and you helped stop Thompson dead in his tracks. He would have gone on for years more had your case not been brought.
>
> Thompson turned out to be a bigger monster than

> was originally publicized. When I spoke with the Tucson cops, I was told that they estimated that he'd molested over 200 kids in his lifetime, including his own grandson . . .
>
> I hope you've come to grips with this episode in your life and moved on. You were a kid, you were a victim, you spoke up and fought back and did everything you could. You should feel good about what you did, because without it, Thompson might have gotten away with what he did in Tucson. He didn't and justice finally prevailed.

When I read this message I started crying. I had never cried about the incident when it happened; I had only felt anger and fear. It felt like a weight had been lifted off my shoulders. I didn't realize how heavy that weight had been all those years. I sat there in front of my computer more than thirty years later, and I cried.

3. San Francisco

By the time I graduated from high school, I knew I was gay. I don't think it had anything to do with Guy Thompson, though. I didn't know if I was gay or straight when I was twelve, but when he showed me straight porn, I was not turned on by it. I've always assumed that being gay has more to do with nature than nurture. Once I came out, it felt like I had been born gay.

The only other gay person I knew in high school was Ron Smith. He hadn't told anyone he was gay, but I don't think he needed to. His bleached blond hair, pierced ears, and camp mannerisms gave him away. I wasn't attracted to Ron physically, but at least we could talk openly about other guys we were attracted to at school. In a lot of ways we were opposites. I enjoyed school and got good grades; he could usually be found smoking cigarettes (or worse) with other students behind the gym. He didn't exactly drop out, he just lost interest in going to classes. When he wasn't smoking grass or taking little speed pills, he was downing diuretics hoping they would help him lose weight so he would look like the guys he saw in Hollywood at clubs like Rodney Bingenheimer's.

Ron had started going to Rodney's in high school. They let minors in if you looked cool enough. I didn't, but Ron and his friend Syd Curry did, and they usually went together. Syd was slightly older than Ron; he had given up high school for beauty school. Later, when I met Paul Lonergan, I discovered that he knew Syd Curry: they had lived together in L.A., both working in the fashion business, before Paul moved to New York. It was such a strange coincidence that Paul from London knew Syd from Simi Valley.

Ron Smith introduced me to the music of David Bowie after I graduated from high school, and that made a big difference in my life. I remember riding with him in his father's pickup truck one afternoon in Simi when the opening notes of a song came on the radio, and he pulled over. "You've got to hear this!" he said as he took out a joint from the glove compartment and lit up. He turned up the radio, and we sat and smoked and listened and were awed. It was "Space Oddity." A couple of days later, Ron took me to Fred Segal's on Melrose, and I bought two pairs of platform shoes and a purple lurex top in another shop nearby. It was all part of the glitter movement—the American version of glam rock. We rebelled against the grey world of our parents through glamor.

Hanging around with Ron meant keeping late hours, and it wasn't long before my parents got fed up with it. After breaking numerous promises that I'd be home by midnight, I was grounded. No more late nights and no access to the car. "Great, you'll have to drive me to and from work. I always wanted a chauffeur," I said, flipping my long blond hair to one side. I was due to start college at San Francisco State after the summer break and had been working at the phone company to save some money for college. I was only seventeen; my parents were still legally responsible for me and, therefore, could ground me.

On one of the evenings that my mother picked me up from work, she said she needed to talk to me and pulled over to the side of the road. I could tell a serious discussion was about to take place. I hated serious discussions with my parents. She parked, turned to me, and asked, "Are you gay?"

"No, why do you ask?" I answered, weakly. (I was dressed in a tight Elton John T-shirt and platform wedgies at the time.)

"Are you bi?" I wouldn't have thought she even knew the term. It was slang Ron and I might use, but my mother?

I told her I thought everybody was "bi"—everyone was born bisexual, including animals—before I interrupted myself by asking why she was asking. "Because I was going through your drawers and found a letter from Ron." I expressed outrage that she had been going through my things. She offered a feeble excuse: "I was worried because you've been acting strangely lately." She had used the same excuse to search my room for marijuana earlier in the year—which, of course, she had found.

I knew what letter she was referring to. Ron had sent it from a family camping trip. It was mostly about all the "foxy" straight guys at the campsite. I didn't know what was worse, my indignation over the invasion of my privacy or my embarrassment about the letter, which my mother had shown to Carol before she confronted me about it in the car. Carol told me about it in London: "Mom read it to me word for word. I guess I already knew you were gay without having to say it, and when I didn't give her much of a reaction, the one she wanted, and I remember this verbatim, she aggressively shouted, 'What?? Does the roof have to fall in on you?' She assumed, by my non-reaction, that I didn't understand the letter."

I ended the conversation with my mother by suggesting it might be best if I left home early. I was leaving in a couple of months anyway. She agreed. We didn't say any more until we got home. As I opened the car door she turned to me and said, "Please don't go into our bedroom. Your father is in there crying."

I couldn't wait to get out of the suburbs. I called Ron as soon as I got into the house, and we left for San Francisco the following week. I paid for our flights and hotel out of my college money; he would be responsible for other expenses until I found a permanent place. The college had a bulletin board where local homeowners advertised rooms for rent; it wouldn't take long to find one. Neither of us had been to San Francisco before. It felt like the beginning of my life.

•

RON SMITH AND I CHECKED INTO the first cheap hotel we found, the Powell Street Hotel at the beginning of the cable car line. We celebrated our new-found freedom by going out on the gay scene. I could look for a room tomorrow. The following day we were too hungover to bother with looking for a room. At night we went clubbing again. We never made it to the college bulletin board.

After a few nights, Ron got homesick for L.A. The gay scene in San Francisco was all guys in flannel shirts and Levis; he missed the glamor of the Hollywood clubs. San Francisco wasn't as wild as he thought it was going to be. He also ran out of money. When I complained about having to always pay the bar bill, he decided to leave. He flew back to Simi, and I suddenly found myself alone in a run-down hotel in a grimy area of a city I barely knew. I finally found a room for rent near the college.

By the time the term started I had spent most of my savings. I found a part-time job at Ripley's Believe It or Not Museum at Fisherman's Wharf. It didn't pay much, but the hours were flexible, and a lot of other students worked there. One of my main duties involved sitting in front of a fake computer in the lobby. Tourists paid $1 for a computerized horoscope. I took their dollar, they told me their date of birth and time if they knew it, I "input" the information, hit a large button on the wall behind me, and all sorts of lights started to flash; a motor whirred, and the machine spit out a preprinted card with the customer's "personalized" horoscope. As it was called the "Believe it or Not" museum," you could believe the horoscope was real or not. It was amazing how many people fell for it, but a bit embarrassing when two people in a family got the same card. I didn't particularly like the job, but at least I got to be around people my own age. I hadn't made many friends at college. The only friends I had were the older men I met at gay bars, whose friendship usually only lasted a night.

Then I met Michael.

I didn't meet him in a bar, I met him through someone else I met in a bar. Michael didn't hang out in gay bars. Before he met me, he probably met most of his sex partners through friends or at a bathhouse owned by the partners of the law firm he worked for, Rick Stokes and David Clayton.

Rick and David lived together as a couple and were well-known in the gay community. Rick ran against Harvey Milk in the 1977 Board of Supervisors election; Stephen Spinella played him in the film *Milk*. Harvey was the radical gay candidate, Rick the centrist. Harvey won.

Rick and David owned a gay bathhouse called the Ritch Street Baths. I'd been there a few times, but I felt uncomfortable walking around in a towel because of my burn scars. I used two towels to hide the scars, one around my waist and one draped over my shoulders. If I had sex with someone, it would be in darkness where, hopefully, they wouldn't notice the scars. They probably weren't as noticeable as I thought they were, but I was self-conscious about them.

A lot of young hustlers hung out at Ritch Street. Occasionally one of them would move in with Rick and Dave, who would treat him like a son, except they'd also have sex with him. After my childhood experience with Guy Thompson, it seemed a bit sick. When I met one of the "sons," he'd give me a knowing glance, thinking I was one of them because Michael was ten years older than me. But I was in love with Michael, even though I continued to have sex with strangers outside of the relationship. The gap between our ages was a lot less than the one between his law partners and their "boys." Michael wasn't quite as square as Rick and Dave. He had been a student in the '60s and still did drugs—in "moderation," his favorite word. He grew his own pot, which he kept in empty peanut butter jars in the fridge, and occasionally took LSD, but he always showed up for work on time in a neatly starched shirt. He specialized in tax law.

It wasn't long before I moved in with Michael. It made sense. He lived in the Sunset District, not far from San Francisco State. It wasn't so convenient the next year after I transferred to UC Berkeley, which took over an hour from Michael's place. I wanted eventually to go to law school at Berkeley—my goal was to become a civil rights lawyer—but it didn't work out that way. I excelled at first, but by my second year I was spending more time cruising the men's restrooms than going to class. The men's room at the campus gym was like a '70s porn film. Students dressed in short gym shorts and tube socks spent hours in the bathroom trying to pick up other students dressed similarly. Having sex with a student in gym gear was almost like having sex with a real athlete, though most of them weren't athletes. Many of them weren't even students.

Every day I told myself I wasn't going to cruise the restrooms—and every day I cruised the restrooms. I fell behind in my work and eventually gave up. I pretended to go to classes; then I just pretended to go to Berkeley. Michael would drop me off at the bus station, and after he left, I'd head back into the city. I hated Berkeley. I went there because I thought it would still be a bastion of student rebellion, but by the mid-'70s it was back to being a prestigious institution for privileged students. I felt out of place among the rich kids; I was on a scholarship funded by a family of wealthy alumni. They thought they were paying for my education but were actually paying me to cruise the toilets.

•

MICHAEL AND I MIGHT STILL BE TOGETHER if it hadn't been for punk rock. It was Ron Smith who turned me on to punk rock, just as he had turned me on to Bowie. My parents gradually got used to the fact that I was gay, and sometimes I'd visit them in Simi. On one of those visits, Ron introduced me to Patti Smith's music. She sounded like the archetypal underground poet—at first a little bit too much of an archetype, like a beatnik you'd see in 1950s movies on television—but I loved songs like "Hey Joe" and the heavy-duty gay imagery evoked by her lyrics. I took Michael to one of her gigs at the Boarding House. He was horrified when she fell off a table and continued to recite her poetry on the floor. I was mesmerized.

Punk reminded me of the glitter days, when we were defined by the rejection of normality and expressed it by the way we dressed. Punk was more serious than glitter; it had a literary aspect, at least in San Francisco. It wasn't uncommon to see a punk carrying a paperback of Rimbaud's poems or William Burroughs's *Junky*. Just as Michael embraced moderation, punks embraced excess. So did I, at least philosophically. By day I dressed "normal" to fit in with Michael's world; at night I changed into a torn T-shirt and black jeans and headed to the punk club, the Mabuhay. When I got home, Michael would be waiting up for me, just like my mother.

On one of my nights out, I met the lead singer of the The Offs, Don Vinil, and went back to his place in Haight-Ashbury, where he lived with a guy named Rico and some other friends. As I was the only one with money, I was sent out to get some beer. On my way back from the liquor store, a strange-looking woman approached me, dressed in psychedelic clothing left over from the previous decade. She stuck something into my mouth and screeched, "I'm giving away hash!" Great, I thought, free hash. There were still a lot of burnt-out hippies living in the neighborhood so I wasn't really surprised.

Back at Don's place, I started throwing up and couldn't stop. I wasn't sure if it was the alcohol or the hash. Don and his friends thought it was hilarious; to them I was just a fake punk from the suburbs. Don tried to have sex with me, but I kept going to the bathroom to throw up. Eventually I collapsed on the floor. When I woke up, everyone else was asleep and it was getting light outside.

By the time I got home, Michael had left for work.

There was a note from him on the kitchen table: "We need to talk." He wasn't aware of the hellish night I'd had, of course, only that I hadn't come home. He had probably waited up. When he got back from work, we sat at the kitchen table, and he told me that he couldn't cope with my lifestyle anymore. He couldn't sleep when I stayed out late, and it was affecting his job. Then came the real shocker—he admitted to having sex with his racquetball partner. It felt like a punch in the stomach. I hadn't exactly been monogamous, but I never expected him to have sex with someone else. Sexual freedom was great as long as your partner wasn't practicing it as well.

I told him that it was probably a good idea that I left, just as I had told my mother that it was a good idea when I left home four years earlier. For me, it was a clear choice: either Michael or "punk." I left the next evening, my most prized possessions squeezed into a big black suitcase, and headed to Polk Street and a cheap hotel, the Broadway, not far from the Mabuhay. On my way to the streetcar, I looked back and saw Michael at the front window with a sad expression on his face. How pathetic, I thought as I waved goodbye with a big smile. I felt like Nora in *A Doll's House*. I was finally emancipated; I was a real punk now.

4. Polk Street

In the late 1970s Polk Street was where the punks hung out when they weren't at the Mabuhay—along with an assortment of hustlers, drug addicts, transvestites, and anyone else who didn't fit in. Michael would have considered them low-lifes, but for me they were a lot more interesting than the Michaels of the world.

The manager of the Broadway Hotel was a large black transvestite who could often be seen out front late at night approaching slow-moving cars to see if the drivers were interested in a $20 quickie. I took her to the Mabuhay, but it wasn't her thing. She craved the secure life I had just rejected. I think she hoped one of the people in the cars would turn out to be a Michael.

It didn't take long to meet some of the other Polk Street regulars. Vince was a gay punk in a black trench coat who later had a sex change and became Dominique. His boyfriend was Beef, a young hustler who reminded me of the birthday present in *The Boys in the Band,* but instead of dressing as a cowboy, he wore black leather. Cabaret artists like Bambi Lake or strippers like Blondine would often be seen wandering down the street after their performances, unable to sleep. Alcohol and downers, usually Quaaludes, were our drugs of choice, although a small clique were into heroin. They weren't street junkies as much as middle-class kids who had the courage to go "all the way."

During the day we hung out at The Bagel, a café on Polk Street. We could usually get enough money together for a coffee with free refills. If we couldn't afford a bagel, the workers at the pizza place next door sometimes gave us leftover pizzas. Vince and Beef used to say they ate fried cockroaches when they were really hard up. If you walked up and down Polk Street long enough, you'd meet someone you knew with money or drugs they were willing to share with a fellow punk.

During one of my daytime strolls down the street, I ran into two punks I recognized from the Mabuhay. Despite the *de rigueur* safety pins holding together her

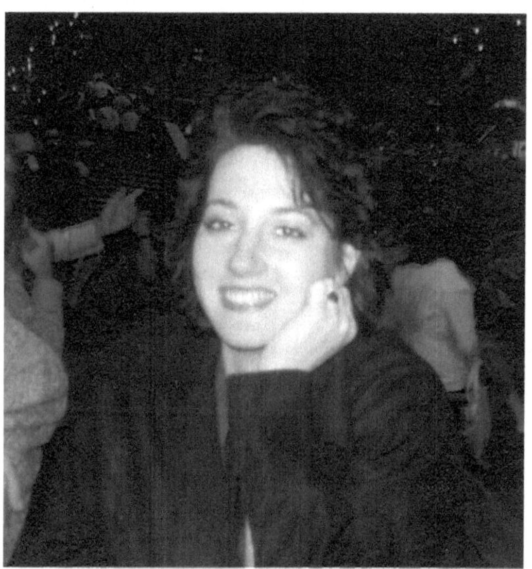

Sally Goldberg

oversized men's dress shirt and tight black jeans, Sally Goldberg was glamorous. With her carefully tousled jet-black hair and dark red lips, she looked like she had stepped out of a 1950s movie magazine. A lot of guys were attracted to her, but she usually wasn't interested in them, which only made them want her more. Her main allegiance was to Georgie, and vice versa. Georgie looked like a demented teenager, short and cute with bleached white hair as artfully disheveled as Sally's. He was gay and had a "straight" punk boyfriend. Sally had a boyfriend as well, a student she treated more like a bothersome brother. He was cute, but he wasn't a punk, and she was embarrassed by that.

We didn't talk long; they were in the middle of a shoplifting spree and didn't want to loiter for too long. They stole new books from a shop on Polk Street and sold them to a shop in North Beach as used books. I saw them later that night at the Mabuhay, and we were able to have a longer conversation. Sally asked where I was living. I told her at the Broadway and that I didn't know how I was going to pay the next week's rent. She suggested I move in with her. She had a studio apartment off Polk Street with a large walk-in closet and said I could live in the closet for free. Her parents back east sent her some money each month to pay her rent. "Would you mind not having a window?" she asked. No, I wouldn't mind not having a window.

I moved the next night when my landlady wasn't around. We found a mattress on the street and managed to squeeze it into the closet. Sally's closet was my home for almost a year. I spent a lot of time writing in my diary there. At night I'd go to the Mabuhay or hang out on the street and then write about it afterwards. I often ran into Ginger Coyote on the street handing out copies of her photocopied zine, *Punk Globe,* which she still does on the web today. A lot of people thought Ginger was a transvestite—that she still had a cock—but she insisted she had had the full operation and was a woman. With her gravely voice and big build, she seemed more like a truck driver in drag. Her five o'clock shadow didn't help. Later, after she moved to L.A., she glammed up and became a minor celebrity. In my diary of summer 1978 I wrote:

So many thoughts have gone through my head between last night and this morning—it feels really early but what time is it? I can't tell without a window—it could be before or after noon or even tomorrow night. I don't know where to start. I'll write about what happened last night during my walk down Polk Street.

It wasn't as cold as I expected—the fog had lifted but it was very dark—there were no stars in the sky. I ran into Ginger on the corner of Polk and Bush Street. She had her thumb out like she was hitchhiking, but I suspected she was trying to attract a john.

A good-looking gay guy in his twenties was trying to pick an argument with her. She was slurring her words so I assumed she was drunk or on a 'lude, probably both. The man was ridiculing her for being a transsexual and into punk rock, like she was a traitor to the gay community. She told him to go back to Castro Street, that "faggot ghetto." He called her a prostitute. She asked him what he was doing out so late.

I went up to her after he left, and we had a much friendlier conversation. She had been to the Rose & Thistle drinking with Vince, where they had gone after raiding the Goodwill box where people dropped off their donations. She showed me some of her finds. I wondered how she would ever squeeze into them.

The other two people I knew on the street were Bambi and Freddy, a guy from England she has been seeing. Everyone is tired of hearing her talk about all the famous people she knows but I like her anyway. I'm entertained as much by her as by most people, which is to say very little.

When I finally got home, Sally was still awake, and we

each had a peach before I went to bed in my closet.

The next day, Blanche came over—Sally and I knew her from the Mabuhay. I listened to their conversation from the closet. Blanche tried to be punk, but she was older than everybody else and never quite got her look right. She looked more like an alcoholic waitress—which she was—than a punk. She was the type of person you talked to at a club when there was nobody else to talk to. Her real name was Karen. An ex-boyfriend had nicknamed her Blanche because she was so tragic—"as in Blanche Dubois in *A Streetcar named Desire,*" she'd say with pride. Her young son lived in Phoenix with relatives but visited her in San Francisco sometimes, a hyperactive kid who craved attention because he rarely got it from his mother. She was too busy trying to get attention for herself. In my diary, I wrote:

> Blanche came over in the morning, From my closet I could hear her complaining to Sally that her mother wouldn't look for her son's birth certificate so she could get welfare. She knocked on my door, and I eventually came out of the closet.
>
> We lay on the bed with Blanche resting her head on my bony leg. She stretched out her arm so that it was perilously close to my cock and complained about how she couldn't get any sex with her kid around all the time. I stayed frozen.
>
> Eventually she left, and Sally and I went shoplifting at the hippie grocery store . . . On the street coming back we ran into Geri and Vincent. He was going to be the gossip columnist of a new street mag that Blondine was trying to put together. Blondine works at the El Cid in the "Love Act" and collects tacky clothes. Who

> knows if she is a real girl or not? . . .
>
> Back at home Sally's boyfriend rang but said not to tell Sally it was him, which was a bit stupid because she was sitting right next to me. He asked if she had booked an abortion yet—he had made her pregnant and she was supposed to get an abortion. She grabbed the phone and said, "Hi, Lawrence."
>
> After she hung up, Sally said he was trying to play the martyr. He had tried to slit his wrists a few days earlier but didn't do it right and just got dizzy and fell asleep. He left the blood stains on the mattress as proof of his attempt. "Such a drama queen," she said.

A few days after that I wrote:

> Sally's getting up. I shut my door guiltily not because of embarrassment for the way I acted (obnoxiously) last night, but because I spent our last quarter on beer and now she has no money for the bus in order to keep her appointment for the abortion doctor. She is over two months pregnant and has an IUD that needs to be taken out along with the dead foetus.

She bled a lot afterwards. She didn't seem to notice that there was blood everywhere. You'd ask her if she was in pain, and she would look at you like she didn't know what the word meant. She was like a robot in a black wig. Nothing affected her. She smiled frequently and occasionally laughed but never cried. Who she was was largely determined by your imagination; you felt that she cared about you because you wanted her to care. The closest she came to a feeling was the smile she made when somebody took her photograph.

•

It was in San Francisco that I first started using heroin. I was turned on to it by Cindy Crayon, a punk who claimed to have been a model in a previous life: she was very tall and thin with boyish good looks. Cindy was friends with two other punks who lived nearby, Geri and Janie, who could have been twins—or dolls. Both barely five feet tall, with short hair (black or white depending on their mood), they tended to dress in similar clothes (mostly black). Geri was the girlfriend of Will Shatter, who played bass with the punk bands Negative Trend and Flipper. Like Cindy they were junkies. Their habit tended to keep them at home, but when they did go out they made a real effort—they didn't just wear the clothes they had slept in the previous night like the rest of us.

One night I asked Cindy if she would score for me. She hemmed and hawed—"I don't know whether I should be introducing you to that lifestyle"—but of course she did it, because I had the cash and she wanted to get stoned herself. She left to score and came back an hour later, her eyes already pinned. I watched carefully as she prepared everything in case I wanted to do it again without her. "Are you afraid of needles?" she asked without waiting for an answer. "You've got such good veins," she drooled as she shot me up, flushing the needle with water before leaving it on the table.

I didn't mind needles, but the dope made me feel ill—not a pleasurable experience. I made my way back to Sally's apartment hanging onto the buildings as I staggered down Polk Street. Fortunately it wasn't far.

Despite that first experience, I was determined to get it right. I wanted to feel what Burroughs felt. It was much better the second time, and even better the third time—and the fourth, fifth, and sixth. When I stopped,

I got withdrawals, but they only lasted a couple of days and felt like a slight cold. Hangovers from alcohol were much worse. Like every other addict, I had no intention of making it a habit. But each time I stopped, the withdrawals got worse, and eventually I couldn't stop. I was hooked.

Sally and Georgie also started using. We supported our habits by panhandling or money from our parents sent by Western Union. We scored from addicts who dealt to support their habits or, if we were particularly lucky, from people who had medical conditions and were prescribed opiates. One guy in a wheelchair got Dilaudid from his doctor. Addicts liked Dilaudid because it came straight from the pharmacy in pill form and was impossible to cut. I don't remember what illness the guy had, but he needed friends, and selling his meds was one way to make them.

Sometimes we found a doctor who was willing to write scripts for imaginary illnesses, but they were rare. Once one junkie knew about them, everyone did; the doctor was inundated by "patients" and stopped writing. As people's habits increased so did their need for money. Some of the girls turned to prostitution. Janie and a girlfriend catered to the white-collar businessmen who frequented Union Square at night. They said they never had sex with the men, they just let them watch, so it was a bit of a surprise when they were busted for prostitution.

So many of those people are dead now, but when we were in our twenties, we didn't think about death. We just thought about fun. We thought we were indestructible. Don Vinil died of an overdose in 1983. Will Shatter died of an overdose in 1987. Geri, his girlfriend, died around the same time of endocarditis, an infection you pick up from dirty needles. Cindy Crayon died in 1991. Blondine was murdered.

At first, becoming a junkie felt like an achievement of sorts, but the success was tempered pretty quickly by a sense of failure and depression. Yes, I had achieved what I wanted to achieve—becoming a real junkie—but there was nothing worse than the depression caused by withdrawals.

•

WHEN THINGS GOT REALLY BAD, I went back to Simi Valley to clean up, convinced it would be the last time—then start using again when I went back to San Francisco. During one of my trips home, Ron Smith came over after my parents left for the Strawberry Festival in Oxnard. I wasn't interested in strawberries.

Ron had just come out of prison and was working as a cashier at Ralph's grocery store. Cops in a police car had seen his car weaving, tried to stop him, and he panicked; the chase ended when he crashed into a railway fence. Things were looking up now: "I'm not getting fucked up anymore . . . oh, you know, I'll do some coke now and then, and I did a load last night, but I haven't had a needle in my arm for almost a year . . ." I had never heard of a "load" before. I assumed it was an L.A. thing. When I asked, he explained that it was a combination of pills that simulated the effect of a heroin high. He said, "Wait a second, I think I have some roaches in the car."

We shredded the roaches into a pipe and got high together like in the old days. I remembered when we lit up a joint and listened to "Space Oddity" in his dad's pickup truck, how excited we had been about the future, when we could finally escape Simi Valley. And here we were, in the future, back in Simi Valley. It wasn't as bad for me as it was for him. I wasn't on probation, and I wasn't staying.

As we smoked, I started to get paranoid. If my parents came home to the smell of marijuana they might not "loan" me the money to get back to San Francisco. Fortunately Rod had his usual can of hairspray in his bag, and we covered up the smell of the grass with the hairspray; then I got paranoid that my parents would know why the kitchen smelled of hairspray. I felt like I was back in high school.

Ron told me about the boyfriend he met in prison: "That fucker, you know what he did to me? I did so much for him." I asked him what happened, and he lit up a cigarette and told me the story: "I got him a job at Ralph's. He quit after a couple of months. Just left for lunch and never came back. And then he had the nerve to get a job at another Ralph's just a few blocks away . . . he ripped them off for hundreds and then disappeared." Hundreds didn't seem that much to me.

He continued as he chain-smoked: "Oh god but he was beautiful. I let him pierce my nipples while we were in prison." He unzipped the orange flight suit he was wearing—he'd had it since high school—and showed me his pierced nipples. I noticed he was still overweight. He zipped himself up and said angrily, "What I should do is let them both heal up. The mother-fucker."

Yeah, that would show him, I thought. Healed nipples. He flicked his cigarette into the ashtray in anger, though there weren't any ashes left; they had already fallen onto the kitchen floor. He continued about his boyfriend: "He ripped off my parents too. He broke into their safe one night and stole all my mom's jewelry and pills."

"What did your dad say?"

"Oh, they really loved him. They were so nice to him. They even went to court and signed some papers so he could live with me, since we're both on parole."

"What did they do when he robbed them?"

"My dad was so pissed. We all knew he did it, but we just pretend it never happened."

I couldn't help wondering if Ron's parents thought he might have had a hand in the robbery and that was really why they ignored the theft. I felt sorry for him. We had such dreams of glamor when we were younger, but there was nothing glamorous about working as a cashier at Ralph's. I used drugs as well, but it was a different scene. In San Francisco we used because we idolized writers and musicians who used and wanted to be like them. Most of the junkies I knew came from middle-class families and had never been in prison—or worked at Ralph's.

That was the last time I saw Ron. I felt sorry for him, but I didn't want to become him. I remembered how superior he seemed when we were teenagers—he could get into Rodney Bingenheimer's! We lost contact after that. It wasn't until years later, after I had moved to London, that I learned he had died of AIDS in a hospice in Los Angeles.

I stayed in Simi for the rest of the week, then flew back to San Francisco, courtesy of my parents. I promised them that this time things would be different: I had no intention of getting involved with heroin again. But the first thing I did when I got back to the city was to score, and the nightmare started all over.

•

AT THE MABUHAY ONE NIGHT I met a girl named Autumn

who was going out with Rozz Rezabek, Negative Trend's lead singer. Years later Rozz popped up in a documentary about Curt Cobain: he was Courtney Love's boyfriend before she met Curt. Autumn had a room for rent, and I took it with Rae Dienstag, a girl I had met at The Stud, a gay bar not far from Autumn's place. Rae wasn't gay, she just hung out with gay guys. She knew I wasn't into girls but didn't mind paying the rent. Maybe she thought she could change me.

On Monday nights we went to the Deaf Club around the corner for "all the beer you can drink for a dollar." It was a social club for deaf people; the manager of The Offs rented it to put on punk bands. Deaf people still went. They couldn't hear the music, but they felt the vibrations, and some of them worked behind the bar.

I met Jim Bresse for the first time at the Deaf Club. He carried me home one night after all the beer I could drink. It wasn't the first time somebody carried me home from the Deaf Club, but it was the first time I fell in love with the person who did.

Jim and I clicked instantly. Talking the next morning, I felt I had known him much longer than one night. We were instantly comfortable with each other. We didn't talk about punk rock, we talked about authors we liked and our future together. Everything was "we" rather than "I." We were a couple the minute we met, it felt that natural.

Originally from Buffalo, Jim was staying with a gay uncle in Palo Alto who didn't know Jim was gay. I'm not sure if Jim knew he was gay at that point. I asked him if he wanted to move in, and he said, "Sure." It was that easy. He left to get his stuff in Palo Alto, saying he'd be back later in the day.

The people we forgot to ask were Autumn and Rae.

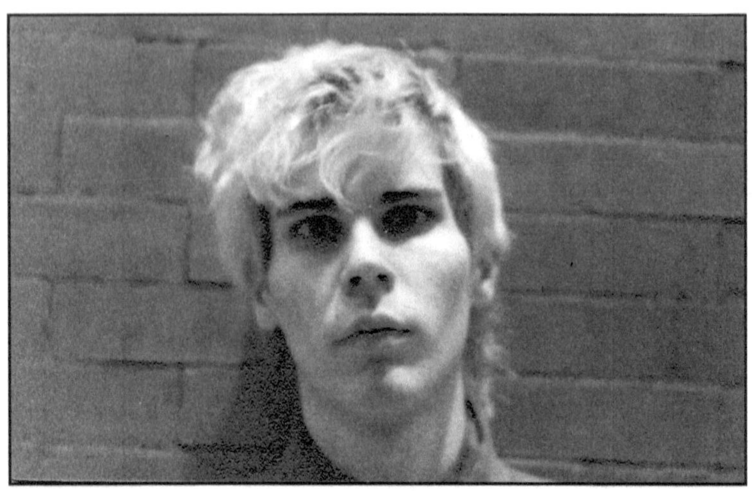

Jim Bresse

Autumn was not happy when I told her Jim was coming back with his stuff to move in with me. Neither was Rae when she got home, having stayed at a friend's house the night before.

"He won't be back," they said, which I interpreted to mean he was too good-looking to be attracted to me.

"Is he even gay?" Autumn asked. I wasn't sure, when I thought about it. I may have been the first man he had sex with. Neither of them worried as the day went by. "Gary, he's not going to show up," Rae repeated in a tone implying that I was stupid for even thinking he would be back. I had felt so comfortable with him, so at one with him, that it felt strange at the end of the day when he wasn't there. Rae comforted me—"Don't worry, there's plenty of other fish in the sea"—and the three of us decided to go to Polk Street.

As we were descending the front steps of our building, we saw Jim walking toward us with a large black suitcase on wheels. He hurried his pace, and when we hugged each other, it was as if he hadn't left. Rae and Autumn would have been happier if their gloomy prediction of my being stood up had come true. The minute we were together, the two of them disappeared. They were still there, but I was no longer aware of them, I was only aware of Jim. We went into the flat while Rae and Autumn carried on to Polk Street.

Although Rae still officially lived in our room, she spent less and less time there, preferring to stay with friends. Eventually she did what Jim and I also wanted to do—move to New York. Jim and I had a lot in common apart from punk rock. In fact, most of what we did together had nothing to do with punk. He was more intelligent than most people on the scene. He loved reading maps, dictionaries, and would have memorized the encyclopaedia if we had one.

Jim wanted to work in the fashion business, and I wanted to write film scripts. But it wasn't long before we were using heroin together—everyone we knew used it by then. When we were stoned, it wasn't necessary to achieve anything; we were as happy as if we already had. Why do the work when you could just shove a needle in your arm? Once again my life revolved more and more around heroin; having someone to share the experience made it easier. Autumn, who was not a user, stood outside our door screaming, "All you ever do is shoot up and suck each other's cocks!"

Jim and I eventually got to the point that all addicts reach at some time. We were fed up with using. It was getting in the way of doing anything with our lives. Rae had moved to New York and kept calling me from there saying how great it was, there was so much happening, I should get there as soon as possible. I could stay with her and her friends until I sorted myself out. When she said "you," I assumed she was talking about both Jim and me. She had never really got on with Jim—but as far as I was concerned, I wasn't going anywhere without him.

The problem was getting the money together for airfares. We made enough money for drugs by working, him as a waiter and me as a typist, but we just couldn't set aside enough for two flights. So first we saved enough so Jim could fly to his parents' home in Buffalo; then, after he left, I tried to save enough money for my flight.

I wasn't very successful. Once he was gone, any money I got went up my arm. I finally got the air fare from my old boyfriend Michael. I had kept in touch with Michael after we split up. He had taken Jim and me out to dinner a few times, usually slipping me some cash afterwards. After Jim flew to Buffalo, Michael invited me over for dinner. When I left his house the next morning, I had the money I needed.

It was the summer of 1980. I was moving to New York.

5. Mr. Chow

JIM TOOK THE TRAIN DOWN FROM BUFFALO the day I arrived. We intended to make a new start in a new city, but it was so easy to score in New York and the dope was so cheap that we started using right away. A dime bag of heroin bought from a street dealer in Manhattan was far stronger than a bag costing twice as much in San Francisco. It was difficult to think of a reason not to use. You could always come up with ten dollars—except that it didn't take long for a ten-dollar habit to develop into a twenty-dollar habit, and so on.

Sally Goldberg and and her boyfriend Fred moved to New York a few weeks after we did, and Jim and I moved into a one-bedroom apartment with them at 12th Street and Avenue D, which we later learned was known as the most dangerous corner in Alphabet City. Fred and Sally took the bedroom; Jim and I had the living room. The only furniture in our room was a mattress and a large naugahyde recliner we found on the street. Sally loved sitting in it after a hit of heroin. She could sit there for hours, staring into a piece of broken mirror and carefully separating her mascara-laden eyelashes with a sewing needle. She had applied so many layers of black mascara over the years that she didn't need false eyelashes—her real eyelashes were fake enough. Eventually she nodded off, holding the sewing needle and mirror gently on her lap.

A few nights after we moved in, the four of us were nodding off in the front room when Sally suddenly screamed. I thought she had seen a flying cockroach: our windows were open because of the heat. A large shirtless black man was in the doorway from Sally and

Fred's room. He must have crawled up the fire escape and climbed in through their window. He came into the room, grabbed the plank of wood we kept for our protection, and ordered us all to sit on the mattress. Memories of the serial killers I had seen on the news as a child went through my head.

"Where's the money?" he demanded.

I took out the seven dollars I had in my pocket and threw it onto the floor.

"Gary! Don't give him your money!" Sally shouted. Then she turned to the thief. "Why don't you go rob rich people? Do we look like we have money?"

He was surprised by her boldness. "Are you a boy or a girl?" he asked. With so much makeup she could have been either.

"A girl!" she told him.

He said, "You're the only one here with balls. You seem more like a guy than these guys," meaning Jim, me, and Fred, who were shaking with fear.

Plank in hand, he quickly checked out the kitchen. Seeing spoons and syringes on the table, he asked, "Are you junkies?" seeming surprised.

Sally said, "I told you we didn't have any money."

He took our ghetto blaster along with my seven dollars. Sally demanded that he leave us some money for food, and surprisingly, he threw us a few dollars. He climbed out the window and back down the fire escape.

We didn't have a telephone so we reached across the airshaft and knocked on our neighbor's kitchen window. "We've been robbed! We need to use your phone to call the cops."

The thief must have heard us and shouted from below: "I'm not gone yet!"

The cops didn't do much. The theft of a ghetto

blaster and a few dollars wasn't a serious crime in New York. The would let us know if they found the thief and good-naturedly warned us to be careful. I liked them. They weren't like California cops, who probably would have searched the place for drugs.

•

JIM AND I SPENT MOST OF OUR NIGHTS at Danceteria or the Mudd Club or lesser-known, word-of-mouth clubs like Rolodex that only lasted a few nights before they were busted. We always got in free. With his bleached blond hair, blue eyes, and chiseled features, Jim was the type of good-looking person clubs wanted, to attract other good-looking people. He looked like a model; I looked like a seedy intellectual with a drug habit.

Eventually I got bored with the club scene. I was more jaded than Jim—I had already been through glitter, disco, and punk. I needed a job. I could still make myself look almost respectable on paper. It helped that I had gone to Berkeley; I didn't mention on my résumé that I had dropped out without a degree. I had worked as a clerk at Michael's law firm for short periods that were easily exaggerated. Résumé in hand, I applied for a job as cashier at Mr. Chow, a high-class restaurant on 57th Street in midtown Manhattan, and to my surprise, after being interviewed by Michael Chow himself, I was hired. They didn't have time to check my references; their last cashier had walked out, and they needed someone immediately. I started work the next night. Jim was over the moon. It was one of the most glamorous restaurants in New York.

Chow's oozed glamor. It was impossible not to make a glamorous entrance. After walking through a set of beautiful Lalique glass doors, you made your way down a series of steps to the main dining area, half-expecting Charles, the French maître d', and the rest of the staff to break into "Hello, Dolly!" Broadway stars would make an entrance and be applauded. It was all about "the entrance"; the food was almost irrelevant—which was probably a good thing, because the food was barely average.

Michael's wife, Tina, was the real star of the show. When she was in town, she was usually at the restaurant, gliding from table to table in a different designer gown each night. She seemed to know everyone.

Innocuous double doors at the back of the main room led to a small VIP section upstairs, where I sat in the shadows behind my cash register. Andy Warhol was a regular; his table was just a few steps from where I sat at the till. The main dining room was brightly lit, but the VIP area was bathed in darkness: VIPs could see and not be seen. Unfortunately, it was one of the most infested areas of the restaurant. I saw a mouse or two running around under Warhol's table and hoped nobody would notice. One night there were so many cockroaches attacking the till that I ran out from behind my counter screaming. The VIPs looked at me screaming, looked at the roaches, and continued eating. Roaches were so common in New York that everyone just ignored them. The bartender kept a gecko at home that ate the roaches in his apartment. It was the only way to keep them under control.

I almost felt sorry for Andy Warhol at Chow's. He sat like a wax figure, barely moving in front of a sparse plate of food and a glass of water. Conversation circulated around him. Jim and I also saw him at clubs—he was very accessible. One night at a party for his magazine, *Interview,* I struck up a conversation with him, mentioning that a friend had some Quaaludes if he wanted any. He said he didn't do them but called a friend over, saying, "Curley loves Quaaludes." According to *Interview* editor Bob Colacello's memoir of the time, James Mellon Curley was Andy Warhol's "latest crush" and "the dashing young son of Nixon's former ambassador to Ireland and Bush's current ambassador to France."[16]

Warhol had a tiny Minox camera with him and took a picture of us. I could see Curley was attracted to Jim, but that wasn't unusual. Jim wasn't attracted to him—again, not unusual. Curley asked Warhol if he could borrow his limo and driver, and we ended up taking it to Curley's apartment in the West Village. When I said something about Warhol drinking water with his meal at Chow's, he laughed: "That's not water, that's vodka."

We were pretty wrecked by the time we got to Curley's apartment, and the three of us ended up in bed together. Curley kept trying to have sex with Jim. When Jim turned to me and complained, I said, "Have sex with him! He knows Andy Warhol!" But nothing happened. Curley eventually fell asleep, and we snuck out the front door.

•

Cocaine was used openly at Mr. Chow's. It was not uncommon to see a customer snort a line at their table after their meal, even on the well-lit main floor. In the private room for special parties one night I saw something I had only heard about before—a gold platter heaped with cocaine set out on the table for guests to

16 Bob Colacello, *Holy Terror: Andy Warhol Close Up* (NY: Harper Collins, 1990).

sample. It was very rock 'n' roll—as it should have been: it was a party Mick Jagger was giving for Jerry Hall. Jim came to meet me when I got off work, and we were invited to join the party. I got drunk and hung out with Keith Richards as he went on a graffiti spree in the bar, which was closed by then, writing all over the marble with a permanent black marker. Michael Chow was furious. He had to hire special cleaners to get rid of the graffiti before the restaurant opened the next day.

I made extra money by selling cigarettes, which I bought for 80 cents a pack at a liquor store and sold to diners for five dollars a pack. They didn't mind paying extra for the convenience of not having to leave the restaurant. Jim often met me after work, and we used the cigarette money to score on the way home, although it was risky to score that late. One night Mama, a dealer we knew, whispered something as she handed over the dope before disappearing into the shadows of a derelict building. Before I could say, "What?" I was hit in the back with a baseball bat and went flying into the gutter. Later we figured out she had said, "Run!"

When I went flying, so did the dope and the paper bag full of cigarettes I hadn't managed to sell that night. The guy who hit me was standing above me, threatening to smash my face with the bat if I didn't hand over the drugs. I tried to get through to him that they had fallen into the gutter when he hit me, but he didn't believe me. He was about to whack me again when someone yelled out that "the man" was coming. At the same time a number of local residents had come out of their apartments and were scrambling for the cigarettes. I took advantage of the chaos to stand up and quickly limp over to Jim, who was at the end of the street by this time. We hurried home without the dope or the cigarettes. We had to wait to score until the next day.

Getting mugged was an occupational hazard for a New York junkie. One time we were approached in full daylight by two Puerto Ricans after we scored. One put his arm around my shoulders tightly and used his other hand to press a hidden knife against my stomach. "Give me your dope," he said with a cheerful expression on his face in case anybody passed. I gave him my dope.

•

WITH MY STEADY INCOME FROM CHOW'S, Jim and I could afford to move to the safety of the West Village. We still went to the Lower East Side to score, but home was now the Marlton Hotel on 8th Street and Fifth Avenue. The last time I saw Sally was on a bench in Tompkins Square Park. She had split up with Fred and had sores on the back of her hands from shooting up. She looked ill. Her face was bruised. When I asked her about her life, a man who looked like a pimp and had been hovering nearby told her to "C'mon," and she stood up and walked away. After the advent of the internet, I searched for her but couldn't find anything; nor could I find a mention of Georgie. They became part of the "disappeared" from my past. I assume they're dead. It's strange how some people can live and die without leaving a mark on the world. I suppose they made a small mark—at least I remembered them.

Jim and I continued to use and continued to try to stop. I was in my late twenties by then, and it felt like time was running out. We cleaned up for short periods, but then one of us would relapse and the other would follow. When one hit could cure all our problems, how could we resist? I had to leave my job at Chow's; I was incapable of keeping to a regular schedule.

We eventually registered at a methadone detox clinic to try to come off heroin. One morning on the way to the clinic, a long-haired guy stopped us and said to Jim, "Oh hi, I'm a photographer, and I'm doing a fashion shoot, and I'm looking for people with your look, you're perfect." We looked at his each other doubtfully. "No, really, I'm legitimate," he insisted. Here, take my card. Will you call me later?" It was Steven Meisel. Jim appeared in a few shoots for Steven, and they became friends. Now when Jim went clubbing he could say he was a model.

We never made it to the end of the detox program. We got behind in our payments and were asked to leave. We became addicted to heroin again to avoid the withdrawal symptoms of methadone, which were far worse than heroin withdrawals.

Once we were back on dope, Jim gave up trying to get a job and was absorbed back into the club scene. I knew I would never clean up as long as I was living with him. The love that we had felt for each other had largely been supplanted by our love of heroin. Human love just couldn't compete. In order to save myself, I would have to leave.

I moved into the Hotel 17 in Gramercy Park, a welfare hotel for drag queens, drug addicts, and petty criminals. I registered at a methadone maintenance program on my own. Maintenance was different than detox. Patients on maintenance were expected to stay on methadone for the rest of their lives. If you felt like using heroin again, the clinic just increased your dose. The State became your connection. It was worth it for them because you didn't have to resort to criminality to support your habit. You could get a normal job and pay normal taxes and become a normally functioning member of the real world.

Although we weren't boyfriends anymore, Jim still visited me at the 17; I'd let him use the room to take a nap while I was at work. I had a new job as a library assistant at a medical library. There were no more late nights for me as I settled into a routine. I'd take a slug of methadone in the morning and spend the rest of the afternoon at the library, filing index cards according to the Dewey Decimal System. At the end of the day, I went back to the 17 and nodded off in front of the TV. The next morning I woke up, had another slug of methadone, and went to work—day after day after day.

•

THE LONGER I WAS ON METHADONE maintenance, the more jealous I became of people who didn't need to be stoned to be "normal." Yes, I could hold down a job now, but I felt like an emotionless zombie. I wasn't unhappy, but neither was I happy—I just "was." After a year or so I decided to quit the program. The clinic staff tried to dissuade patients from detoxing because they usually relapsed. I knew I wouldn't go back to using heroin. I had said that before, but this time I meant it. I didn't ask myself how many times before I had said this time I meant it.

It wasn't easy coming off the program. Methadone stays in your system longer than heroin. Withdrawing from it takes months instead of weeks. I managed it by gradually decreasing my dose from over a hundred milligrams a day to less than ten and finally to none. At last I was clean. When I picked up my last dose at the clinic, the woman behind the counter wished me luck, adding. "Don't be embarrassed to come back if you need to." There were no hugs or kisses, no fanfare, no congratulatory cake. It felt like I was the only person who thought I had actually accomplished something.

A few days later Jim stopped by to invite me to Sam's place and the Palladium.

Part V

I. The stalker

As Carol and I reminisced during her visit, I realized there was a lot she didn't know about me. She knew about my addiction and my relationship with Jim, but she didn't know I had worked at Mr. Chow. She knew that I had moved to London with Kate, but I never mentioned Cleveland in our sporadic emails to each other in the years before my heart attacks. There were some periods, like the years I worked at Island Records, when I lost touch with my family altogether. I had never told my father I was HIV positive, and Carol only learned about it when I was in a coma. I enjoyed her visit and was sorry when she and Anne-Marie left to return to the States. I was also worried. Having them in the flat made it easier to sleep. If I had a heart attack in the middle of the night, somebody would be there to call an ambulance.

My health continued to improve after they left, but a few months later my recovery seemed to stall and then stop altogether. Then it felt like I was getting worse. I started to have palpitations in the middle of the night and a few times rang for an ambulance and stayed overnight in the hospital.

One night the inevitable happened: I had another heart attack. This time I was conscious as the ambulance blared its way down Tottenham Court Road and thought back to what the pharmacologist had told me after my first heart attacks—that if I had another one, there was little chance I would survive.

This attack led to my having an ICD—an

implantable cardioverter-defibrillator. The pacemaker would help steady my heartbeat and the defibrillator would send an electrical charge to my heart if it stopped beating. Usually it took three hours to put in an ICD; my operation took seven: my heart was so damaged that they had difficulty connecting the leads. I had to be awake as they cut into my chest, although I had a considerable amount of diamorphine (pharmaceutical heroin) during the procedure—I overdosed twice and had to be injected with an antidote. Afterwards, lying in my hospital bed recovering, still stoned from the diamorphine, I noticed the light fixture on the ceiling above me. It was the same one I noticed in my Dwell delusion and thought was decorated with live, miniature people. They weren't miniature people at all. The metal surround reflected the staff around my bed. In my delusion the previous year, I remembered the fixture as being on the floor, which is why I thought the reflections were tiny people.

I didn't get many visitors this time around. My hospitalization had not been announced on social media; there were no "likes" to be won by reporting on my health. I became one of those patients I used to feel sorry for because they rarely got visits. Kate didn't come at all. Cleveland made a short appearance with his latest boyfriend to get the keys to my flat. My illness was old news now. Maybe I should have died the first time.

•

When I got home from the hospital, I emailed Bill in New York telling him about the implant. I felt better as a result of having it, although I expected to be catapulted from one side of the room to the other when I got zapped by the defibrillator. He wrote back that he was happy I was feeling stronger. A sentence at the end of his email caught my attention: "I'm still being stalked, and now have an email telling me that she'll be where I am going tonight! I see now what famous people undergo." I didn't recall his mentioning a stalker previously.

He emailed the next day, "She stalked me tonight at Drawing Center! I'M IRRESTISTIBLE . . ." But when his stalker showed up at another event, she didn't seem so harmless:

> . . . I'm being stalked by a young woman who misunderstood my impersonal work on her methods of thinking as my personal response to her—so as an 82-year-old cripple I have twice had a woman try to stick her tongue into my mouth. Thurs, at the Museum of Modern Art, she snuck in a kiss on my cheek before I could stiff-arm her without losing my balance. In case you think I have nothing to do! I have an ethic of attention which she is damaging with her destructive mis-attentions to me.

Bill was working on a book about Ray Johnson—he had received a grant of $40,000 from the Warhol Foundation to help fund it. But the stalker was a serious distraction. Over the next weeks he forwarded her crazy-sounding emails. When I advised him to report her to the police, he responded in such a light-hearted way that I felt guilty for suggesting it. "Well, she doesn't need to be totally crazy to 'love' me," he joked. "I carry a cane to beat off droves of the enraptured."

When I wrote back saying that the woman sounded mentally ill, he replied:

> . . . I was teasing about the "love": the situation is

> absurd; I get my exercise by pushing my hernias back in; I so misread her responses, and so under-read the suggestions of my behavior as a "mentor," that I will be more careful. She adds pain to my pain, and damages my ability to work—& now has sent a long note about rage . . .

He misinterpreted my comments to mean that his stalker must be crazy to be in love with him. But that wasn't what I meant. I had grown very fond of him myself over the years, although I rarely expressed my feelings. We didn't talk about feelings, we talked about ideas.

•

WHILE BILL DEALT WITH THE CRI DE COEUR of his stalker, I was dealing with my own heart problems. I had not expected the ICD to be so heavy or to move around the way it did. A day didn't go by when I was not aware of it. In bed I was constantly having to adjust my position so as not to apply too much pressure to it. I continued to have problems breathing, unsure if that was because of my heart condition or my COPD. I forced myself to go to my regular café each morning to get me out of the house at least once a day and give me a sense of purpose.

The first public event I went to was Sam's sixtieth birthday party at Tramp. I hadn't been to a club in a long time, but I had promised Sam and Lilli I would be there. Lilli helped me into the main room, hobbling along on my stick, squeezing past Lesley Chilkes in the hallway. I couldn't believe it was her.

"Do you remember me from New York?" I asked. She nodded nervously, looking at the stick. "You look exactly like you used to look back then."

"I know," she replied, "everybody says that."

"You're even wearing the same clothes." She had on a black dress that looked exactly like the one she used to wear in the Mike Todd Room every night. She laughed but seemed distracted. I later found out Paul Lonergan was hovering behind me.

Paul had stopped talking to me. I was never sure why. While I was at St. Pancras, I had emailed him asking if he would donate to a charity bike ride Jo and Bruce were doing for the Heart Association. When I didn't hear from him, I asked again and got this response: "Are you all right? What's the panic? With respect I prefer to make my own decisions in my own time . . . I've had a hard week Gary." And that was the last I heard from him. We had been friends for nearly three decades. During that time I had seen him cut off friendships with other people for fairly trivial reasons, but I had never expected him to do it to me. At the time I was so focused on my own medical problems that I had forgotten about his. His cancer would return soon, if it hadn't done so already.

Unaware that he was behind me when I was talking to Lesley, I continued to hobble through the club, mingling as best I could among the relics of the past—and future. I hardly got to talk to Sam that night. I gave him a copy of Andy Warhol's *Wild Raspberries* as a gift, but the party was business for him. He stood in the entrance hall talking to journalists and well-wishers like the fashion royalty he had become. As I passed him on my way out, he cried out in surprise, "Gary, you're still here!" It was midnight, late for me; in the old days, the night would have just been beginning.

•

MEANWHILE BILL'S STALKER had returned:

> Sylvie pushed her way into my house a few days ago, terrifying me—I can't think fast, and get overwhelmed. Fortunately my daughter Kate heard my screams and came to handle her. Sylvie and a bronchial infection (for a month) make work difficult, but I don't give up. The "art world" grows so repulsive to me that I start to lose inspiration as work doesn't seem worth doing. I will now count a few blessings and a few achievements in order to try to get back up on my high horse to look down with disdain at the harsh hustlers who are clawing their way into the bottom third.

It was clear that, as much as Bill tried to escape into new ideas, he was becoming increasingly worn out by Sylvie's unwanted attentions. In August he wrote:

> As I gasp in wonder at some of my work, I am slow and weak, but persisting, trying to figure out how to find a hands-on take-charge get-up-and-go doctor. Don't worry about me; I don't feel sick, merely weak, less inspired to wash dishes and to put out the garbage in my 75th or so year of hauling. I wash toilets to tell myself that I haven't given up: "You can do this."
>
> Kitty litter can go another day, and nobody is likely to see my underwear as I hide it under the trash in the bucket of grunge. I do have strength to work, & less interest in the activities that squander my attention. As I repeat to anyone who will listen, I remain ready to die without self-importance or self-pity, yet with a tinge of mild regret if I don't get some statements out there . . .

> London on the tv makes me nostalgic. I've lost the strength to loathe royalty, though I have enough venom for "royal-watchers" exuding a bland English sauce on tv.
>
> We'll both work on being strong men crossing through slaughter-houses:
>
> Love, Bill

The description of his life was depressing. It wasn't like Bill, who had always kept his, and often my, spirit up. When I first met him I was impressed by his youthful energy, and now he didn't even have the energy to go to the doctor. He had led such a gregarious life, but where was everyone now? His mention of London made me nostalgic as well; I didn't want to contemplate the possibility that we would never see each other again.

Meanwhile his stalker was threatening violence and suicide. I emailed him immediately and told him again to contact the police. Somebody needed to intervene immediately: "Please, Bill, call the police. NOW."

I didn't get a response. I waited. What was going on? He usually responded the same day. I left it a few days, assuming that if something was wrong, Michael would email me, as he had done before. But was Michael still working for him? He never mentioned him anymore. I sent another email, and still no response.

Finally he wrote back. There was no text, just an empty email with a message on the subject line: "quite a week—now in the old Village Nursing Home—someday I'll explain."

I wrote back: "What on earth has happened?"

He replied the next day. It wasn't exactly an explanation of what had happened, but at least I knew he was okay.

> Gary: I'm still in Village Care, working on an accumulation of physical problems, quite hopeful that I'll have more strength for my work, when I can return to it. I'll spare you my attempts to make amusing anecdotes out of Beth Israel, now a medical dumping ground (my near neighbor had been in jail for 23 years).
>
> Village Care is on a different level of care, with about as much physical therapy as I can tolerate, decent food, and a reasonable "hospital" atmosphere. Maybe I go home Nov. 4th, but that has its own problems (my son wants to make "improvements" I don't want at all).
>
> The injury to my body coinciding with a severe injury to my mind by the threat to kill me has been a shock, but may force me to clarify the process of my work. (Her next e-mail was morally even more offensive).
>
> I'm OK, eager to work, maybe better focused on the realities for an 83-year-old in 2015: Bill

Later he wrote again, treating me to a humorous description of his life at Village Care:

> My room-mate is a repulsive self-pitying Mama's boy long after Mama has died—he whines and uses weakness and demonstrations of incapacities to get what he wants. I won't speak to him. His brother visits because he wants to get the money Mama left to baby her baby. The only use of him is to strengthen resolutions not to become like him.
>
> Hence I am sitting up in a chair studying Heidegger on "presence" (I have a computer here in room 6006A), but the omni-present television blares of noise and forced laughter make thinking difficult. This place does

not believe in QUIET: HOSPITAL ZONE, with nurses loud enough to be heard by the deaf and to awaken the problematic dead.

here come de pills!!

•

AROUND THE TIME THAT BILL was writing about Village Care, I heard that Anita Sarko, the DJ and door-person at the Mike Todd Room, had died. The news brought back so many memories. What made it extra shocking was that she had killed herself. I couldn't understand that. Her friend Michael Musto described her death in *Paper*: "On Sunday October 18, her husband came home from a trip to Canada, saw a note she'd left, and found her on the bathroom floor with a rope around her neck. She'd also hung her red wedding dress. Her note expressed appreciation to her husband, me, pal Kohle Yohannan, and her childhood friend Linda."[17]

It was such a strange way for somebody like Anita to kill herself. How would she even know how to hang herself? Her fellow door-person from the '80s, Haoui Montaug, had also killed himself, but that almost made sense. It was 1991, he had AIDS, and he had begun to get ill. He arranged for a small group of his friends to be at his apartment. After they left he took the pills and put a bag over his head so he would suffocate as he fell asleep. Unfortunately, when his friends returned to the apartment to find the body, he was still alive; they had to leave and come back again. Anita had been one of the friends.

I was surprised to hear that Anita had a husband. He made his presence known after her death as he

17 Michael Musto, "R.I.P. Anita Sarko," *Paper*, 27 October 2015

took to social media to berate what he referred to as the "shitty '80s NYC crew." When the subject of a memorial came up, he wrote, "I'll tell you 99% of the people that inquired about a memorial did not give a shit about Anita when she was alive and def did not give a shit about what I was going through. Everyone loved the rich Anita Sarko of the '80s, but hardly anybody loved the Anita Sarko I met in 1999 who was down and out. All these people care about is making themselves look good and having a fuckin' party."[18]

It was painful to think of Anita being ignored by the people who had once clamored for her attention to get into the Mike Todd Room. The New York '80s left a lot of casualties. I almost became one myself; I was glad I left when I did. By 1988 the *New York Times* was reporting that the Palladium was considered "over the hill by downtowners" and the Mike Todd Room was being turned into a no-alcohol club for minors.[19]

•

ON NOVEMBER 6TH BILL WROTE, "I'm home, rather shaky on my feet, but eager to work, hoping to endure as effervescently as you do: Rehabilitated Love: Bill."

A week later he told me his stalker was "under surveillance and care—forbidden to communicate with me—but I remain terrorized . . . I was worried about hurting her, but now am angry . . ." He was only getting angry now?

A few days later he sounded desperate:

18 Posting in "New York New York" group, Instagram via Facebook, 17 August 2016.

19 "No Liquor but Still Exotic: A Night Life for the Young," *New York Times*, 26 April 1988.

> . . . Sylvie is back, terrorizing me, wrecking my attention, with the meretricious destructive "interest" that a psychopath can have (I waste my own time thinking about & fearing her—and only try to reach anger for my pitiful attacker) . . . I have sympathy for the very stalker who is preventing me from doing the thinking/ writing that is me . . . me . . .

That was the last time Bill mentioned his stalker.

2. Let's face the music and dance

BILL AND I CONTINUED TO CORRESPOND almost daily as we had before. Then, on December 20th, I received a worrying email from him. The main text was about a "Love Book" he had found by Ray Johnson, but what caught my attention was a note he had tacked onto the end of his message:

> Wed. we schedule surgery. You have endured so much, so I'll think of your ordeals while I face the music and dance: Bill

Surgery? I wrote: "Hope that it goes well, whatever it is, but what is it?" He replied:

> Gary: on Wed. the 23rd I meet with Dr Pacholka who about 6 years ago performed surgery on my cancerous large colon. I now have had the tests—CT scan barium enema—which should clarify the results of a colonoscopy a few weeks ago. The cancer has been seen as a recurrence, now recent tests can guide the surgery which is to be scheduled. I am horrified, but have been through this operation before, so I can hope that the horrors are limited to the physical.
>
> This season I am rather weak, without much spirit for my work, so maybe I can improve. I don't need a full colorful life—I need energy for my work. Thus at least a month of disaster, with dangers to my brain from anesthesia and pain medications, so I'm trying to organize my notes so that any future work can be more like editing than creating. I am satisfied to die now, but will work to earn a gift of time to complete some work on both Ray and Andy (the Andy stuff is in better shape).

> Please don't be upset. I'm 83, now with a panoramic view of my life. But I plan to go on going on to be able to share my work with you, my fittest audience: Bill

The fact that he was telling me not to be upset gave me even more reason to be upset. I clung onto the positive aspects of his email, but doubts lingered. If he was going to continue to share his work with me in the future, why was he telling me not to be upset and that he was "satisfied to die now"?

The day after Christmas he wrote:

> As of today, I am scheduled (January 21st) to enjoy two operations at Lenox Hill Hospital, where my twin daughters were born in 1962, thereby focusing Ray's appreciative study of identity and difference. The twins bodied forth one of his governing themes—they functioned like axioms made visible. My visit may have fewer aesthetic implications.
>
> The surgery will be two operations—first to treat a hernia which is in the way, then, without cutting through muscles (the horror the last time) to perform a laparotomy (if that is the word). If all goes well, my walking won't be affected, and I might be able to come home after 4 or 5 days. I am much relieved of specific anxieties based on the earlier emergency operation which hacked through muscles.
>
> I'm planning as though all will go well, while more and more eager to get it over with so that I can settle down to my work. I hope to prepare my sketchy notes so that I can edit them into coherence, without needing fresh inspirations. I have to figure out how to "use" these events—so will compose questions for myself about Ray's disagreements with conventional

agreements: Love among the ruins: Bill

I was reassured when he said he would be home so soon after the operation. The day before he went into hospital I sent him a message of support:

> It's Wednesday morning here and you're going into hospital tomorrow so I wanted to wish you the very best. If the nurses don't treat you properly, ask to speak to the head nurse (called the Ward Sister over here) or the doctor. They can't deny you that and it will scare them into action. And sit in the chair next to the bed as soon as you can.
>
> I'm sure you don't need this advice—but I'm not there to boss the staff around so I am offering it anyway.
>
> I don't express my emotions very well—but I am thinking about you and thinking about you and thinking about you,
>
> Love always—for the past and the future.
>
> gary

He wrote back the same day:

> You have fortified me. I do feel that we have a "special relation." Now I'll try to be strong for "us": Bill

I sent him an email after the operation but didn't get a response. It didn't surprise me. A few days passed. I tried not to worry. After a couple more nights, I woke up in the dark and, for no particular reason, checked the emails on my phone. There was a message from Bill Wilson's daughter Kate: Bill had suffered a heart attack in recovery from surgery and died on February 1st.

I was devastated. I still am.

3. The gift

WHEN BILL WILSON DIED, I felt like I had lost my only friend. In a way, I had. I continued to work on the website sporadically, but my heart wasn't in it. I missed my morning emails from Bill. I prayed to a god I didn't believe in for a sign of some sort; something that signified "goodbye." I hadn't had the chance to say goodbye to him.

I tried to keep to my normal schedule. I began each day by having a coffee at the same café I had been going to for the past couple of years, but each day seemed longer than the previous one, and I felt lonelier as each day passed. A Brazilian member of staff at the café sensed my depression and asked me what was wrong.

I laughed a fake laugh and said, "Nothing, I'm just tired."

He looked at me and said, "Something is wrong."

A couple of weeks after Bill's death, the manager of the café told me that she and her team were leaving. The powers-that-be were transferring them to another branch. I told her I'd miss everyone and put out my hand; instead of shaking it she reached out to give me a hug and said, "Goodbye." I watched her lips mouthing the "goodbye" without connecting the lips to the person speaking. They were the words I wanted to hear. It was silly really—the moment only lasted a few seconds, the manager hadn't said the words as part of a sentence. She just said, "Goodbye."

As she hugged me, I could feel tears forming in my eyes. She looked at me puzzled. Why should the absence of her and her team affect me so much? I sat down at my usual table and looked the other way while she got on with her work. It was nothing, just a random "goodbye" instilled with extra meaning because of circumstances she knew nothing about.

•

I WROTE AN OBITUARY FOR BILL for my website, hoping that writing about his death would help me cope with it. When Cleveland saw it, he told me that Bill had said some nice things about him when I was in a coma—could he read them to me? Hoping to avoid histrionics, I told him to forward the emails to me. He hemmed and hawed but eventually agreed, muttering something about ignoring the mention of money. I had no idea what he was talking about.

The emails came in dribs and drabs. They were mostly thanking Cleveland for everything he was doing for me, the "thanks" usually preceded by Cleveland's own boasts. I was shocked to read in one email a reference to £2,000 that Bill had given to Cleveland because he wanted "everything to do with Gary to be comfortable." Cleveland had never told me about Bill's gift. I was furious. It wasn't the money that bothered me, it was the fact that Bill had died without my being able to thank him. And why had Cleveland accepted the money in the first place? I was in a coma. Flowers were forbidden in intensive care. My medical expenses were paid for by the National Health Service. I didn't need the money. Cleveland didn't tell Bill that. Instead he wrote to him:

> I am still lost for words about your gift but I have carried the weight and been the correspondent to everyone for Gary. I am thankful that I know Gary as well as I do and that I know him well and who he is

> fond of. As you said in your first email to me any friend of Gary's is a friend of mine and I feel the same way.
>
> Everyone thanks me sincerely and endlessly for tirelessly keeping everyone informed and updated on Gary's state. It makes me cry to know what you have kindly done and maybe you had an idea of the extent to what I have done and will continue to do for my dear friend Gary.

I was grateful for Cleveland's help, but describing himself as "the correspondent to everyone" in his email was ridiculous. "Everyone" thanks Cleveland "sincerely and endlessly" for "tirelessly" keeping "everyone" informed? Who was this "everyone"? Even worse was the way Cleveland arranged to pick up the money. Bill offered to send the money by bank transfer, but Cleveland insisted on cash. So Bill contacted Alex Sainsbury to arrange for an envelope of cash to be waiting for Cleveland at Raven Row. It seemed so tawdry, more like extortion than a gift.

Cleveland tried to excuse his actions by saying that he had already begun his "slippery slide into the depths of hell" by then. The "depths of hell," I learned, was an addiction to crystal meth that he developed while I was in the hospital—the reason he became so undependable as time went on. I didn't judge him for his addiction, I judged him for his hypocrisy. He had made himself look like an angel while he was ripping off Bill for £2,000. Yes, Bill could take care of himself, but he was still an elderly man, and it was clear that Cleveland had taken advantage of his worries about my health in order to make a bit of cash for himself.

I emailed Alex, apologizing for what Cleveland had done. Alex told me not to worry about it: "Cleveland came to Raven Row to collect the money. I can't remember how much it was and I can assure you that it is water under the bridge for me now. Bill was led to believe that you were at death's door." I told him it was true that I was at death's door but that wasn't the issue. Cleveland had taken advantage of both him and Bill. Bill never knew that the money went toward Cleveland's drug addiction, and there was no way to tell him now that he was dead.

•

A MONTH AFTER BILL DIED, Paul Lonergan died. I always expected Paul and I would become friends again before one of us died. I had stopped speaking to him because he had stopped speaking to me, but I didn't know why he had stopped speaking to me in the first place. Both of us probably expected the other one to make the first move. Although Lilli had said he was hovering behind me at Sam's birthday party, I didn't see him—I was too busy trying to stay upright.

I thought I saw Paul once on a street corner near my flat after I came out of the hospital the second time. He was standing in the doorway of a deli near to where I lived. It didn't seem particularly strange that he was there as there were quite a few companies in the area related to the fashion business—Paul was still working for Premier. I crossed the street to avoid passing him but thought I saw him smiling at me out of the corner of my eye. I didn't stop. I was tired and wanted to get home. Later I regretted it. If it was Paul, that was the last time I saw him—as a smiling image in the corner of my eye.

Kate and Paul had remained friends after he stopped talking to me, but then he turned against her as well.

She had brought up his illness, and he told her that if she did that again, he would have to end their friendship. She brought it up again—and he stopped talking to her, just as he had done with me. They almost reconciled in November, the year before he died, when she ran into him at Fat Tony's birthday party at the Café de Paris. As she was leaving, she offered to buy him a beer. But when she got to the crowded bar, she had second thoughts. Why should she buy a beer for someone who had treated her badly? She left without buying the beer. And that was her last contact with Paul. The fact that it happened at Tony's party reminded me that it was at the Dime a Dance party in New York, DJ'd by Tony, that I first met Paul. Kate tried to visit him when he was on his deathbed in the hospital, but his sister had a list of people who could visit, and she was not on it.

Strangely, I learned of Paul's death through Syd Curry, the hair stylist friend of my high school buddy Ron Smith. Syd had moved to Mississippi, but we were in touch through social media. At 2 a.m. London time, on 22 March 2016, Syd sent me a message: "Hey kiddo, what's going on with Paul Lonergan?" I had heard that Paul was ill again and told Syd, "He's in hospital with cancer. Have you heard something?" Syd told me that there were people leaving comments on Paul's Facebook page, "but nobody saying much except they hope he's feeling better." I contacted a couple of people and found out that Paul was dead. I sent Syd a message telling him the bad news. He wrote back, "I hate that . . . fuck."

•

A FEW MONTHS AFTER THAT, Billy Name died. I had not heard much from Billy over the past two years and knew he was in poor health. An interview in *The Guardian* began like this: "Billy Name is lying in a bed in a ward of Mid-Hudson Regional Hospital in Poughkeepsie, upstate New York, hooked up to a saline drip. He is not looking good: his face is pale, his skin sallow, his voice almost inaudibly low."[20] In addition to having had a stroke, he also suffered from diabetes. Sean O'Hagan, the journalist who did the *Guardian* interview, was a friend of Regine's: I had met him a few times when I worked at Island.

The interview was to publicize "Billy Name: The Silver Age," a London exhibition of Billy's photographs from the book Dagon James had produced for Billy. Sean Carrillo had written to me about the New York opening in 2014: "The gallery was packed to overflowing and then some. There was a line literally down the block when we arrived and the gallery was already full. I am at work so I don't have access to any pix but it was a HUGE success. Billy was there and so was Bill Wilson. Tons of others. I am sure you are getting reports from everywhere. Dagon, Anastasia, and Tony deserve all the credit for shining a light on Billy's beautiful photographs." Bill Wilson wrote that "hugging Billy was like saying good-bye to a scarecrow—but a brave, cheerful one . . ."

Billy outlasted Bill by about six months. I thought back to how excited I was when Billy first contacted me nearly fifteen years ago. It seemed like yesterday. I wrote to Dagon to express my sympathies. He responded: "Hi Gary . . . This is a day I had hoped was still a long way off . . ." An official statement would be forthcoming for the site. As sorry as I was about Billy's death, I was glad

20 Sean O'Hagan, "I shot Andy Warhol: photographer Billy Name on drugs and shootings at the Factory," *The Guardian*, 27 September 2015.

he had managed to find a good agent before he died.

Bill Wilson's stalker, Sylvie, started a website about him after he died. Her obsession with him outlived him. I couldn't help but wonder if he would have lived longer if he hadn't had to deal with the stress of being stalked during the last year of his life. I know he would have been happier. It felt like Sylvie had first stolen his life and was now stealing his soul.

•

THE OBITUARY I WROTE FOR BILL was also seen by David Gates, a young English artist who had stayed in Bill's house in New York during the Raven Row exhibition. He contacted me and then contacted Alex Sainsbury to see if Alex would host a memorial dinner for Bill. I suggested inviting the young artists who had helped to hang the Raven Row show. But the memorial ended up as a small gathering—David, Alex, Clive Phillpot, the artist Luke Dowd, and myself. Bill had known Luke and his artist father, John Dowd.

We met at the gallery. Clive passed around a small book he had edited, *Ray Johnson on Flop Art: Fragments from Conversations,* and we all signed copies for each other to commemorate the evening. Alex gave the others a tour of the current exhibition while I waited at the same table at the front of the gallery where Bill and I had sat during the Ray Johnson show. Because of my heart condition I wasn't able to go with them—too many stairs.

We went to one of the trendier restaurants in the gentrified East End and hardly spoke about Bill at the dinner. Alex referred to his own writings several times—his "body of work." I didn't know he had a body of work. His wife had a small publishing company that was linked to the gallery; maybe that had something to do with it. Clive and I talked about Ray Johnson; when I expressed doubts about the suicide theory, to my surprise he agreed with me. I had not met Luke before but knew from Bill that his father had died from AIDS. I asked him what it was like for a son to have a father who died that way. He said he didn't remember much about it, it happened when he was very young. He did remember how embarrassed he was when he took his school friends to his house and his father's S&M gear would be out.

After a few glasses of English champagne, I felt increasingly tipsy. The wine was interacting with my meds. Every time Alex said something, Bill's complaints about him popped into my head, comments in his emails about Alex being "self-promoting" and that "he has money that does his thinking for him . . ." Instead of listening to Alex, I was listening to Bill. Had Alex "bought" himself a position of importance in the art world? The more "champagne" I drank, the more jumbled my thoughts became.

I left early. I don't think I missed much; everyone was on their best behavior. Alex helped me find a cab. As it headed toward the West End, I couldn't help thinking how great it would be to email Bill when I got home with all the gossip from the dinner: "Hi Bill, Just got back from the memorial dinner Alex Sainsbury gave. Clive Phillpot was there. And that guy David who stayed at your house when you were in London. And John Dowd's son, Luke."

He'd write back asking, "Who was the memorial for?"

"For you, Bill. The memorial was for you."

And then, there he was: Bill, coming out of Liverpool

station, wearing the same dark suit he wore when we went to the British Museum, with the same walking stick that I had bought him from James Smith & Sons. I turned to look back at him as the cab moved forward, and of course it wasn't Bill. It was just another old man with a black stick and white hair and a beard.

As we drove through the city, I realized that this would be where I would end up dying: London. My trip to London had turned into a lifetime. I had lived here for more than thirty years. Yet it still felt like a visit. I had never really connected with the city—but had I ever connected with anything? I had tried to become a "real" this or a "real" that but had ended up drifting through life without becoming a real anything.

I wished I hadn't drunk that "champagne." My mind wandered as I thought how wonderful it would be if, when the cab arrived in front of my building, the people from my past would be there and I'd be able to see them one last time; Andy Warhol people like Bill and Billy and Callie and Ron Tavel; and the druggie friends I had outlived like Paul, Lee, and Ray. I thought of Sally Goldberg and how she used to spend hours separating her eyelashes with a sewing needle, and how Ron Smith and I had sat in his dad's pickup truck and listened to Bowie for the first time. And how nice it would have been to tell my mother what my life was like in London. When she died I was still addicted to heroin.

The cab pulled up in front of my building, and of course nobody was waiting. I paid the fare and took the lift to my flat. Inside the flat, I walked to the kitchen, poured myself a glass of water, and sat in my darkened front room looking out onto the balcony. The curtains were open, and I could see the lights of London outside. I thought about being a kid looking down on the lights of

Hollywood from the freeway and the glamorous world they represented. Whatever happened to that world?

I looked around the room and remembered how happy I had been when I first got this flat. How happy I was when I returned to it after four months in the hospital. How grateful I was to the doctors and nurses who had kept me alive. I tried to hold onto that gratitude—but I felt so tired. And old. For the first time in my life I felt old. So many of my interests had died with the deaths of my friends. I still kept the phone next to my bed in case I had another heart attack, but did it really matter anymore? My life had become a series of medical appointments and memories of the past. Would it ever be possible to overcome the past to arrive at a future?

Sitting in the darkness I noticed a small light flashing on my laptop on my desk. As usual, I had left my computer in sleep mode before leaving for Alex's dinner. I walked over to it, tapped on the space bar to wake it up, and started typing.

www.ingramcontent.com/pod-product-compliance
Lightning Source LLC
LaVergne TN
LVHW091118080826
845145LV00008B/1966
9780998279367